The Teaching of Saint Gregory

An Early Armenian Catechism

TRANSLATION AND COMMENTARY BY
Robert W. Thomson

HARVARD UNIVERSITY PRESS
Cambridge, Massachusetts
1970

TO JUDITH

Distributed in Great Britain by Oxford University Press, London
Library of Congress Catalog Card Number 78–115482
SBN 674–87038–7
Made and printed in Great Britain by William Clowes and Sons, Limited
London, Beccles and Colchester

Preface

The *Teaching of Saint Gregory* is one of the most interesting and complex early Armenian theological compositions, yet it has never attracted much attention nor ever before been translated into any other language. The reasons for its neglect may be partly the enigmatic character of the work in which it is found, the *History* of Agathangelos, and partly the general emphasis in contemporary Western scholarship in Armenian theological studies on the Armenian attitude to Chalcedon and attendant Christological questions. The purpose of the present work is therefore twofold: to bring an interesting text out of the obscurity which has enshrouded it for too long, and to introduce to the world of Armenian scholarship a document whose main emphasis is scriptural exegesis in the hope of restoring a better balance to the study of the early Armenian church and its literature.

The idea of this translation was first suggested to me by Professor G. Garitte over five years ago. A first draft was ready in 1965, but in the meantime my work became somewhat sidetracked by other interests. However, Professor H. Chadwick encouraged me to annotate the translation, and the present work is the result of these two suggestions. In its preparation I have greatly profited from discussion of some of the obscurities in the text with Professor Sirarpie Der Nersessian in Paris, Professor A. K. Sanjian of U.C.L.A., and Mr. Aram Ter Ghevondian at the Matenadaran in Erevan. Professor John Strugnell of the Harvard Divinity School gave some useful hints which have been incorporated in the notes. But the sole responsibility for the translation and the notes is my own, and I am only too well aware of the many imperfections which remain in the former, and of the omissions in the latter.

In the more material aspect of the preparation of the book I am very grateful to Miss Carol Cross for typing the final version of the translation.

Harvard University R. W. Thomson
January 1968

Contents

The Teaching of Saint Gregory: An Early Armenian Catechism

Introduction

Note on Transliteration

In the transliteration of Armenian I have followed the system used in the *Revue des études arméniennes*: a b g d e z ē ə t͑ ž i l x c k h j ł č m y n š o č͑ p j ṙ s v t r c͑ w p͑ k͑, ու = u. Only for the two common names John and Moses have I kept the English forms.

The Teaching of Saint Gregory is a long catechism which is included in the *History of the Armenians* by Agathangelos.[1] This History is a complex document: it purports to be the account, written by an eyewitness, Agathangelos,[2] of the conversion of King Trdat and the Armenians to Christianity at the beginning of the fourth century through the efforts of Gregory the Illuminator. The book brings together many episodes of diverse origin, and it may be helpful briefly to summarize the story in order to place the *Teaching* in its context.

Xosrov, king of the Armenians, is murdered by a Parthian noble, Anak, at the instigation of Artašir the Sassanian. Anak is killed, but his two young sons escape and are taken one to Persia, the other, Gregory, to Caesarea in Cappadocia. The Persians occupy Armenia, and the murdered king's son, Trdat, takes refuge in Greek territory; he later gains the attention of the emperor Diocletian and is restored with the help of Roman arms to the throne of Armenia. Gregory, brought up as a Christian, takes service with Trdat without revealing his parentage. When requested to offer to the goddess Anahit he refuses; after a series of tortures, and when he is revealed as Anak's son, Trdat orders him to be thrown into the pit at Artašat, from which no one ever emerged alive.

Our historian now turns to the story of Rhipsimē (Hṙip͑simē), who fled from Rome with her abbess Gaianē (Gayianē) and thirty-five companions to escape a forced marriage to Diocletian. They take refuge in Armenia, but there Trdat falls victim to Rhipsimē's beauty. He is rejected and orders all the nuns to be martyred. But as punishment for this wickedness Trdat is turned into the form of a wild boar, and his household and the citizens are afflicted by demons. The king's sister is informed by a vision that only Gregory can save the country from these torments. To the amazement of all he is discovered to be alive after fifteen years in the pit. Brought to court he orders the bodies of the martyrs to be buried and instructs the court in

1. Agat͑angełos, *Patmut͑iwn Hayoc͑*, critical edition by G. Tēr Mkrtč͑ean and St. Kanayeanc͑, Tiflis 1909, the text without apparatus reprinted in the *Łukasean Matenadaran*, 15, Tiflis 1914. There are translations in Italian (*Storia di Agatangelo, Versione italiana illustrata dai monachi armeni mechitaristi riveduta quanto allo stile da* N. Tommaseo, Venice 1843) and French (V. Langlois, *Agathange*, in his *Collection des historiens anciens et modernes de l'Arménie*, I, Paris 1867), but they both omit the *Teaching*.

2. §12. The paragraph numbers are those established by the editors of the 1909 edition and retained in the reprint of 1914.

Christian doctrine. Here follows the catechism, or *Teaching*, which is a little longer than the total "historical" section.

After the catechism and a further sixty-five days of instruction, Gregory orders the building of three *martyria* for the martyrs, in accordance with a vision he had enjoyed. The king and his court are converted and cured of their afflictions, then in the company of Gregory they proceed to overthrow the pagan temples of Armenia. Gregory is then sent to Caesarea to receive consecration as bishop. On his return Gregory founds churches and baptizes Trdat, his household, the nobles, and more than four million Armenians.

Gregory later retires from public life, his younger son, Aristakēs, becoming bishop[3] and head of the Armenian church. Gregory joins Trdat on a visit to Rome to see the emperor Constantine, after which he regains his solitary cell. Agathangelos ends his *History* with a brief account of the presence of Aristakēs at the council of Nicaea, and an even briefer reference to the death of his hero Gregory.[4]

Within the *History* the *Teaching of Gregory* does not play an essential role; the story would be as coherent, or incoherent, without it. The manuscripts give the catechism a separate title and clearly mark its end and the return to the narrative. Yet the narrative before and after the *Teaching* consists of speeches by Gregory which make direct reference to the content of this section. Gregory's first sermon begins at §226. In it he speaks briefly of God the Creator, the Son who calls all who worship the Father his brothers, and the Spirit who gives the firstfruits of his love to those who are converted. The Armenians must repent, he says, of their sins committed in ignorance; he himself was saved by God to preach the gospel which the Armenians rejected by putting the martyrs to death. At this Trdat and the crowd ask if there is any hope of forgiveness and request further instruction. Gregory then begins a second, shorter sermon (§247) explaining that he has been preserved in order to save the Armenians from idolatry and bring them to repentance, and he then elaborates the subject matter of the catechism to follow (§252–258).

It is clear that the *Teaching*, marked in the manuscripts as a separate section, cannot be dissociated from the final Armenian redaction of the *History*. But there is no indication that the content of Gregory's sermons forms part of the earlier traditional material woven by the final redactor into the *History* as we now have it.

That the *Teaching* forms an integral part of the *History* is indicated by the various versions made from the Armenian.[5] Paradoxically, they all omit this catechism. However, the Greek version of the *History*, as published by Lagarde,[6] translates faithfully the sermon of Gregory in which he announces the main lines of the catechism (§252–258), and also the remarks of Gregory immediately following the catechism in which he refers back to it (§716);[7] the translator was evidently aware of the existence of the *Teaching* which he chose to omit. This translation has been dated to between A.D. 464 and 468.[8]

Two other Greek versions of the *History* are also known in addition to the Life of Gregory adapted by Simeon Metaphrastes, one from a manuscript at Ochrid, one from a manuscript in the Escorial.[9] The former, on which depends in large part the Arabic translation, is a different recension from that published by Lagarde, translated from the Armenian and not adapted from the Greek text. It dates to, at latest, the early eighth century, as it was known to George, Bishop of the Arabs, in 714. The Greek version in the Escorial gives a text similar to that of the Ochrid manuscript but has its own independent witness to the traditions concerning Gregory's life. The importance of the Ochrid version from our point of view is that it contains three paragraphs from the *Teaching* (§652–654). Two of these paragraphs are also incorporated, with some adaptation, in the Arabic version.

From internal evidence it seems clear that the *Teaching* formed part of the text of Agathangelos as it was known by the 460's. It is impossible to push this date further back from the witness of quotations from the *Teaching*, for it is not quoted in Armenian until the seventh century.[10] A Georgian reworking of some extracts from the *Teaching*, passing as a treatise of Hippolytus, has been recently published by Garitte, but the text is undated and the

3. §862. Aristakes becomes bishop and succeeds to the see of the catholicos (Ֆատաւ յաթոռ կաթողիկոսութեան ٭այոց Սَهۀաց). Gregory himself is called catholicos (§884), but when referring to his consecration at Caesarea Agatʻangeɫos speaks of the rank of "chief-priest" (պատիւ քահանայապետութեան §793), of priesthood, and of episcopacy (§805).

4. The tradition concerning Gregory's burial place (Tʻordan in the *gawaṙ* of Daranaɫikʻ) is first mentioned by Pʻawstos Buzandacʻi, *Patmutʻiwn Hayocʻ*, III 2.

5. See G. Garitte, *Documents pour l'étude du livre d'Agathange* (*Studi e Testi*, 127), Vatican 1946, reviewed by Toumanoff, *Traditio*, 5 (1947), pp. 373–383; also G. Garitte, *La Vie grecque inédite de saint Grégoire d'Arménie* (*ms. 4 d'Ochrida*), *Analecta Bollandiana*, 83 (1965), pp. 233–290.

6. Paul de Lagarde, *Agathangelus*, *Abhandlungen der königlichen Gesellschaft der Wissenschaften zu Göttingen*, 35 (1888), pp. 1–88.

7. The break in the Greek comes at §106 line 91 of Lagarde.

8. P. Peeters, *S. Grégoire l'Illuminateur dans le calendrier lapidaire de Naples, Analecta Bollandiana*, 60 (1942), pp. 108–109.

9. See note 5 above.

10. In the *Knikʻ Hawatoy* (Seal of faith) published by K. Tēr Mkrtčʻean, Ējmiacin 1914. The quotations are collected in Garitte, *Documents*, pp. 354–356. The full title of the *Knikʻ Hawatoy* claims that it was compiled by the Catholicos Komitas (610–628); cf. G. Garitte, *La Narratio de rebus Armeniae*, CSCO *Subsidia* 4, Louvain 1952, p. 268), though it contains extracts from works by John Mayragomecʻi who did not die until at least 668 (cf. Garitte, *Narratio*, p. 346).

two manuscripts in which it is found are from the tenth and twelfth or thirteenth centuries.[11]

Before analyzing the ideas of the *Teaching*, we may present the general lines of its argument.

It begins with a declaration of belief in the Trinity—the Father who created us, the Son who saved us, and the Spirit by whom the world was made and who acts in the world. Being and eternal existence belong only to God; there is no one before Him and no other creator beside Him. The whole universe was made by Him and depends on Him; everyone and everything regardless of his rank, angels and men, the stars of heaven, the earth and its creatures, all take their continued existence from Him and are established by his power only.

God cannot be described, for no created mind can grasp the absolute, and God is absolute light, power, and glory. He is without beginning or change, infinite, beyond speech or thought. We earthbound creatures who had a beginning cannot scrutinize or examine the unfathomable—the Godhead must remain a mystery. Within the single nature of the Godhead can be distinguished three Persons, Father, Son, and Spirit. The author of the *Teaching* never ceases to emphasize the unity, the one divinity and hypostasis of the Trinity; for him the foundation of the Christian faith is this unity of the Trinity.

God is complete and perfect in Himself, yet He wished to bring creatures into being for a purpose: that everything might glorify the Creator in its own way. But of all creatures God had a particular care for and interest in men. He created them with his own hands and blew into them the breath of intelligence, that men might become familiar with God and have knowledge of his benevolent activity.

Creation can be divided into two kinds: the visible and the invisible. The invisible creatures are the angels. They are made of fire or light and are not corporeal; they ceaselessly watch and praise, and also serve as God's messengers to men, sometimes appearing in human guise. In addition they protect mankind from the evil spirits, fallen angels, who attempt to deceive men and lead them away from the true knowledge of God.

The visible creation our author describes in some detail, following the order of Genesis. All creatures, animate and inanimate, have their fixed courses. By God's command the stars follow their set paths; the winds and the rains cause the plants to blossom and flourish, and all creation adheres to its measure. By contemplating this wonderful order of the universe, the regularity of the movements of the celestial bodies and the recurrent changes of the seasons, man can appreciate the goodness of the Creator and glorify Him.

Man has a special place in God's scheme. He alone, with the angels, has independence of will and a rational mind, and this is how we are to understand that he has been "made in the image of God." By exercising his power of choice he would have been able to gain greater knowledge of God. But by choosing evil and disobeying God's command, aided by the deceit of the devil who was jealous of his virtue, man introduced evil to this world, and as a consequence, death.

Even after the fall of Adam and his expulsion from Paradise, God did not abandon men. He wished all to gain immortality by a good life, and as a token of this the just Enoch was raised up to immortality without mortal death. But after the eighth generation men forgot God and descended to impiety. God therefore chastised men and purified the earth by means of an universal flood, again making a covenant with the only just man, Noah, to show his love for men to the future generations. But foolish as ever men once more abandoned their Creator and attempted to build a tower to heaven, in punishment whereof God scattered mankind over the face of the earth and divided them into seventy-two mutually unintelligible tongues. Seventy-two patriarchs were set over the various tribes, and each tribe was established in its own lands. The gathering together again of these seventy-two tribes to the worship of the only God is the task of the church, begun by the seventy-two apostles who traveled to the farthest ends of the earth.

But after the destruction of the tower of Babel not all men deserted God, for Abraham was found worthy to receive the great gospel and promise of God: that his Son would come in the flesh of the seed of Abraham to be the father of righteousness for all believers. From Abraham also descended the inspired prophets, the disciples, and the evangelists. So God did not abandon men, but by signs, visions, and appearances revealed Himself and his commands to them, taking particular care of the race of Abraham in their pilgrimage to a greater understanding of Himself. The *Teaching* follows the fortunes of Israel in Egypt, the deliverance by Moses, the lawgiving in Sinai, and the arrival in the promised land. Our author then describes some of the revelations of the prophets whose task was to urge their people to keep the commandments of God; they were sent to warn Israel not to neglect their Creator, but they were unheeded, stoned, and killed. And then each time that the Hebrews turned to false gods and wrongdoing God punished them by means of those whose gods they were worshipping, but later he would free them from their oppressors or captors and restore Israel.

These preliminary reflections on the history of Israel bring our author to the central theme of his discourse—the Incarnation of the Son of God as the fulfillment of the prophecies and types of the Old Testament and the

---

11. G. Garitte, *Le Traité géorgien " Sur la foi" attribué à Hippolyte*, *Le Muséon*, 78 (1965), pp. 119–172. For the date of the composition of the *Teaching* see below, pp. 37–38.

continuing mission of the church in bringing back all men to the cross, the antitype of the tower of Babel. But before describing the earthly life of Christ and explaining the details of the prophecies fulfilled by Him and the meanings of the types of the Old Testament, our author points out that the Incarnation was not a sudden idea of God's, but that it was part of his eternal plan of redemption. The corruption which was the lot of Adam and his seed came about through the foreordained will of God to set men free in Christ. Thus there is no change or alteration in the eternal being and will of the Creator. But the mystery of the Incarnation was hidden from time and was revealed in auguries to the just and the prophets according to their ability to understand it. And so the Son did not immediately come to earth after the first transgression, lest men having no previous warning might not receive Him. Before He came all races and ages were given indications of the future.

The focal point of history is the Incarnation of the only begotten Son of God. The historical events of the Old Testament are prefigurings of Christ, brought about by God as preparation for the fulfillment of his eternal plan. In the life and death of Christ this plan was completed and men were reconciled with God, released from death, and made heirs of immortality.

Before describing the earthly life of Christ, the author of the *Teaching* indicates that He fulfilled all the promises concerning Him in the Old Testament. And not only did Christ fulfill the prophecies, but He is in a special sense heir to the tradition of Israel. An important stage in Jesus's life is thus the Baptism, at which moment He took over his heritage from John the Baptist. But our author first describes the birth and childhood of Christ.

The signs at Christ's birth indicated the divine glory and the divine humility, the mystery of the revelation of the Godhead, just as the prophets had indicated the birth of Christ in the flesh and the birth of the Son from the Father before all ages. This mystery of the Incarnation was an eternal mystery, hidden with God until it was revealed to angels and men at the birth from the Virgin. Then Christ took a true form, a real beginning, and was not a phantom or appearance. He was born of the seed of Abraham as promised by the gospel; He was circumcised to fulfill that gospel; He grew up according to the law of human nature, and hid Himself for thirty years before submitting to baptism by John. Just as in the time of Moses God ordered the Israelites to purify themselves with water in order to become worthy to receive the revelation of divine glory, so also John was sent to wash the people with the water of repentance that they might become worthy to hear the teaching of Christ and receive Him in their hearts. This baptism was not that of regeneration to eternal life, but a washing of repentance and holiness.

John the Baptist is the link between the old covenant and the new. The tradition of the priesthood, kingship, and prophecy of the seed of Abraham

descended to him, and he was the keeper of this tradition and its heir, at once priest, prophet, and king. He passed on this tradition, the priesthood, the prophecy, and the kingship, to our Lord Jesus Christ. Our author will later develop this theme to stress the continuity from the old covenant through John and Christ to the disciples and the church.

The *Teaching* devotes very little space to describing the earthly life of Jesus. Its author is more interested in the fulfillment of prophecy, the exposition of biblical types, and the continuity of tradition through Christ from the Old to the New Covenants. So the episodes on which he concentrates are the Nativity, the Baptism, the instruction to the disciples and their appointment as his heirs, and the Passion and Resurrection.

After his Baptism our Lord exhorted all to strip off the old man and the heavy weight of sins through the bath of baptism and repentance. Baptism is now more than a means of repentance as it was with John; it is an effective means of regeneration. Jesus then called his twelve disciples and made them worthy of the mystery of the divine tradition which they were to inherit. He demonstrated his power to heal and cure diseases and began to teach the truth about Himself. He revealed his Divinity by his miracles and through parables and prophetic parallels. He foretold his Passion and the future fate of those who plotted against Him. The twelve disciples and the seventy-two He instructed, telling them of his resurrection and the coming of the Comforter. Their leader was Peter, and he was made the foundation stone of all the churches, since he first recognized that Jesus was Christ, the Son of the living God. Jesus gave the keys of the kingdom to all the disciples, He Himself being the gate. Then the disciples received the grace of priesthood, prophecy, and apostleship, knowledge of the mystery of the old covenant with the seed of Abraham, which tradition John had given to Christ and Christ had handed on to the apostles.

The death of Christ on the cross and the prophecies which foretold it are next briefly narrated, followed by the resurrection on the third day. The *Teaching* stresses the fact that Christ willingly underwent this death; He was neither forced nor under any obligation in Himself. Being free from sin, by his death He effaced death which held all men in its power. He died for the dead, and by his resurrection proved his victory over death, giving an example of the future resurrection of the just.

On the cross of Christ is based our author's theology of redemption, for the theme central to the whole of his discourse is the antithesis between the tower of Babel, with the consequent scattering of all peoples, and the cross which draws all men together again and brings them back to God. In place of the tower which soon fell to ruin has been set up the cross; instead of the wood which men worshipped, the cross has been raised; from the one was scattering and expulsion, from the other gathering and an approach to

the kingdom of heaven; and in opposition to the darkness which reigned in men's hearts is the light which radiates from the cross as from a candlestick. The shape of the cross itself has a special significance for it has four corners just as the altar of the Old Testament. The base fixed in the ground shows that the Lord walked on earth and that He established the church on a firm foundation. The top points upwards and reveals the nature of Him who was nailed to it. The right arm shows the power of God's right arm and points to the future joy and rewards of the just while the left arm indicates the torments of the sinners. The four corners of the cross are the four corners of the altar which received the sacrifice of the Lord's body which was offered to the Father; they are the four corners of the earth, signifying the whole of mankind who rejoice at the victory over death demonstrated by the cross planted in the ground.

After his resurrection our Lord appeared to his disciples, not only giving them much joy, but confirming that He had been in no way restrained by the tomb, and that the Son of God was the same before, during, and after his suffering. He revealed to them the meaning of the Scriptures concerning Himself and commanded them to go and baptize all the gentiles. Our author then recalls the ascension of Christ and the descent of the Holy Spirit at Pentecost.

The Spirit was revealed as fire, signifying the flames to which the wicked will be consigned and the burning away of sins. As the tower of error was destroyed by fire from heaven so will the Spirit burn away our sins, for unless the impurities of sin which cling to our bodies are removed, we cannot fly up to heaven. The fire of the Spirit also acts as a furnace, testing first the disciples (of whom one was consumed and destroyed—Judas), and then, through them, the world.

Of equal importance to our author as the theme of fire is the idea of the cups of joy and bitterness of the Spirit. The apostles are cupbearers giving drink to the world. There are two kinds of drink: the one is the sweet wine of joy for those who drink it in faith and virtue, the other is the gall of bitterness for the wicked; the one brings life to our souls, wisdom and illumination, the other, poison which destroys the unbelieving. The fire of the Spirit burns away the impure and preserves the sanctified, as the bodies of the sons of Aaron burned yet the robes of their priesthood were not consumed. The Spirit is like the living fire of the sacrifices of the Old Testament. Just as it turned into water when the priests cast it into a well at the time of the captivity, and on their return changed back to fire, so the Spirit has diverse forms and different powers.

The consideration of the life of the Spirit in the church brings our author to the final section of his discourse. Having explained God's eternal plan for the redemption of mankind and its fulfillment in Christ, he turns to the

continued activity of the missionaries bringing knowledge of the possibility of salvation to all peoples of the earth. For man's personal salvation is dependent on repentance for his past life and belief in Christ, the rejection of which entails eternal damnation.

The history of the world can be divided into seven periods of a thousand years, the last of which is rest for the just, for each thousand years corresponds to one day of God's creative activity. We are now in the sixth period of a thousand years, in which God effected the renewal of his creation and in which will come the end of the world, so that in the seventh age those who have travailed on his behalf will have eternal rest with Him. The present time is one of trial for the testing of the just, and this testing is accomplished by the fire of the Holy Spirit. Just as the Apostles were themselves tested, so they test the world. They have become trumpets, speaking all tongues, to announce the dispensation of the Word to all nations, to call all men to baptism.

The example of the first Apostles was followed by many who became martyrs and witnesses to the faith of Christ. The martyrs whom Trdat had put to death had been the first to bring the gospel to Armenia, and now that the gospel has been preached, the Armenians must decide to accept or reject it. By the intercession of the martyrs' prayers the Armenians can be reconciled with God, says Gregory, for just as the Son of God died and lived, so the martyrs live and intercede for them. The martyrs loved the Lord more than themselves and gave themselves in return for his death for them. The Son of God accepted their sacrifice and drew them to Himself, and through them the whole world.

Gradually the world is reunited to God as men hear the gospel and repent. The author of the *Teaching* emphasizes the importance of repentance, for without it no one can be saved. He has Gregory warn his audience that repentance must be made during a man's lifetime, for there can be no repentance in hell; one's fate is fixed at death. Our author returns to the Old Testament parallels of the backsliding of the Jews, the warnings of the prophets, and God's punishment of the impious, and contrasts the harmony of the church of Christ with the variance of the races scattered at the tower of Babel. The tower and the cross are for him the dominant symbols of the old and new dispensations.

Our author finishes his sermon with an account of the tradition of the church. Just as the prophets improved on the teaching of the Mosaic law, God gradually introducing his people to higher things, so the apostles at first introduced the neophytes to easier things. In their instruction they added oral explanations to the apostolic letters, they committed the gospel to writing, defining the one tradition in four accounts, not adding elaborations of their own, but informed by the Spirit. And its truth is proved by its accordance with the foreordained parables in the law of Moses and the

prophets. The holy faith was revealed in a mystery to our fathers; it was announced by the prophets and preached by the Son of God; it is confirmed in the scriptures and the canons of the church, the canons being fixed by the apostolic synods.

The *Teaching* thus ends as it had begun—on the theme of unity. The unity of the Trinity is imitated in the unity of the church and her faith. The church is in the direct tradition of the Old Testament priesthood, and her mission is to restore that unity lost at the tower, as Christ has restored the unity of God and man destroyed by Adam's sin. The time for final judgment approaches as the gospel has now spread to all regions of the world and men must make their decision. The historical events of the last six thousand years are the gradual revelation of God's eternal plan. In this last millennium that revelation has been completed, and soon the just will be at one with God in the everlasting peace of the kingdom. But woe to those who reject Christ, for there is no repentance in hell.

In its general lines the *Teaching* thus falls into the category of a catechism, instruction before baptism, which from the earliest days of the church was an indispensable preliminary to the administration of that sacrament. In the development of the catechism two factors played a parallel role: dogmatic considerations and moral exhortation. The latter is uppermost in the *Didache* which elaborates the doctrine of the two ways, one of life and one of death, indicating the moral decision those to be baptized must make, while the importance of dogmatic instruction is obvious from the development of the creeds recited before baptism.

Catechetical instruction was oral, and its emphasis would naturally shift depending on whether those being instructed were Jews or Gentiles. In the development of literary forms, the apology addressed to Gentiles similarly differed from the genre which depended on proof texts from the Old Testament. Irenaeus's *Demonstration* (*Epideixis*) marks an important stage in the literary development of traditional material based on the idea of the continuation of the old dispensation into the new and its fulfillment in Christ, with the prophecies and types of the Old Testament as proof (hence *Epideixis*), rather than on the Hellenistic tradition of the refutation of idolatry and polytheism. This traditional material is interwoven with exposition of the creed in the *Catechetical Orations* of Cyril of Jerusalem. It is to this type of literature that the *Teaching* is directly related.

The three main facets of the *Teaching* are thus traditional in such works: dogmatic instruction based on a creed; exposition of the types and prophecies of the Old Testament as proof of the New; and moral exhortation to repentance. We may now turn to a more detailed examination of these themes in the *Teaching*.

The author of the *Teaching* expresses his doctrine of God in terms common to all early Armenian writers. He starts from the statement in Exodus 3.14: *Եւ եր Աստուած որ էն, ἐγώ εἰμι ὁ ὤν.*[12] This term *էն* is used at §377. It is also the terminology of Eznik, who uses *է* both as a verb and as a substantive.[13] Similarly in the first homily of those attributed to Gregory the Illuminator, the *Yačaxapatum*, we read: "the unbegotten begat the eternal *էն.*"[14]

Derived from *է* is the adjectival form *էական*, frequently found in the *Teaching*, for example §325 *բնութիւն էականին Աստուածոյ.*[15] From the adjective an abstract noun is formed, *էականութիւն*, which is used only once in the *Teaching* (§458, with reference to the Trinity). The denominative verb *էանալ*, also known to Eznik, likewise only occurs once in the *Teaching* (§711), where it is used to render the *τὸ εἶναι* (*ἴσα Θεῷ*) of Philippians 2.6 in place of the *լինել* of the Armenian vulgate. The substitution is in accordance with our author's careful distinction between "being" and "becoming."

This distinction between the eternal existence of God and the transitory becoming of the created world is well expressed in the *Teaching* by the contrast between the two terms *էութիւն* and *լինելութիւն*. The former describes the nature of the *է*, the only uncreated, eternal being. It is a common expression in Armenian, first found in the New Testament as the rendering of *ὑπόστασις* in Hebrews 1.2. It is frequent in Eznik, in the works attributed to John Mandakuni,[16] and all later writers. Of similar meaning are *գոյութիւն*[17] and *գոյացութիւն*. The former occurs in §705 with reference

12. Cf. John 8.58.

13. L. Mariès, *Etude sur quelques noms et verbes d'existence chez Eznik* (extrait de la *Revue des études arméniennes*, 8), Paris 1928, p. 51.

14. *Yačaxapatum*, p. 9; *իրք անծին զէն անսկզբն ծնեալ*; cf. ps.-Eliše, *On the Passion of Christ*, p. 311; *խնամամ է, զխոսելոյ ճշմարիտ զէ զոյ Աստուած.* On the *Yačaxapatum* see note 82.

15. See also §326, 420, 702. It is used as a substantive at §263, 271, 284; cf. Mariès, *Etude*, pp. 51–52. The expression *էակից*, "sharing in the same being," is used by John Mandakuni (*Girkᶜ Tᶜltᶜocᶜ*, p. 30), and the substantive *էակ* is used in the translations of Aristotle's logic to render *τὸ ὄν*.

16. Cf. M. Tallon, *Livre des lettres: Mélanges de l'Université Saint Joseph*, 32 (1955), p. 101. The *Čaṙkᶜ* published under John Mandakuni's name, Venice 1860, were attributed to John Mayragomecᶜi by K. Tēr Mkrtčᶜean (*Knik Hawatoy*, p. xxvi; cf. Garitte, *Narratio*, p. 348), but they do not give much evidence of Mayragomecᶜi's polemical style or ideas in Christology.

17. An abstract noun derived from *գոյ* (3. p.s. verbal form). The addition of the suffix *-ութիւն* to a conjugated verbal form is foreign to Armenian practice; cf. A. Meillet, *Altarmenisches Elementarbuch*, Heidelberg 1913, pp. 28–29. If *է* is considered as a substantive, not as the 3 p.s. verbal form, then *էութիւն* is regular. The model of *ʾitutāʾ* in Syriac may have influenced the formation of these two terms.

to the Trinity, the latter in §391 with reference to the eternal hypostasis of the Word. But զոյութիւն does not necessarily imply uncreated existence, for in his *Demonstration* John Mandakuni writes that God brought us into զոյութիւն from աննիւթութիւն.[18] Similarly in the *Questions on Genesis* attributed to Eliše we read that darkness is not a զոյ[]թիւն, whereas light is an էութիւն.[19] More usually the term լինելութիւն expresses "created being."[20] The concept of nonexistence is rendered by չգոյ (§275) or ոչինչ (§439, 620).[21]

The same root գոյ is used twice in the *Teaching* as a substantive with the meaning "essence": no man can see God գոյիւ—in his essence (§356, 382). The adjective զոյական occurs once, predicated of God's nature (§332). Of similar meaning are խակութիւն and խակական, which are frequent in the *Teaching*, in the *Yačaxapatum*, and other Armenian theological treatises.

The most common term in the Teaching to denote "hypostasis" is զաւրութիւն. This is an ambiguous expression, for it means basically "power," ἐνεργεία, and as our author is not always very precise in his exposition, in some passages it is not clear whether զաւրութիւն should be translated as "power" or "hypostasis." In this latter meaning it is used only with reference to the Trinity, not one of the three Persons individually. A further expression, ինքնութիւն, is common in the *Teaching* and is used in much the same context as զաւրութիւն. It means "individuality" and is applied either to God and the Trinity (§259, 380) or to the Son (§439).[22]

The author of the *Teaching* had a large vocabulary at his command with which to express abstract concepts of being, essence, hypostasis, and other philosophical ideas. But by overloading his explanations with synonymous terms and parallels he blunted the effectiveness of his presentation. He was not a rigorous thinker like Eznik and did not always take care to correlate his various sources. Such ambiguities reappear in his exposition of the doctrine of the Trinity.

The *Teaching* begins and ends with reference to the Trinity, and no subject is more frequently stressed than the consubstantiality of the three Persons, Father, Son, and Holy Spirit. The vocabulary used to describe their interrelationship is varied: at least eight different adjectives are compounds of

18. *Girkᶜ Tᶜltᶜocᶜ*, p. 33. This negative աննիւթութիւն does not occur in the *Teaching* or in Eznik.

19. Elisée Vardapet, *Questions et réponses sur la Genèse*, publié par N. Akinian, traduit par S. Kogian, Vienna 1928, pp. 38–39.

20. E.g., §262. In the translation of, and commentaries on, Aristotle's logic it renders γένεσις. Unlike էութիւն it does not occur in the Armenian bible.

21. See also note 7 to §259 of the *Teaching*.

22. The inherent ambiguity of ինքնութիւն was avoided by most Armenian writers by the use of անձնաւորութիւն, "personality." The substantive անձն, "person," is used frequently in the *Teaching* to distinguish the three Persons of the Trinity, §362, 702, 705; once երկու §623. The adjective երիքանձնական occurs at §383, 623, 662.

մի, "one." The expressions միական, միարան, միարանական, միաւորական, միասնական emphasize primarily the unity. More interesting are the terms միաբուն, "of one nature," միակամ, "of one will," միախորհ "of one council or mind," whose content is further emphasized by their reappearance as nouns in such phrases as "one will," "one council," "one nature."

In its first paragraph the *Teaching* speaks of the Father as creating through the Spirit, an idea repeated in §362 and elsewhere. But our author is at pains also to associate the Son with the Spirit in the work of creation. He applies the terms "co-author" (արարչակից) and "co-worker" (համագործ) to Them both; and this not only in connection with his interpretation of the biblical "let us make" (Gen. 1.26, 2.18, at §260, 275), which he interprets as referring to both Son and Spirit, but explicitly at §443: all things established by the Father are through the Son, as the credal δι' οὖ τὰ πάντα ἐγένετο.

A greater inconsistency is apparent when the *Teaching* discusses the procession of the Spirit. The concept of "procession" is expressed by our author in various ways. In addition to the use of a simple ablative case with the preposition ի (as §362: the Son is from the Father, the Spirit is from the being of the same, or the Spirit is from them both), four verbs are found in the *Teaching*. One of these, ելանէ (§207), occurs only in a quotation from John 15.26 to render the Greek ἐκπορεύεται, the Spirit proceeds from the Father. The verb ծագեաց (§566) also has a biblical origin: "the Son arose from the Father" is a reminiscence of Hebrews 7.14 and Isaiah 11.1. Similarly բղխէ (§707, "flows from") has parallels in John 4.14 and 7.38, and առաքեցաւ (§665, "was sent") is also taken from John.

What is inconsistent, however, is not the vocabulary but the interrelationship between the three Persons. Two different ideas are expressed: the Son is from the Father[23] and the Spirit is also from the Father,[24] or the Son proceeds from the Father and the Spirit[25] and the Spirit from the Father and the Son.[26] The idea in §443 that the Son distributes[27] the grace of the Spirit does not bear so directly on the problem. The first of the two propositions is the older and was enshrined in the creed known as that of Constantinople,[28] whereas the second reflects a post-Ephesus usage.[29] There is no need to assume any interpolation in the *Teaching*, which on other grounds can hardly be earlier than the 440's.[30] It is

23. §362, 566, ablative case and ծագեաց.

24. §362, 707, ablative case and ելանէ, բղխէ.

25. §665, առաքեցաւ.

26. §362, 665, ablative case and առաքեցաւ.

27. The term բաշխէ and the passive verb բաշխի are taken from Galatians 3.5.

28. But see J. N. D. Kelley, *Early Christian Creeds*, London 1950, pp. 298 ff.

29. B. V. Sargisean, *Agatᶜangelos ew iwr bazmadarean Galtnikᶜn*, Venice 1890, pp. 372–373. Cf. Cyril of Alexandria, *In Isaiam*, quoted in note 2 to §486.

30. On the date of the *Teaching* see below, pp. 37–38.

typical of its author to use sources of varying date without reconciling any discrepancies.

A further apparent ambiguity arises when the doctrine of creation is discussed. The emphasis on the role of all three Persons in the creation of the world has already been noted, and in general there is no doubt that creation ex nihilo (*ի չգոյէ*, §275, *յոչընչէ*, §439, 620) is assumed. But in one passage our author's lack of rigorous terminology is confusing. At §272 we read that creatures took their origin (*լինել*, becoming) from matter (*նիւթ*) which is described as immaterial (*աննիւթ*), undifferentiated (*չբաւոր*, literally "lacking"), and formless (*անկերպարան*). The inference might be that creation was the act of imposing order and form on a preexistent matter, but this would be out of harmony with the rest of the *Teaching*, and we are left with the conclusion that "immaterial matter" is a periphrasis for "nothing."

Concerning the nature of this created universe, our author shares in general the notions of his Armenian contemporaries. The matter (*նիւթ*) of which creation is composed can be analyzed into four elements (*տարր*). These elements are not enumerated in the *Teaching*, but Eznik mentions the classical four: earth, water, air, and fire, whereas the homilies in the *Yačaxapatum* describe the four examples of elements (*զտարերս ամենայն չորից միգանակաց*) as height, depth, length, and breadth, and the four kinds of matter (*ի չորից նիւթոց զիրակելեաս*) as the wet and dry, the cold and warm.[31] Eznik and the *Teaching* have similar accounts of the position of the earth in the cosmos. For both it is set in the void; underneath extends the unfathomable chaos, while above the earth is the solid vault of heaven. The luminaries circle on their fixed paths, returning every day to mark the passage of time. Eznik considers that the sun and moon are independent and have their own light, but the *Teaching* (§566) is content to explain that the luminaries shine in imitation of God's own light. Like Ełišē[32] our author emphasizes the inability of the revolving luminaries and recurring seasons to alter their course; they are unconscious in their obedience to the will of the Creator.

The only exception to this order and harmony is the behavior of men. They are not forced to obey the will of the Creator but have freedom to act as they choose. From this freedom came the fall into sin, and its natural consequence, death and corruption. But God knew that men would sin, and therefore his plan for creation involved more than starting this world on its course.

Eznik (§52) explains that God did not abstain from creating Satan and mankind, although He knew that they would turn away from the good, because He wished to reveal his goodness (*բարերարութիւն*) and mankind's free will. This desire for good God has always had (Eznik, §247) and has now, as part of his nature. The *Yačaxapatum* does not elaborate on this theme, but merely points out that evil and vice did not exist in the beginning; they came about as a result of sin (for example, see p. 48) and man's free will (p. 64). The Incarnation is thus explained as a demonstration of God's love (p. 147) and the death of Christ as a sacrifice which removed men's sins (p. 155). God has foreknowledge, but does not force anyone to choose good or evil (p. 166). The *Teaching* develops this argument with more rigor. The consequence of sin was foreseen by God from the beginning; He did not therefore have to devise a remedy after the event. "For not after the Omniscient had taken thought did the Son come and appear to the world . . . but according to his resolution in the beginning He accomplished it in the end" (§342). God had the eternal intention of setting men free in Christ (§350). So in addition to the evidence of nature for God's love for his creatures, our author sees in the witness of the Bible a further proof of God's interest in his handiwork, a token of which is his continuous participation in the historical fortunes of Israel.

God's eternal plan was not revealed as soon as mankind had fallen from grace. Rather, God gradually taught mankind through special revelations, the law of Moses, and the prophets, about Himself and his commands. Because of the inability of any creature to bear the complete vision of the Creator, He took on various occasions a visible form and used an audible voice (§272). Sometimes He appeared as fire or smoke, or on a high throne surrounded by cherubim, or sometimes as a man. He used the same likenesses to several different generations, in order that people would become familiar with these appearances and not be terrified by strange and unknown forms (§328). These likenesses are not material forms, but passing visions, for God's nature is invisible and inscrutable; and by calling God light, for example, we merely show our incapacity to express the invisible by means of the visible (§358). Since the full vision would be impossible for men to bear, God veiled Himself in his appearances with a cloud, and without this cloud no man ever saw Him (§558).

Before the manifestation among men of the Son, God appeared in a mystery. This mystery (*խորհուրդ*, §625) is not the direct revelation in visible guise, but the indirect adumbration of the divine truth, the type (*աւրինակ*). These two terms are common to all Armenian theologians,[33] but in the *Teaching* several synonyms are also employed. In §354 we read the forceful image: "we creatures are nailed to types" (*տիպս*). From the noun the denominative verb *տպաւորիլ* is formed. It occurs twice in the *Teaching*,

31. *Yačaxapatum*, pp. 23–24, 146.
32. Ełišē, *History*, p. 34.

33. Cf. Eznik, §407.

in §407 and 589 where a pattern of life is intended, as in Łazar,[34] whereas Eznik (§407) and Ełišē[35] use it in the technical sense of "to be a type." In this latter sense the *Teaching* also has ղուշակ (augury, §342), նմանութիւն (likeness, §346), առակ (example, parable, §373, 431, 450, 557, as also Ełišē, *History*, p. 107), but most frequently աւրինակ. This may refer to the prophecies (§423, 505), to types (§332, 371, 431, 432, 435), or to a pattern of life (§452, 687). In this last sense the verbal form աւրինակեալ is also found (§407, 583). Աւրինակ also occurs as a synonym for the "image" of God (§264, explaining Gen. 1.27), and as the Trinitarian "pattern" of triple immersion at baptism (§662).

The idea of a "type" in the *Teaching* is not confined to tangible realities or historical events; more abstract principles also could indicate the future. So the whole law of Moses can be said to foreshadow Christ (§348). But in view of man's weakness even this example had to be graduated according to his ability to comprehend it. Therefore, at first simpler commands, such as sacrifices, festivals, and Sabbaths, were enjoined, and later God separated them from these and led them to better things through the prophets (§696).

The preparation of mankind for the complete revelation is frequently discussed by other Armenian theologians. Eznik points out that Christ did not come when the world was young, but at the most opportune moment, after men had been instructed by the prophets and informed by the witnesses to the future continually sent by God (§345–349). Similarly the *Teaching* says that these forewarnings were necessary in order that Christ might not come as one unexpected and unknown. For if He was not received on earth after such indications, how much less would men have realized who He was without such warning (§352). Ps.-Ełišē also says that Moses taught the people and the prophets, the just men of Israel, that the mystery of the secrets of God would be revealed at the coming of Christ.[36] The *Yačaxapatum* takes the theme of types of the future a little further. Not only did the prophets, apostles, patriarchs and other scriptural figures warn and teach men about God's will, but the whole universe was a school (դպրոց)[37] in which his creation revealed the solicitude of the Creator (p. 57). And likewise in the world of affairs, the secular lawcourts are patterns of the divine laws proclaimed by the prophets and scriptures (p. 75). The author of these homilies had a lively sense of the value of material illustrations for the spiritual

life, but he was not so concerned with the types of the Old Testament and their fulfillment in Christ.

If the author of the *Teaching* is careful to explain the meaning of the indications of the coming of Christ given through the prophets, he is not so clear in his explanation of the theology of the redemption and atonement accomplished in Christ. He has a wealth of ideas on this subject, but he presents them in a rather unordered fashion. However, one can see that he has a few central themes to which he frequently returns. These are: the revelation of the Father to men; the destruction of Satan and the freeing of men from sin; and the raising of men to immortality and incorruption.

The first of these themes is the necessary corollary to our author's arguments concerning the partial revelation of Himself which God imparted to the just of Israel. This revelation was a gradual one, made more and more explicit as men's understanding was developed. The process has its culmination in the revelation of the Son in the flesh, for no one has ever seen God in his essence save the Son. Therefore, since the Father and the Son are one, whoever has seen the Son has seen the Father. It was only He who could illuminate the darkened spirits of men and bring joy and light to the souls fallen into the shade (§566), just as it was necessary that He by whom creation was made should hallow it. The shade is the darkness of death, and to the overcoming of death and sin our author devotes the major part of his exposition of men's redemption by Christ.

Men were perishing because of sin. This sin first committed in the body of Adam involved all men and brought them into slavery to Satan and under the debt of death. The author of the *Teaching* seems to have regarded physical birth as the means whereby the debt to death was transmitted from Adam to posterity ("Christ liberated men from birth in sin," §364), but he does not develop this particular argument. Christ healed us from sin, as a doctor heals those perishing from some infirmity; He freed our flesh from sin by Himself taking human flesh;[38] his body released men from slavery to sin as the body of Adam had first brought sin into the world. By his flesh He destroyed Satan and paid the debt for sin. The payment of the debt was effected by the sacrifice of Himself in death as an offering of reconciliation to the Father (§593, 675); by the sacrifice the sentence of death was abolished, and so Christ raised up to life those who had fallen into death (§588). Death, caused by sin, had brought about a breach between men and God. No man could breach this gap since men were in the power of death; only the Son of God, by taking the form of Adam and becoming like one of mankind, could build up what was destroyed and reunite men with God (§591).

---

34. Łazar, *History*, p. 109.

35. Ełišē, *History*, p. 107.

36. Ps.-Ełišē, *On the Passion*, p. 246. On the date of these theological works attributed to Ełišē see H. Lewy, *The Pseudo-Philonic De Jona Part I*, S. D. VII, London 1936, pp. 9–24, and N. Akinean, *Ełišē Vardapet*, III, Vienna 1960, p. 420.

37. Cf. the world as a παιδευτήριον in Clement, *Quis dives*, 33.

38. There is only one word in Armenian, մարմին to render both "flesh" and "body," σάρξ and σῶμα, but occasionally մս is used in the context of communion, e.g., Agatʿangełos, *History*, §719.

To the development of this theme, the reunion of men with God, whose archetype is the scattering of the races of men at the tower of Babel and their gathering together by the cross, our author devotes much attention. He uses a number of expressions to elaborate this idea. Christ's redemption made men like the angels, sons of God, and similar to the image of the Godhead (§364, 587, 588). Men were raised to the divinity of the Son of God, were elevated to heaven, and brought to immortality (§590, 595, 679). Mankind has been completely reborn and renewed, and the earth has been saved from the curse put upon it at the time of Adam's sin (§391). This renewal was effected once and for all by Christ; those who died before his coming He rescued by descending to hell in his body (§368), while those who have not yet been born will by baptism receive a new life and be born again from the womb of baptism as children of the kingdom. But the benefits of this renewal and elevation to heaven are only for the just. They and they alone will share the joy of Christ, since only the righteous are members of the Lord's body (§595).

The *Teaching* describes the reunion of men with God by means of three technical expressions. Christ humbled Himself and joined his divinity to our humanity in order to *link* (անբակ առնել,[39] §385) all mankind to the immortality of his divinity, that they might be *submerged* (ընկղմեալ, §595) in the Godhead, and that He might *join* (խառնել, §385, 679) men to his divinity. This last expression is fundamental to the *Teaching* in the context of both redemption and Christology. It is also used by other Armenian writers with regard to the reunion of men with God,[40] or questions of Christology.[41]

This terminology is paralleled in the discussion in the *Teaching* of the union of God and man in Christ. Some of the frequent references to the human body of Christ have already been noted. It was in the flesh that Christ destroyed Satan, paid the debt for sin, and descended to hell to rescue those there imprisoned (§368, 387). Christ, therefore, was truly born as a man, and this humanity is described in various ways. Most usually our author says that Christ "became man" (եղեւ մարդ, §382, or the verb մարդացաւ, ἐνηνθρώπησεν, §390, 675) or "was born in the flesh" (մարմնով ծնաւ, §391). We also find such expressions as: He took flesh from the virgin (առ զմարմին ի կուսէն, §387, 587), He was enveloped in our human flesh (ի մարդկեղէն մարմինս պատեցաւ, §364), He put on flesh or manhood (զգեցաւ մարմին, §377, 381, զգեցաւ մարդկութիւն, §663), He was restric-

ted or contained in flesh (ամփոփեցաւ ի մարմին, բովանդակեցաւ ի մարմին, §377, compare 379). But the most common such expression in the *Teaching* is: He joined his flesh to his Godhead (խառնեաց զմարմինն ընդ իւր Աստուածութիւն, §369) or vice versa (խառնեաց զ Աստուածութիւն ընդ մարդկութեանս, §385). This term խառնեաց is rather imprecise. It means "to mix, or join," and can be used in various contexts. As noted above, our author employs it often to describe the reunion of men with God effected by Christ, and he finds this expression so congenial that he interpolates it into a quotation from John 14.16: "I shall pray the Father that He may send the Holy Spirit the Intercessor to you, the pledge, *who will join you to the Deity*, who will dwell among you for ever" (§590). In more strictly Christological contexts խառնեաց is frequently combined with other verbs of similar meaning, for example: "He joined and united" (խառնեաց եւ միացոյց, §592), or "joined, united and submerged his flesh to his divinity" (խառնեաց, միացոյց, ընկղմեաց, §378).

The *Teaching* continually emphasizes the flesh or body of Christ (մարմին has both senses), because it was by means of this human body that human nature was saved from sin and reunited to God; in so far as Christ's body was similar to men's, they will be taken up to heaven on account of their being members of the Lord's body (§595). Our author speaks occasionally of the Son of God descending in our likeness (նմանութիւն, §377) and of his moving about in human form (մարդակերպ շրջեցաւ, §390), or of his taking the form of the weakness of human flesh (§381). But this humanity of Christ was no mere appearance; He became a true man (ճշմարիտ մարդ եղեւ, §377), a perfect man (մարդ կատարեալ, §368), and took upon Himself all the circumstances of the flesh (զամենայն անցս մարմնոյն յանձն առեալ, §379). But only once does he say: "He put on our earthly *nature* and joined it to his unmingled divinity" (զմեր հողեղէն բնութիւն զգեցաւ եւ խառնեաց յանխառն Աստուածութիւն, §515), and once: "He was united to the flesh by *nature*" (միացաւ ի մարմին բնութեամբ, §369).

These two uses of the term բնութիւն are exceptional and do not imply any understanding of "two natures," the divine and the human. Such terminology was foreign to fifth-century Armenian theology and was expressly rejected at the first council of Dvin in 505.[42] So we may briefly examine our author's use of the word in other contexts before returning to his Christology.

Nature (բնութիւն) in the *Teaching* refers to "substance" in the secondary Aristotelean sense. Water and fire have their own nature (§453, 544); there is a nature of the fruit tree, that is, a genus, in which individual species are distinguished by taste and smell (§643). One can also refer to the nature

---

39. The abstract noun անբակութիւն is used in §706 to describe the inseparability of the three Persons of the Trinity. It is notable that the *Teaching* frequently uses the same terminology in the different contexts of the Trinity, Christology, and redemption.

40. E.g., Pᶜawstos, III, 14, IV 6.

41. As in the *Yačaxapatum*.

42. The correspondence at the time of this council is preserved in the *Girkᶜ Tᶜłtᶜocᶜ*, pp. 41–51. See also E. Ter Minassiantz, *Die armenische Kirche* (*Texte und Untersuchungen*, n.F., XI Band, 4. Heft), Leipzig 1904, pp. 152–157.

of a specific species, for example of trees (§646), which remains unalterable because trees of that species do not give fruit or bear leaves of a different kind of tree. But "nature" does not refer to an individual tree, nor to an individual man. Hence when our author says: "Christ put on human nature," he does not envisage so much the individual humanity of the historical Jesus, as the characteristics of manhood which the Son of God willingly took upon Himself.

In only one case can "nature" and individual be equated—in God. For the Trinity is a single nature, a single being, and a single hypostasis, who is unalterable and unchanging. So the nature of Christ is his divinity which He does not abandon at the Incarnation. "Although He came down for our sake to humility, yet He remains in his own nature, as He Himself said: 'I am the same and have not changed'" (§378). "Although He came down to our likeness, yet He remains in the glory of his divinity of the Father's nature. As He was, He is, and He remains eternally with his Father on high in his own nature with the flesh which He put on of ours" (§381). "He became a true man and descended to humility that He might raise us up, but in his own divinity He is in heaven and on earth, beside the Father and with the Father" (§377). So those who were scandalized at his flesh denied his nature (§369).

Thus our author does not consider the Incarnation to involve a union of two natures, but he does not deny the reality and completeness of the humanity which Christ took upon Himself for our sake. He insists that Christ became a true and perfect man with all the attendant circumstances of the flesh. But his nature is his divinity, and to this divinity He joined human flesh, which was united to Him naturally (§369). "Christ remains in his own nature with the flesh which He put on."

No other Armenian composition of this period deals so fully with the theology of redemption as the *Teaching*. The three themes discussed above (the revelation of the Father, the destruction of Satan and the freeing of men from sin, and the raising of men to immortality and incorruption) are frequently touched upon in other works but rarely elaborated. In the *Yačaxa-atum*, for example, the same few ideas are repeated in different homilies and can be resumed in the following terms: by removing sin, Christ renewed mankind and opened the door to life (pp. 147, 155); He saved the world from bondage to Satan and by his death destroyed death (pp. 17, 18); by the death of Christ we thus gain immortality and are raised up to live in glory (pp. 18, 65). In addition to the forgiveness of sins, the author also mentions that Christ came to reveal God's love. But these homilies do not pretend to be a complete exposition of the Christian faith; they are primarily concerned with exhortations to a Christian life, and none of these themes is developed to any extent.

Similarly the homilies attributed to John Mandakuni,[43] in contrast to his *Exposition* on the problem of the definition of "nature" as applied to Christ, are primarily devoted to moral exhortation. A few hints in the works attributed to Ełišē point the same way as the *Yačaxapatum*. The redemption of mankind effected by Christ is regarded as the defeat of death whereby everything is made new and we are raised up to God.[44] In his *History* (p. 39) Ełišē explains the purpose of the Incarnation: God came into our humanity in order that we might enter his immortality. Eznik's *De Deo* is a philosophical rather than a theological treatise and does not discuss this question, while the fragment of his letter to Maštocᶜ is concerned only with the Incarnation as a Christological problem.[45] Nor are the replies of Sahak to the letter of Acacius and the *Tome* of Proclus of much help in this regard. In these short letters,[46] which echo each other in several respects such as the opposition of the wood of the cross to the wood of the tree in Paradise, Sahak speaks of the renewal of the old man corrupted by sin through the Incarnation of Christ. But he does not develop any theology of redemption beyond this theme.

We do not find in the earliest writers any detailed exposition of the mode of the Incarnation or of the question of the nature, or natures, of Christ. On this point the homilies attributed to Gregory, the *Yačaxapatum*, are almost silent. They merely tell us that Christ put on our nature and all the circumstances of human nature both of body and soul, save sin (pp. 16, 147). The Word was joined to the body (*իաոռնեայ ի մարմին*, p. 147), as He was united to God by the Spirit. In the early letters preserved in the *Girkᶜ Tᶜłtᶜocᶜ* this subject is only discussed in detail by Eznik and John Mandakuni. The short fragment of Eznik's letter composed shortly after the council of Ephesus insists that Christ was perfect God and perfect man, born as Logos of the Father and as man of the Virgin, and that when the Logos put on human flesh He in no way changed his divine essence (*էնքունթիւն*). These ideas are paralleled in the *Tome* of Proclus, an exposition of faith in the instigation of which Eznik had a hand.[47] Proclus' key motif is "one hypostasis of the incarnate Word," and he emphasizes that when Christ took flesh and appeared as a man (*մարմնացաւ . . . կերպարանացաւ իբրև զմարդ*), there was no diminution of his divinity; Christ remains one and the same.

---

43. Or John Mayragomecᶜi, see note 16 above.
44. Ps-Ełišē, *On the Passion*, pp. 287, 297.
45. *Girkᶜ Tᶜłtᶜocᶜ*, pp. 1–2 line 3; Tallon, *Livre des lettres*, pp. 52–53.
46. *Girkᶜ Tᶜłtᶜocᶜ*, pp. 9–13, 16–18; Tallon, *Livre des lettres*, pp. 34–38, 72–77.
47. Cf. M. Richard, *Acace de Mélitène, Proclus de Constantinople, et la grande Arménie*, *Mémorial Louis Petit*, Bucharest 1948, pp. 393–412; Tallon, *Livre des lettres*, p. 51; K. Sarkissian, *The Council of Chalcedon and the Armenian Church*, London 1965, p. 227.

Half a century later, when the controversy over the use of the term "nature" was more acute, John Mandakuni composed his *Demonstration* in which he analyzed the meaning of this word and the legitimacy of its application to Christ. This is one of the most sober and erudite of the many such works composed by Armenians, and John brings several nuances to the discussion which the *Teaching*, for example, had not distinguished. The use of the expression "two natures" is foreign to the first Armenian writers, but it is interesting to follow through some of the earlier ideas to the more developed theology of John Mandakuni.

John recognizes that the term "nature" has different connotations. One can speak of the natures of the body, of the soul, and of the mind, and these are all different; yet man is not many, but one. Similarly, the many names of Christ do not involve several persons (*երիւք*) or natures, but only one Lord. Ecclesiastical tradition, summed up at Nicaea, speaks of the single nature of the Son who is of the essence of his Father, so John can say that the Son is of the same nature as the Father. Hence the name of the Son is his divinity. But this term is not scriptural, so John suggests that "life" would be more appropriate to indicate the single personality of Christ (*Girk Tᶜltᶜocᶜ*, p. 34). John thus realizes that "nature" does not necessarily mean "person," but this traditional identification of the two terms is still influential enough to lead him to stress that the acts of Christ can be ascribed to only one nature, for the Lord is one. The Incarnation is thus to be conceived as the indivisible union of Logos and flesh, but the subject of discourse is always the divine Word. The Logos was incarnate, became a man, and was united to the flesh, and this flesh is said to be the flesh of the Word by a true union (p. 39). But the Word did not become flesh by nature, for then the flesh would be the Word, which is ridiculous (p. 37). So Christ was by will and not by nature in the flesh; He is God with the flesh, and with this same body (for Armenian does not distinguish "flesh" and "body") He will come again.

The *Demonstration* is more closely reasoned than the *Teaching* or any of the other works mentioned above, but its author has not parted from the usual view of the earliest Armenian writers. "Nature" is a term applicable to the condition of being a mortal, and so it is permissible to say that Christ put on human nature, meaning that He took upon Himself all the characteristics of a man. But Christ is a unity, a single Person, the incarnate Word, and since "nature" means the subject of discourse, He is one nature and that nature is his divinity. These ideas are echoed in Ełišē. He insists that Christ was true God and true man without detracting from either his divinity or his humanity. Christ is a unity and not a duality (*միութիւն եւ ոչ երկութիւն*); He took our complete nature, with body, soul, and spirit, and united it with his divinity.[48]

48. Ełišē, *History*, pp. 37, 87.

The expression "united" was traditional in Armenian theology, but John Mandakuni explicitly rejected any idea of "natural union." "If the Word became flesh by nature, the flesh would be the Word." For him the union can only be said to be a true one: "The flesh is the flesh of the Word ... not in appearance but by a true union" (*ճշմարիտ միաւորութեամբ*, p. 39). The early Armenian theologians did not go further than this.

In its theology of redemption and in its Christology, the *Teaching* is typical of early Armenian Christian thought. It is also typical in its emphasis on repentance as the means whereby the benefits for men gained once and for all by Christ at his death can be appropriated and each man's salvation assured. Here two ideas are interconnected: the idea of the church and the idea of repentance and forgiveness. We may first examine the former.

We have already mentioned the importance of the Old Testament types for the author of the *Teaching*, not only prophetic utterances but also historical events in the life of Israel. Of these types none is more central to his thought than the contrast between the tower of Babel and the cross: from the one came confusion and scattering, and by the other the scattered races are reunited and brought back to God. But this reunion is at the present moment a potential one only; it will be realized in the future, before the end of the present millennium, which is the sixth after the creation. But even then not all men will be united with Christ to enjoy the seventh millennium of rest and peace, for some will reject Him and be cast into eternal hell. The great importance of the church, therefore, is in making the potential actual, in bringing the message of salvation to all men so that they will have the opportunity to accept it and be saved. So it is not surprising to find parallels in the *Teaching* between the scattered races and the role of the apostles. Since at the tower mankind was divided into seventy-two races each with its own patriarch, seventy-two disciples were chosen by Christ to go to the ends of the earth and preach the gospel.[49] The scattered races all spoke different languages, so the disciples were given the gift of tongues by the Spirit. And our author stresses frequently the unity of the church in opposition to the confusion of disobedient mankind.

The significance of the Holy Spirit is to be seen in this work of the church, which is a true continuation of Christ's own work. The Spirit was revealed in the Old Testament and spoke through the prophets, but not until Pentecost was He made fully manifest. From then on the Spirit guided the church in the true path and explained the complete significance of the life and deeds of Christ (§505). The way in which the Spirit was revealed at Pentecost is also significant, for the fire is a symbol of the fire preserved for the wicked (§507), of the fire which burns away sins to purify the bodies of the just

49. On the number 72 see note 1 to §503.

(§586, but compare 602), and of the furnace in which first the disciples and then all men are tested.

In one sense the church is a new creation, begun at Pentecost when the disciples became vessels of the Holy Spirit. This life of the Spirit in the church appears as a new phenomenon in the history of mankind, although the Spirit had not been inactive before. But the *Teaching* emphasizes the continuation of the old Israel to the new rather than the novelty of the Christian church. The vital link in the continuation of this tradition is John the Baptist.

In times past the prophets had revealed God's will to the Israelites in so far as they had been able to comprehend it, but John was greater than any of his predecessors. He was sent immediately before Christ revealed Himself in order to prepare the people for the manifestation of the Son of God, and this preparation he effected not merely by preaching, but by baptizing his hearers with the baptism of repentance. Just as in the time of Moses God ordered the Israelites to wash and purify themselves before He appeared to them, so when Christ revealed Himself after waiting thirty years from his birth, John was commanded to purify the people that they might become worthy to receive the Lord. Christ Himself submitted to this baptism, setting an example for the Christian baptism into eternal life. But Christ's baptism had a greater significance than this for it marked the transition between the old and the new covenants.

Because of his role as forerunner of Christ, and because he was entrusted with the tradition of prophecy which belonged to the race of Israel, John can be called the greatest of the prophets. But he was more. For being of the tribe of Levi, he was heir to the priesthood of Israel and also to the kingship. The tradition of prophecy, priesthood, and kingship had been first given by God to Moses; Moses then made the silver horn of unction from which were anointed in succession the prophets, priests, and kings of Israel. The mystery of this unction, a type of the anointing of Christ, was preserved in the seed of Abraham until John, who thus became the keeper of the tradition handed down over successive generations from his forefathers. This tradition of prophecy, priesthood, and kingship he gave to Jesus Christ at his baptism.

So three factors combine to give Christ's baptism a very special significance. It is the first revelation to the world of Jesus as the Son of God, confirmed by the descent of the Spirit and the voice of the Father; by his own baptism Christ purified the water of Christian baptism, making it an instrument of salvation, a visible symbol of invisible rebirth (§412–415, compare 552); and at his baptism He received the tradition of prophecy, priesthood, and kingship, the special grace of God to the old Israel, which He then passed on to his disciples and they to the new Israel, the church. The church,

therefore, is both new and old, being the heir to the ancient promises and gifts of God, and being the means whereby the Spirit now works in the world completing the work of Christ.

But the church does not merely look forward to the time when all scattered races will have been reunited by the cross and the seventh millennium will have arrived. Already in their present lives Christians are members of the body of Christ and at their death share in his joy, for Christ loves his church as a groom his bride. Furthermore, the church is the guarantee of the authentic faith taught in the holy scriptures by the Spirit (§361). The apostles, basing themselves on the gospel and prophets, composed letters to serve as future norms for the church and elaborated on them with oral explanations (§700). The tradition of the gospel was established in four accounts by the evangelists, who did not add anything of their own but were illuminated by special revelation (§701–702). No one may add to the inspired books; they now form a closed collection. The only other source of authority in the church is canon law as established by apostolic synods (§389, 699).

The church was founded by the apostles, who received the grace of prophecy, priesthood, and knowledge of heavenly mysteries from the Lord. Their leader was Peter, and because he realized that Jesus was Christ, Son of the Living God, he was made the rock on which the church was founded. But the *Teaching* does not elaborate on the primacy of Peter; its author is more concerned with the whole college of apostles and their universal missionary work. The keys of the kingdom were given to *all* the apostles (§468); they divided the nations among themselves and spread throughout the world. In the course of their journeys the apostles worked many signs and miracles, but the real purpose of their preaching was twofold: to inform their hearers about the dispensation of the Word, and to test them as in a furnace.

The apostles were the first to be freed from this earthly order and to be given knowledge of the heavenly mysteries. The special knowledge which was vouchsafed to them was an understanding of the Trinity, of the three Persons in one consubstantial being, worshipped as one Lord (§623, 662). In the name of the Trinity they baptized all peoples, thereby bringing forth the world anew by water and the Spirit. By baptism they delivered all men from the bonds of darkness, sealed all nations as Christ's, and united the world in saying "Abba, Father"; then by eating the flesh of the Son of God and drinking his life-giving blood, all could become fellow heirs of Christ and sons of God by adoption. This teaching the apostles introduced gradually, having regard to the ability of their hearers to understand it. Just as Christ first instructed with simple words and symbols and with miracles of healing and afterwards spoke the truth quite frankly, so did the apostles proceed in Gentile lands (§696, 698).

But the message of the gospel was not confined to an exposition of the Trinity and baptism. More vital for those to whom the apostles were preaching than their passive acceptance was their repentance, for without repentance there could be no salvation.

Repentance was the keynote of John the Baptist's message. The preaching of Christ began with the same theme: Repent, for the kingdom of God is at hand; unless you are converted you cannot enter the kingdom of God; the times are now fulfilled, so believe in the gospel (§446–467). Christ opened the doors to repentance, instituting baptism as the means of entry to the kingdom. Whoever does not believe in the Son of God is condemned and has no second chance, nor is there any possibility of renewal a second time by baptism (§454–455). The urgency of the message is stressed in the *Teaching* for a man can only make his decision once, and he must make this decision as soon as the choice is offered him.

This choice our author describes in an involved and frequently repeated simile of two cups: one is the cup of joy, of sweet wine of the Spirit, the other is a bitter cup of fire, of retribution for sin, and of death.[50] The latter is prepared for the wicked to drink, that their lips and souls may burn and be consumed in hell. The first cup gives wisdom, not foolishness, mercy, not anger, faith, not unbelief; it also is fiery, but its fire burns away the rust of sins and purifies the soul (§508–510). The wine pourers are the apostles and their successors. Christ sent his twelve throughout the world as cup bearers, and the apostles sent witnesses to the Armenians, thirty-seven who were martyred. So this is the opportunity that the Armenians must take to cast off their former ignorance and drink the cup of salvation. They will be aided by the prayers of the martyrs, whose bodies are temples of God in their midst (§564, 572), and who showed the truth of their message not only by mere words but by miracles—that is by the torments which fell on the king and his country as punishments for their death. The Armenians can be reconciled with God by the intercession of the martyrs and the Spirit who dwells in their bones, for their sacrifice of themselves is an imitation of the sacrifice of the Son of God, and they gave themselves to death in return for his death on behalf of all mankind.

The position of the Armenians may be particularly critical, our author suggests, because they had put to death those who had brought the gospel to them. But all men's condition is the same, for as soon as they have been warned of the fearsome fire which awaits them, they must cast off the bonds of paganism and free themselves from past sins. God certainly wished all men to become his heirs; He invites everyone to the kingdom and Himself frees them from slavery to sin, guides them on the right path, and helps all

to know Him (§573–574). He opened the door of forgiveness to all kinds and conditions of men, without distinction of race, including the worst sinners like tax collectors, harlots, and brigands—even his own crucifiers (§695).

So men must take care not to abandon what has been promised, for there will be no hope for them if they do. Before they can receive the seed which will give fruit, they must root out from their souls the weeds of sin, take account of themselves, and give up idolatry (§520–522). If they are obstinate and persist in their ignorance, eternal torments will be their lot. For if they do not repent now, when they hear the message, it will be too late. There is no repentance in hell (§535). The time of this world is drawing to a close. Within the present millennium the gospel will have been carried to all corners of the earth, and all men will have had an opportunity to repent and be converted. Then will occur the second coming of the Lord, when He will usher in the seventh millennium of eternal rest for the righteous and eternal torments for the wicked.

But before considering our author's conception of the last things, we may turn to other Armenian theologians' doctrines of repentance, for repentance is a constant theme of early Armenian theology. It was a necessary theme, for it signified the rejection of a heathen past and the turning to Christ. In later times repentance and confession became a more disciplined aspect of Armenian church life[51] but continued to form one of the most notable branches of Armenian theological writing. The beginnings of a systematic approach to the subject may be seen in the homilies attributed to Gregory, the *Yačaxapatum*, the nineteenth of which contains instructions on repentance and confession in a schema of ten stages. But of more direct interest to our present enquiry is the attitude of the author of these homilies to repentance in general, for his thought shows many similarities to that of the *Teaching*.

He speaks of repentance in two contexts: baptism, and confession for sins committed after baptism. He cannot conceive of salvation without repentance and confession and usually considers these as the necessary prelude to baptism and communion; only by sincere repentance with tears (and the importance of tears as the outward guarantee of inward contrition is often emphasized) can a man escape from the anger to come. Although a man can only be baptized once, and it is in connection with baptism that most of this author's remarks about confession are made, he may again fall into sin; and if any one die in sin, then the laws of God do not forget his evildoing, and he is condemned for ever. For there can be no repentance in hell, and if a man has not confessed his sins on or before he comes to his deathbed, he has no hope. Only those who die in childhood, exempt from the temptations of earthly souls, will be saved without repentance.

---

50. On the origin of this simile see note 1 to §508.

51. See the Introduction to C. J. F. Dowsett, *The Penitential of David of Ganjak*, CSCO 217, Louvain 1961.

The dire consequences of an unrepentant death are frequently mentioned in the *Yačaxapatum* and have a direct connection with the author's views on the judgment of the last day. Man's salvation depends entirely on his conduct in this world and his confession of sins committed during his life on earth. Although the prayers of the saints are efficacious in several respects, they cannot sway the judgment of God on a sinner. At death a man's body is laid in the ground where it awaits the general resurrection while his soul is taken up to heaven. If he has been virtuous his soul will be led before God by the angels and saints with psalms and spiritual songs; such souls will rest in Christ, enjoy the vision of God, and have a dwelling place in heaven according to their individual merits. These disembodied souls wait in the hope of the future glory which they will attain when, at the general resurrection, their bodies will rise from the earth; reunited to these glorious bodies they will become as the angels and be admitted to eternal light and felicity. On the other hand, the evil are condemned to torments the moment they die, and when their bodies also arise at the general resurrection, the judgment on them that day will merely confirm their assignment to eternal punishment. The importance of repentance and confession, therefore, can hardly be overemphasized, for there is no second chance after death. These ideas were common to all early Armenian theologians. In the homilies attributed to John Mandakuni there is a similar stress on the fear of hell and the urgency of repentance.

We have already briefly touched upon the doctrine of the last things in the *Teaching* and shown how closely it is connected with the author's emphasis on repentance. We may now develop this in more detail and describe the ideas of the *Teaching* on the second coming and the general resurrection.

God's creative activity as described in Genesis is paralleled by the efforts of men on earth to attain the goal reserved for the righteous. Just as creation began on the first day and was completed on the sixth, so God has measured six thousand years for the toils of the world. This parallel was clearly seen by the prophet who said: "A thousand years in the eyes of the Lord are as the passing of a single day." During the sixth age God's plan for his creation was fulfilled by the renewal of the world effected by the coming of Christ and the descent of the Holy Spirit. In the same period of a thousand years the end will come, but the exact time of this is a mystery. Then for those who worked in the six ages of the time of the earth there will be the seventh age, an age of rest for the just which will be without limit or end (§670).

The seventh millennium will be ushered in by the second coming of Christ. The moment of this is unknown to men; it will be sudden and unexpected, but there will be warnings in the form of signs. Our author quotes the predictions of Christ and adds that the special sign of the Son of man in the heavens will be a shining cross which will fill the whole earth with its light. Then Christ will come with fire and anger to judge all races and make retribution (§471). He will take his beloved by the hand and bring his own to heaven (§713–714). When the Creator will be revealed again (Christ is called creator in as much as all three Persons of the Trinity acted together in creating the world), then the apostles who were tested and proved will reign with Him in an eternal kingdom. At the second coming of Christ will also occur the general resurrection. Then men's minds and bodies, which had been lying in tombs, will spring up; each one's spirit, which after his death had been separated from his body, will return to him and he will receive his original likeness, bones, flesh, sinews, and all other parts of his body being clothed with skin and hair. All men's good works will be apparent, as they will show them in their crowns, flowers for the just and thorns for the sinners. Likewise in the tombs before the resurrection flowers will have grown around the just, but thorns around the sinful.

Our author does not explain what form the judgment will take, but he clearly regards it as based on the works of men while they were still alive. There can be no repentance after death, and there is a strict dichotomy between the good and the wicked with no hope of rehabilitation or improvement in their fate for the latter. They are consigned to eternal torments. But the just will strip off all ephemeral impurities from their bodies as a snake sloughs off its skin, and like doves they will fly up to heaven (§602 ff.). This idea is combined with the conception of the last day found in Paul's first epistle to the Thessalonians, where those who are still alive at the second coming will be caught up with the dead in the clouds to meet the Lord in the air. Then the saints will fly up to heaven, and the angels will not recognize them. But the Lord will explain that they are those who hoped in Him and will lead them to his hill of holiness and to his temple to rejoice. The just will enjoy eternal felicity in paradise near to God in both a physical and spiritual sense and be admitted to those ineffable gifts which God has prepared for those who love Him.

We have noted in the preceding pages the intertwining of the three themes prominent in the *Teaching* and typical of early Christian catechetical instruction: dogmatic instruction, proof by Old Testament exegesis, and exhortation to repentance. We have also seen some parallels, both in terminology and in substance, to the main ideas of the *Teaching* in other Armenian writers of the fifth and sixth centuries. It remains to examine more closely the immediate sources of the *Teaching* and to attempt to date it more precisely.

Our author never mentions by name, nor does he even allude to indirectly, other Christian writers. The only sources to which he refers specifically are books of the Bible. Here he names a majority of the books he uses: Moses

(for the Pentateuch), Joshua, the books of Kings, Job, the Psalter,[52] the book of Wisdom,[53] Ecclesiastes,[54] Isaiah, Jeremiah, Ezechiel, Daniel, Amos, Micah, Zechariah. A quotation from Baruch is ascribed to Daniel (§398), and six of the minor prophets are cited simply as "the prophet" (Hosea, Joel, Nahum, Zephaniah, Haggai, Malachi). Of the New Testament, the four evangelists are distinguished but only Luke and John by name.[55] The book of Acts is ascribed to Luke, and Paul is frequently mentioned as author of the epistles;[56] of the Catholic epistles Peter and John are named.[57] It is noticeable that in quoting the scriptures our author very frequently assimilates several passages into one. His memory confuses similar quotations, especially from the prophets and psalms, and he naturally runs together different accounts of the same episode from the gospels.

But if the author of the *Teaching* often takes a free hand in assimilating scriptural quotations, when it comes to exegesis his interpretations are usually traditional. Only once does he hesitate and suggest that "perhaps" his own explanation is intended.[58] But his originality does come out in the development and expansion of his borrowed material.

The first part of the *Teaching* is concerned with the history of Israel up to the coming of Christ (§259–368). But its author does not deal equally with all periods as reflected in the books of the Old Testament; he merely takes those episodes which are important for his larger theme. The period from Adam to Moses he expounds in greatest detail; the judges and kings are dismissed in two paragraphs; and then the visions and sayings of the prophets receive greater attention. In this first section the author of the *Teaching* has relied primarily on the commentaries of John Chrysostom on Genesis, but only as background material helpful in the interpretation of

---

52. At §560 the tenth psalm is mentioned by number, at §500 the forty-ninth.

53. As at §523; at §278 its author is called "the sage."

54. §658: "the hymns of inspired wisdom of the Song of Solomon." The Song is not elsewhere mentioned by name, though quoted at length in §440.

55. The four gospels are but one tradition, §701. At §710 John is called "the theologian," see note ad loc. Lyonnet notes that the references to Luke and John may be interpolations, and that "tout se passe à peu près comme s'il utilisait pour ses citations évangéliques un diatessaron," *Les origines de la version arménienne et le Diatessaron, Biblica et Orientalia,* 13, Rome 1950, pp. 68–71. The suggestion is plausible, but our author did not use Tatian's *Diatessaron* as a model for his account of Jesus' life (see below, p. 31), and a comparison between the tables of gospel quotations in the *Teaching* (below, pp. 191–197) and in the *Diatessaron* (Leloir, *Commentaire,* S.C. 121, pp. 415–424) shows that the *Teaching* uses many verses not found in Tatian.

56. Including III Corinthians; see note 1 to §280. By name are mentioned: (I) Corinthians, (I) Thessalonians, Hebrews. Quoted, but not by name, are: Romans, II Corinthians ("the Gentiles" §439), Galatians, Ephesians, Philippians, II Thessalonians, II Timothy, Titus.

57. I and II Peter are quoted, but only I John. James is quoted, but not by name.

58. At §486, commenting on Isaiah 26.19, see note ad loc.

---

certain themes. He has made his own choice and ordering of material and has drawn on a wide range of reading in the Greek Fathers, notably the *Hexaemeron* of Basil and the *Catecheses* of Cyril of Jerusalem.

At §392 the faith is summarized in apparently credal form. But the clauses used refer only to the three Persons of the Trinity and are far more full and more varied than any liturgical creed. However, it is noticeable that when referring to the Father the *Teaching* follows the credal order: God, Father, Lord, Creator. But with reference to the Son no such clear order is followed, and many different expressions for the Incarnation are employed. Since the descent into hell is mentioned, but not the burial, our author cannot have been strictly influenced by the creeds of Nicaea, Jerusalem, or Constantinople. His varying ideas on the procession of the Spirit[59] also indicate that no one model was paramount in his mind. His thoughts on the church, baptism, the resurrection and life to come are expressed in noncredal form, and so although most clauses of the three creeds could be paralleled in the *Teaching,* it would be impossible to reconstruct a hypothetical creed which its author might be considered to be expounding.

From §391 to 497 the *Teaching* follows a chronological order in describing the earthly life of Jesus from his birth to ascension. The exposition is eclectic, but there is no trace of the use of the *Diatessaron* as a model. Not only does the *Teaching* include episodes (as the circumcision) omitted by Tatian and omit others included in the *Diatessaron* (as the temptation), but it omits all but a few details between the baptism and the passion and expands at great length those episodes its author considers important for his own argument.[60] As in the first section he relies particularly on Cyril of Jerusalem. His wide acquaintance with patristic traditions is indicated by the parallels not only with the Cappadocian Fathers and Origen but also with the earlier Apostolic Fathers and Irenaeus.

From §489 to 586 the *Teaching* concentrates on the coming of the Holy Spirit and the activity of the apostles as missionaries. Central to this section is the simile of the two cups, which depends on a combination of Origen's exegesis of Jeremiah 25 with the theme of the "two ways,"[61] interwoven with exhortations to repentance and warnings of God's punishment of sinners. Again the closest parallels are with the *Catecheses* of Cyril of Jerusalem. From §587 our author recapitulates in slightly different ways the main lines of his previous argument. From §685 to the end he gives further details of the apostles' missionary journeys and the writing down of the gospels

---

59. See above, p. 13.

60. Although the *Diatessaron* of Tatian did not serve as the basis for the chronological exposition in the *Teaching,* its *text* was certainly influential in the gospel quotations; see the important work of Lyonnet, *Diatessaron.*

61. See note 1 to §508.

and epistles. In these sections he continues to draw on the sources he had used previously.

Although parallels can be found for much of the subject matter of the *Teaching*, the ordering of the whole is highly original. It is usually difficult to point to specific sources for most of the author's ideas, as he often drew from traditional material common to many writers. However, certain works do seem to have exercised a discernable influence upon him. Foremost among these are the *Catecheses* of Cyril of Jerusalem.

These catechetical homilies were delivered in the church of the Holy Sepulchre at Jerusalem in the year 348. The introductory lecture and the first eighteen were given in Lent before baptism on Holy Saturday; a further five (if authentic) were delivered to the newly baptized during the following Easter week. These homilies form an inestimable source for the traditional teaching given to catechumens, being a consecutive exposition of the creed of Jerusalem. They were known in Armenia and translated into Armenian. The last five, which have been challenged as not being authentically Cyril's, were not included in this translation.[62]

The influence of Jerusalem, however, was greater in Armenia with regard to the development of liturgical practice, notably the lectionary.[63] It is therefore primarily as the authority in establishing festivals and lections that Cyril is mentioned by Armenian theologians. But it is remarkable that he is only once named before the latter half of the sixth century. Łazar in his letter to Vahan, when speaking of his Greek studies, lists Athanasius, the two Cyrils of Alexandria and Jerusalem, Basil of Caesarea, Gregory Nazianzenus (the theologian), and the Armenian Gregory the Illuminator.[64] In this context the *Catecheses* are more likely to be in Łazar's mind than the lections. Three extracts from these *Catecheses* were included in the seventh century *Knikc Hawatoy*.[65] John Awjnecci in his *Synodal Oration* delivered at the council of Dvin in 719 noted that Cyril correlated his *Catecheses* with the

order of scriptural readings.[66] With these exceptions Cyril seems to have been known only for his role in ordering the lectionary, which is first mentioned in Armenia by the Catholicos John II (557–574) in his work *On the Epiphany of Christ*: "Cyril of Jerusalem, versed in rhetorical skill and full of the Holy Spirit, who inveighed against and reproved all sects and their lawless synods from Simon Magus to his own day, and confirmed the festivals and lections and psalms set by the holy apostles, and authoritatively established the memorials of prophets, apostles, and martyrs, and set as chief of the feasts the Epiphany, which had been established by the holy apostles, did not say that the Nativity [was] before the Epiphany, but that they were one and the same."[67]

The reference to Cyril's antiheretical activities may be a reflection of his attendance at the second ecumenical council (Constantinople 381). Moses Xorenacci mentions this (III 13), and also knows of Cyril's vision of the luminous cross over Jerusalem. Moses Daxuranci echoes the remarks of John II, that Cyril prescribed readings and celebrated the Nativity and Epiphany on January 6; he also mentions Cyril's vision and his letter to Constantine.[68]

In view of this dearth of early references to Cyril one may doubt whether his *Catecheses* were commonly known in Armenia before their quotation in the seventh century *Knikc Hawatoy*. But that the translation predates the catena is probable, for the text of the latter shows various corruptions of the Greek most easily explicable from a previous Armenian text.[69] This Armenian version has been dated to the fifth century by its editors and by Akinean.[70] Lyonnet notes the similarity of language between the Armenian versions of the *Catecheses* and of the homilies of Chrysostom on Matthew, both of which he attributes to the earliest period of Armenian literature.[71]

---

62. See W. J. Swaans, *A propos des "Catéchèses mystagogiques" attribuées à S. Cyrille de Jérusalem*, Le Muséon, 55 (1942), pp. 1–43, and the review of Peeters, *Analecta Bollandiana*, 61 (1943), p. 270; also Lyonnet, *Diatessaron*, pp. 111–114.

63. See B. Botte, *Le Lectionnaire arménien et la fête de la Théotocos à Jérusalem au Vᵉ siècle*, Sacris Erudiri, 2 (1949), pp. 111–122; A. Renoux, *Un Manuscrit du lectionnaire arménien de Jérusalem*, Le Muséon, 74 (1961), pp. 361–385; idem, *Lectionnaires arméniens et commémoraison de la sépulture du Christ le vendredi saint*, L'Orient syrien, 7 (1962), pp. 463–476; idem, *L'Epiphanie à Jérusalem au IVᵉ et Vᵉ siècle d'après le lectionnaire arménien de Jérusalem*, Revue des études arméniennes, n.s. II (1965), pp. 343–359.

64. Łazar, *History*, p. 192. But Łazar is implying that he read Cyril in Greek, though presumably the Armenian text of Agatcangełos. A Cyril is mentioned in the canons attributed to John Mandakuni, *Kanonagirkc*, I, p. 496, but it is not clear who is meant. Since Zenob is named in the same canon, it can hardly date before the eighth century.

65. *Knikc Hawatoy*, p. 22 = Cyril, *Cat.*, XI 17, p. 264 = XIII 18, p. 306 = XIII 5–6. On the *Knikc Hawatoy* see note 10 above.

66. John Awjnecci, *Opera* (Armenian and Latin), Venice 1834, p. 27: Cyrillus Ierosolymitanus episcopus catechumenorum canonem (կանոնն) illustravit, et iuxta singula fidei verba lectiones ex divinis scripturis item una simul coniunxit apposuitque. John goes on to say that these rubrics had fallen into disuse because of the increase in infant baptism and urges their reintroduction.

67. *Girkc Tcłtcocc*, p. 88.

68. *Sic*, a common confusion for Constantius, Moses Dasxuranci, II 33 (see also II 50, III 14). On this letter see J. Vogt, *Berichte über Kreuzeserscheinungen aus dem 4. Jahrhundert n. Chr.*, Annuaire de l'Institut de philologie et d'histoire orientales et slaves, 9 (1949), pp. 593–606.

69. E.g., Cyril, XI 17 νομίζειν: Arm. version կարծել, Knikc կարել. XIII 6 πιών: Arm. version արբեալ, Knikc առեալ.

70. N. Akinean, *Hay Matenagrutcean Oskedarə*, Handēs Amsorya, 46 (1932), col. 121. But Peeters doubted this early date, without giving his reasons for doing so, Analecta Bollandiana, 61 (1943), p. 270.

71. Lyonnet, *Diatessaron*, p. 111.

Whether or not this Armenian version of the *Catecheses* was known to the author of the *Teaching* is impossible to say, as he never quotes them verbatim. But since he evinces such a wide acquaintance with patristic literature he must have had a good knowledge of Greek, and so we cannot prove that the Armenian version was already made by his time from his knowledge of Cyril's ideas. It is, however, noteworthy that the parallels in the *Teaching* are only with passages from the first eighteen homilies, not with the five "mystagogical" sermons, which are included in neither the Syro–Palestinian nor the Armenian versions, and whose authenticity is suspect.

In addition to Cyril, the author of the *Teaching* had a special debt to John Chrysostom. As with Cyril, it is surprising that Chrysostom is rarely mentioned by name by early Armenian writers. Many of his commentaries were translated into Armenian in the fifth century,[72] and quotations appear in the *Knik° Hawatoy*. He was also known from excerpts in the catena of Timothy Aelurus, translated into Armenian before 555,[73] but his name does not appear in the *Girk° T°ltoc°* before letters of the seventh century. The enigmatic Moses Xorenac°i (III 57) has Atticus, Patriarch of Constantinople (405–425), write to Sahak bishop of the Armenians, accusing him of neglecting the teachings of John Chrysostom. This letter follows one supposedly sent by Theodosius the Emperor to Sahak in which he blames Sahak for turning to the Syrians for help in inventing the Armenian alphabet and announces that he has enrolled Mesrop among the foremost teachers. The letter of Atticus expands this to say that Mesrop was ordained ἐκκλησιαστικός. Moses here depends on Koriun (IX 2), and the reference to Chrysostom is most implausible, as Atticus was shunned by the followers of the late patriarch. Whatever the date of Moses' *History*,[74] it is slim evidence for the popularity or otherwise of Chrysostom's works in the entourage of Sahak and Maštoc°.

In fact there is very little direct evidence of which works were translated by the first school of translators, the disciples of Maštoc° who were sent to Syrian and Byzantine centres of learning to study Syriac and Greek and to make translations from the Fathers. Koriun is cryptic in his remarks (XVI 1): Sahak and Mesrop "set to work translating and composing according to their previous custom, being anxious to improve the standard of education of their nation." He adds (XVI 2) that Sahak and Mesrop sent Joseph and Eznik to Edessa to translate the traditions of the Syrian Fathers from Syriac

72. Akinean, *Handēs Amsorya*, 46 (1932), col. 119–120.
73. *Timotheus Älurus' Widerlegung*, ed. K. Ter-Mekerttschian and E. Ter-Minassiantz, Leipzig 1908. On the date of its translation into Armenian see Garitte, *Narratio*, pp. 163–165.
74. On the disputed date of Moses see C. Toumanoff, *Studies in Christian Caucasian History*, Georgetown 1963, pp. 330–334.

into Armenian. Joseph and Eznik then proceeded to Greek territory, where they became translators of Greek. Later Łevond and Koriun went to Constantinople (XVI 4), where they met Eznik. They returned to Armenia with accurate copies of the scriptures and traditions of "many" Fathers and the canons of Nicaea and Ephesus. From these copies Sahak corrected the first translation of the scriptures (XVI 5) and translations of scriptural commentaries were made. But Koriun does not say whose commentaries these were. Nor does Moses Xorenac°i, in his account of the translation of the scriptures and patristic works from Greek and Syriac, give any clue as to which Fathers and which works were translated. It is indeed remarkable that no Armenian writer before Łazar mentions by title or author translations of any of those Fathers who were regarded as authoritative. Dating of the many translations made in the fifth century depends on internal criteria of style and language and on the traditions preserved in manuscript colophons.[75]

But so far as the *Teaching* is concerned the lack of precise information about the translated Fathers is no disadvantage. There is no doubt that our author was personally acquainted with Greek, and with little question Syriac also, witness the wide range of borrowed material which has been reworked in his own fashion.[76]

Such extensive knowledge of Greek and Syriac literature in an Armenian author of the fifth century is neither surprising nor unusual. From the moment of the final elaboration of the Armenian alphabet schools were established, pupils trained, and a concerted drive begun to make available in Armenian the principal treasures of earlier and contemporary Christian literature. This activity was directed by Sahak and Maštoc°, but the key role was played by younger men, the elite of contemporary Armenian intellectuals, who were sent to the centers of Greek and Syrian Christian culture in order to learn Greek and Syriac. The activities of the most famous of these are known to us from the biography of Maštoc° composed by Koriun, himself one of that band of scholars. There must have been many others who collaborated in the work for such a large body of translations to have been made in so short a time. The similarity of style in much of this translated material points to a common training among these men, a centralizing influence attributable to Sahak and Maštoc°. Among this group of scholars, the first school of translators, most probably should be included the author of the *Teaching*, in which case the catechism cannot predate the thirties or forties of the fifth century.

Such a date is compatible with the internal evidence of the sources used

75. A list of fifth-century translations, based on criteria of style, has been drawn up by Akinean, see note 70 above.
76. Cf. L. Mariès, *Le De Deo d'Eznik de Kolb* (extrait de la *Revue des études arméniennes*, 4), Paris 1924, pp. 34–92.

by our author, yet it is surprising that the *Teaching* contains no obvious reflection of the debate raging among Armenian theologians of the time concerning the propriety of reading Theodore of Mopsuestia, and the successful efforts of Acacius of Melitene and Proclus of Constantinople in bringing the decisions of Ephesus to bear in Armenia.[77] Such questions of Christology as disturbed Eznik[78] were of no concern to the author of the *Teaching*. Only in the matter of the procession of the Holy Spirit are influences discernible in the *Teaching* of contemporary thinking.[79] In other respects its theology is pre-Ephesus.

The precise purpose of the *Teaching* is not immediately apparent. It is clear that "Agathangelos" has remodeled earlier material (oral tradition rather than written sources) which consisted of the life of Gregory and the martyrdom of Rhipsimē and her companions. It is also clear that the *History* is designed to glorify the site of the national cathedral at Vałaršapat, to link Gregory with the place of the martyr's shrines, although the center of Armenian Christianity in Gregory's own day was in the West at Aštišat. By means of the famous vision (§731–755) divine authority for the building of the main cathedral and the two churches of St. Rhipsimē and St. Gaianē was obtained; consequently, the site of the cathedral was later named Ējmiacin ("the Only-begotten descended"). It is no coincidence that the only two fixed dates in the *History* are the martyrdom of Rhipsimē and Gregory's vision. The *History*, therefore, must be subsequent to the establishment of Vałaršapat as the see of the Armenian Patriarchate in the early fifth century. Its purpose was to give this see a divine foundation.[80]

Within this framework the *Teaching* plays no integral part, yet it is difficult to suppose that a section which is longer than the rest of the book together was included fortuitously. A solution to the problem may be found, however, in the debt owed by Agathangelos to Koriun. This dependence was first emphasized by Gutschmid nearly a century ago,[81] and the editors of the critical edition of the *History* have established the extent of the correspondence.[82] Agathangelos clearly used material from Koriun in order to present Gregory as a forerunner of Maštoc᷄ and to give his hero the credit for

77. It was the younger generation of Armenian scholars, including Eznik, who urged Proclus to send his *Tome* to the Armenian bishops, which arrived as a surprise to Sahak and Maštoc᷄; cf. note 47.

78. In his letter, to Maštoc᷄, *Girk᷄ Tᶜłtᶜoc᷄*, pp. 1–2 line 3; cf. Tallon, *Livre des Lettres*, pp. 50 ff.

79. See p. 13 above.

80. Cf. Peeters, *S. Grégoire l'Illuminateur, Analecta Bollandiana*, 55 (1942), p. 117.

81. A von. Gutschmid, *Agathangelos, Zeitschrift der deutschen morgenländischen Gesellschaft*, 31 (1877), pp. 1–60; reprinted in *Kleine Schriften*, ed. F. Rühl, Leipzig 1892, vol. III, pp. 339–420; see esp. pp. 371–379.

82. A list of the parallels is printed in the 1909 edition, pp. xiv–xv.

far greater influence than he had in fact enjoyed. One may therefore suggest that the *Teaching* is another facet of this influence, and that it represents, in an expanded version, an epitome of the missionary preaching of Maštoc᷄ as known from Koriun's account of his master's sermons.

If this is so, a key passage is Koriun XVI 7, where he speaks of the *čaṙk᷄* delivered by Maštoc᷄: ". . . blessed Maštoc᷄ began to compose (կարգիլ եւ յաւրինիլ) many homilies (ճառք), difficult of language, profound parables, easy to listen to, full of grace, varied, [drawn] from the power and matter of the prophetic scriptures, full of all subtleties of the truth of the faith of the gospel. In these he put and ordered many similarities and examples from our transitory world, especially concerning the hope of the resurrection for the future [life], that they might be intelligible and easily understood by the ignorant and those occupied with worldly affairs, in order to awaken and arouse and urge them on firmly to the promised good news."

A problem here is the translation of կարգիլ եւ յաւրինիլ, rendered above as "to compose." The first verb means "to put in order" and is used by extension of both oral and written compositions. The second verb means "to elaborate, to construct, to arrange, or to compose" and in the last sense is used of songs, speeches or writings. Nothing compels us to the conclusion that Maštoc᷄ put his homilies into writing; the Armenian is ambiguous. But whether or not Maštoc᷄ did write down his homilies, it is clear that there are many parallels between them and the content of the *Teaching*: the complexity of the language, yet the interesting sidelights and rhetorical passages; the importance of argument from prophecy; the parables from the physical world; the emphasis on the hope of the resurrection; and the extended passages of exhortation.[83]

It has sometimes been supposed that the Teaching was written by Maštoc᷄, and that it is to be identified with these *čaṙk᷄*. However, the proponents of this theory[84] do not explain whether the *Teaching* is merely one of these homilies, or a distillation of them all. But in view of Agathangelos' dependence on Koriun the reverse is rather the truth. The *Teaching* was composed in conscious imitation of Maštoc᷄ known style as an epitome of the traditional Christian teaching. The purpose of this pious fraud, as of the whole *History*, was to give the authority of Gregory's name to the position of the Armenian church in both authority and belief.

In other words, Sahak and Maštoc᷄, aided by their disciples and pupils, through the invention of an Armenian alphabet had given a new life and cohesion to the Armenian church, and by indefatigable missionary journeys

83. The homilies attributed to Gregory, the *Yačaxapatum*, have also been identified with the *čaṙk᷄* of Maštoc᷄; see A. N. Srabian, "*Yačaxapatum*" *čaṙeri helinaki harcᵊ, Telekagir*, 1962 no. 5, pp. 25–38.

84. As Akinian, *Koriwn*, p. 107.

had extended its influence throughout the Caucasus. As a corollary to the authority given the national church with its new see at Vałaršapat by the association of Gregory with the cult of the martyrs there as elaborated in the *History* of "Agathangelos," the *Teaching* was an attempt to sketch the lines of the Armenian theological tradition and gain for it the authority of the Illuminator.

The composition of the book of "Agathangelos" was no mere academic exercise. After the collapse of the Arsacid monarchy the only national focus for the Armenian people in their struggle against the encroachment of the Sassanians was the church, and in the fight for the allegiance of the people to the church edifying mythology was an important weapon. At the same time that foreign danger threatened the strength and unity of the church, internal dissensions began to exercise a divisive influence as the newly literate Armenia became aware of the theological quarrels which were rending the Byzantine empire. The quest for authoritative tradition led "Agathangelos" to enshrine the teaching of Maštocᶜ as the authentic message of Gregory, now transformed into the hero of the whole Armenian people.[85]

In sum, the author of this enigmatic *History* is unknown. He was probably a member of the circle of pupils trained by Sahak and Maštocᶜ, certainly familiar with the work of Koriun and Eznik, yet of very different cast. He was widely read and original, though hardly rigorous in thought, but in his attitude to history the complete reverse of his predecessors. He did not describe but recreated the past, and in so doing left an indelible stamp on the whole development of his country and his church. He was only equaled in importance as the shaper of the Armenian past by that other obscure historian, Moses Xorenacᶜi.

85. In this regard it is interesting to note that Pᶜawstos speaks of Gregory as the first Catholicos of greater Armenia (առաջի կաթողիկոս Հայոց Մեծաց, III 10), and Łazar says that he taught the whole country (*History*, p. 37). But curiously enough Eliše and the original Koriun do not mention Gregory at all. In Łazar we find the first frequent references to Gregory as an example and national hero, and the first invocations of his intercession.

The Teaching of Saint Gregory

Notes on biblical references

References to Old Testament books follow the numbering of the Armenian Bible and the Septuagint.

(For abbreviations used in the notes see below, pp. 184–190.)

The Teaching of Saint Gregory

259. [*The creation of heaven and earth*] The Lord God is unique in essence,[1] and there is no one before Him. There is no other creator of all that is visible and invisible, except the only-begotten Son who is born[2] from the Father, and the Spirit of the same who is from the being[3] of the same, by whom was made this world in the beginning [Gen. 1.1], created by the single power of almighty will, one essence of united thought, will, and nature of the consubstantial Trinity;[4] and everything was made by Him, heaven and earth. He made the heaven domed[5] and solidly vaulted,[6] and the earth firm, enclosed and compact; and heaven He suspended in the void,[7] and the earth He set above the void, and in the void the vast abyss, dark, invisible, unordered, formless and shapeless, diffuse and shadowy [Gen. 1.2].

1. In essence: *ինքնութեամբ*. For this term see Introduction, p. 12.
2. Son born from the Father; see also §382.
3. Being: *էութիւն*. See Introduction, p. 11. The Holy Spirit from the being of the Father; see also §362.
4. See also the more elaborate credal statements about the Trinity in §362, 705. For the procession of the Son and the Spirit see especially §362 note 1, 665, 707, and Introduction, p. 13.
5. Domed: *խորանաձեւ*, a reference to Isaiah 40.22 (διατείνας ὡς σκηνήν). In Job 38.38 *խորանաձեւ* renders κύβος.
6. Solidly vaulted: *հաստատայարկ*, not an Armenian biblical term, lit. "with a firm roof." Cf. the καμάρα of Is. 40.22 (*կամար*, see Hübschmann, p. 164) and Basil, *Hex.*, I 8E.
7. Void: *ունէս*, not an Armenian biblical term. It has an exact parallel in Eznik §271; see Mariès, *Etude*, p. 69.

260. And then with his creative word to the co-creator[1] Son and co-worker Spirit, who moved over the waters [Gen. 1.2], the Father commanded to come into being below the waters the orderly ranks of creatures. The Father said to his co-workers,[2] who share and carry out his counsel, that there should be light [Gen. 1.3]; and then was created the light, ubiquitous, darkness-scattering, day-bringing. After this [was created] the firmament [Gen. 1.7], covered with water, icy, dividing the seas, separating the waters, from which appeared the dry land, mother of all, fertile in flowers and plants.[3] And after this the power of the consubstantial Trinity said that there should be luminaries in the watery,[4] domed firmament of heaven, as lamps, globes, markers, time-measurers [Gen. 1.4]. And then [He created] the race of breathing birds and reptiles and lively fish [Gen. 1.20–21].

1. Co-creator: *արարչակից*; see also §275.
2. Co-worker: *համագործ*. This is a conflate of Gen. 1.3 and 26. See §275 note 1.

41

3. The author of the *Teaching* is greatly interested in flowers, plants, and trees; see also §644–649.

4. The firmament separates the upper and lower waters. That heaven was made from water was traditional doctrine; cf. Cyril Jer., *Cat.*, III 5. Origen, *In Gen. Hom.*, I 2, had supposed that there was a difference between the upper and lower waters: above was the "spiritalis aquae intellectum et participium capiens eius quae est supra firmamentum," while below dwelt the prince of this world and his angels. This opinion was violently attacked by Basil, *Hex.*, III 9: τὸ ὕδωρ ὕδωρ νοήσωμεν.

261. Afterwards sprang up from the earth all the four-footed kind, each in its own order [Gen. 1.24], wonderfully established by the predisposed readiness of the will of the Deity for the honor of man, who was to perform what befitted the Creator. Willingly He thus revealed his own goodness in creating the rational, wise, speaking creature in the midst of speechless, irrational, ignorant creatures, that the wise one might know the honor of the Creator, and understanding the wonderful grace of the glory of the Creator, might know to offer back praise in return, and that with him and through him all creatures and visible works might offer praise.

262. In the midst of the invisible creatures He created the invisible glori-fiers[1]—the hosts of angels, spiritual and fiery,[2] multitudes of watchers. These dwell in the upper air, above the water-covered firmament. But to us men has been given a place below, in the terrestrial dwelling place of this earth. For benevolent God has created everything, establishing the ranks of created being.[3] But evil, entering from independent will, destroys each individual, whereas everything was made and established as good by the Creator.[4]

1. The creation of the angels is not mentioned in Genesis, but cf. Col. 1.16. According to Basil, *Hex.*, I 5, the spiritual world was created before the physical and temporal world.

2. The angels are spirit and fire (հոգեղէն, հրեղէն): Ps. 103.4, Heb. 1.7. Eznik, §114, develops an explanation of these two predicates.

3. Created being: լեսելութիւն; see Introduction, p. 11.

4. That God's creation is good and that He is not responsible for evil are especially important and recurrent themes in Armenian theologians, who were extremely sensitive to suggestions of dualism. This is partly explained by the religious persecutions which formed part of Sassanian policy towards Armenia, and which came to a climax in the mid-fifth century when the *Teaching* was composed, and partly by the influence of Gnostic sects, especially the Marcionites; cf. R. P. Casey, *The Armenian Marcionites and the Diatessaron, Journal of Biblical Literature*, 57 (1938), pp. 185–194. The main emphasis in Eznik's *De Deo* is the refutation of Zoroastrian dualism and the vindication of freewill, as also in the theological passages of Eliše's *History*. On later dualist theology in Armenia see N. Garsoian, *The Paulician Heresy*, The Hague/Paris, 1967.

263. [*The creation of man in God's image*] In making man, He set him in most wonderful order as the leader,[1] and here one can see this wonderful

and amazing and incomprehensible angelic being. "Let us make," He said, "man according to our image and likeness" [Gen. 1.26]. According to whose image then, does He mean, or according to whose likeness, that He would make man? For the essential Deity is known to be incorruptible, uncreated, and immaterial. How could what was to be created become like the truly existent, or the dust, in some little respect, like the real hypostasis[2] of God? God is neither limited by space nor finite in extent but has fullness without beginning and is inaccessible to anyone, eternally the same, simple and unmoving without distinction.

1. Leader: իշխան; see also §264, Adam became aware of his ruling (իշխել) all things created from the earth. The same phrase occurs in Eznik, §348. In the Bible իշխան usually renders ἄρχων. Cf. Chrysostom, *In Gen. Sermo*, IV 1: ἐποίησε βασιλέα καὶ ἄρχοντα τῶν θηρίων τὸν ἄνθρωπον ὁ Θεός.

2. Real hypostasis: իւրաքանչիւր զաւրութիւն; cf. Introduction, p. 12.

264. So how could He set Himself as an image for the created, or form and fashion clay in the image of God, according to the saying: "In the image of God He created him" [Gen. 1.27]? First he spoke words predict-ing the history of the future, then He turned to the present and alludes to what is to come into being. And by indicating present things, He thereby shows the future.[1] For the Lord made him in the image of God—on the one hand because of [man's] wisdom,[2] rationality, intelligence, life, spiritual breath, which He bestowed in abundance, that he might know, realize, understand, and become aware of all the divine, God-given wisdom of grace, and his rationality, knowledge of God and leadership, and his ruling over all things created from the earth, and knowledge of preknowledge. And He made him ruler of all; and God said: "All the sweet seeds of the earth will be food for you" [Gen. 1.29]. And then all the wild beasts and animals and birds He led before man [Gen. 2.19] and tamed them. Then with godly wisdom he understood according to the forms of each particular one to recognize and indicate its name.[3] For the Lord introduced knowledge and through his knowledge he [Adam] recognized his creatures and was called similar to Him.

1. The sentence is very obscure in the Armenian but seems to mean that God fore-shadows the future through present events.

2. The *Teaching* here seems to refer պատկեր (image) to man's rationality and in §265 նմանութիւն (likeness) to man's freewill. In general the *Teaching* is primarily concerned with freewill, but this distinction is close to the patristic distinction between εἰκών and ὁμοίωσις, the former being the natural image of God in man, the latter the supernatural likeness resulting from grace and spiritual perfection. Cf. also Clement, *Str.*, II 22: τινὲς τῶν ἡμετέρων τὸ μὲν κατ' εἰκόνα εὐθέως κατὰ τὴν γένεσιν εἰληφέναι τὸν ἄνθρωπον, τὸ καθ' ὁμοίωσιν δὲ ὕστερον κατὰ τὴν τελείωσιν μέλλειν.

3. See §273 and note 1.

265. And on the other hand He says "similar" because of his power of independent will. For from the activity and all-creativeness of God two honorable and precious creatures were made and established by the benevolent one—mankind and angels. So He left man to independence of will, in order that by his own free will he might be able, in return for good works, to merit grace from the benevolent Lord and Creator.[1] And He placed before him the knowledge of the commandments pleasing to God, that he might know to flee from the evil and to choose the good by the probity of his will, as by his own virtue, through his independent will; and that receiving from the Creator the reward for his labors, he might honor Him.

1. Although the *Teaching* gives the impression that man is "similar" to God because of his freewill and "in the image" because of his knowledge of God, its author is not consistent; see also §264, 271. But for him the two ideas are closely associated. Cf. J. S. Muckle, *The Doctrine of St. Gregory of Nyssa on Man as the Image of God, Medieval Studies,* 7 (1945), pp. 55–84. For the freewill of the angels, see §277–278.

266. The similarity must be understood thus: all creatures are forced under the obedience of servitude, so that they are not able to effect anything more than the limit which has been commanded them, each being placed in the necessity of fulfilling the command. But God especially honored man alone, and enriched him with a mind,[1] and made him inspired, a more humble companion to the angels [Ps. 8.5; Heb. 2.7].

1. Mind: *միտք,* i.e., the faculty of rational thought and choice (διάνοια or διανοητικὴ δύναμις; cf. Gregory of Nyssa, *Or. cat.,* 6, 7) rather than the faculty of intuitive reason (νοῦς).

267. See the sun and moon and stars. So much greater than man they are, yet they stand under God's will, constrained by the requirement of the command.[1] The sun does not linger on its course, nor does the moon cease to wane and wax; the stars do not overstep their paths, nor the mountains change their place. The winds do not cease to blow, nor is the sea, in its confines of deep and furious swells, in its violence of raging and turbulent waves continually amassed, able to pass its fixed boundary and destroy the earth, nor does the earth cease to support and carry all. By his command is all arranged; his holy and heavenly angels stand in ceaseless praising. He made the height of the heavens and the number of the stars, the waters of the sea and the sand of the earth, the balance of the mountains. He raises up the clouds and restrains the winds, and brings back the evening, and makes green the arid dried-up grass, and gathers the raindrops. Concerning Him the spirit of prophecy relates: "Who measured with his palm all the waters, and with his span the heavens, and all the earth with his fingers? Who placed the hills in a scale and weighed the plains with measures [Is. 40.12]?" Which

is the place that holds up Him by whose word all creatures are suspended? He knows the paths of the courses of the heavenly bodies, which circle above the air and are not deflected, which spread out and do not go astray. They come and stay as laborers hired for a year, they go out and are relit from day to evening and from evening to day,[2] giving compensation to each other impartially,[3] freely returning to the measure of their times, changing at the four seasons of the year, just as God arranged.[4]

1. This paragraph is reminiscent of I Clement 20; *Apostolic Constitutions,* VII 34 and VIII 12; Aphraates, XIV 36 and XXIII 55. Cf. Job 38.
2. Ełišē also, *History,* p. 166, considered that the sun had no light of its own. Cf. Heraclitus, fragment 6: ὁ ἥλιος . . . νέος ἐφ' ἡμέρῃ. In a different sense, *Teaching,* §365 note 1.
3. Cf. Anaximander, fragment 1: διδόναι γαρ αὐτὰ δίκην καὶ τίσιν ἀλλήλοις τῆς ἀδικίας κατὰ τὴν τοῦ χρόνου τάξιν.
4. Cf. Ełišē, *History,* p. 34: զրշագոյութեաւթբ Հորթէբ յեզանակաւթ կատարեաւ զորҍեն զաւարիւոր սպաաւատրութիւն; and Cyril Jer., *Cat.,* IX 6, 8; Athanasius, *C. Gentes,* 29; Basil, *Hex.,* VI 8.

268. And how do the powers of the stars of the firmament of heaven travel, keeping balance in their paths continuously, without passing over the measure?[1] Or whence come the gusty breezes of violent winds, and whither do they go and die down, and what are the seasons of each one of them? One nourishes the plants with its sweet breeze; another brings on and opens the buds; another weaves garments, decorates the earth with multicolored flowers in diverse hues, clothes the naked trees and adorns the leafy tops.

1. Balance and measure: *կշիռ, չափ;* cf. Job 28.25: *զկշիռ Հողմոյ եւ զչափ ջրոց* — ἀνέμων σταθμὸν ὕδατός τε μέτρα. Cf. Athanasius, *C. Gentes,* 29, the limits (ὅρους) of the seasons. The natural limit (thumā') of the physical world is the main theme of Aphraates, XIV 36.

269. Whence come into our ken the cloud-bearing winds in which[1] the rains, born from the sound of thunder, are scattered by the lightning storm? And where the Lord commands them to go, they descend and water the earth, they make the plants to grow and ripen the fruits which fatten the body. From whose womb come the rivers with their sources, unceasing in their course, yet not overflowing in their passage?

1. In which: *որ եւ ի նոսին,* probably a Syriacism, but see Meillet, *Altarmenisches Elementarbuch,* §157, quoting Agathangelos §75. See also *Teaching,* §315 note 1, 376 note 1, 386 note 3, 406 note 2, 588 note 1, 663 note 2.

270. Heaven and earth, sun and moon and multitudes of stars, seas and rivers, beasts and animals, reptiles and birds, swimming fishes, created things and things to be, all show their fixed order, following the command to each. Only the will of man has been left independent to do whatever he wills. And

he has been constrained in nothing more than what was warned: not to eat of the tree [Gen. 2.17], that thereby He might make him worthy to receive greater things in return for lesser, and that by virtue of his having grace for his task, he might receive from the Creator, as recompense for lesser deeds, greater grace.[1] For this reason He commanded him to have power of independent will.

1. See also §277 and 713 note 2. This is the theme of Athanasius, *De Incarnatione*, 3 (cf. also Cyril Jer., *Cat.*, XII 15), but the idea of greater compensation for obedience is not found in Chrysostom's homilies on Genesis which are one of the main sources for this part of the *Teaching*. (The greater grace is immortality, not naturally possessed by man as a created being.)

271. But how could man, sprung from the earth, come into the world in the image of the Creator and, but recently created and finite, take his being in similarity to the inaccessible, essential one? For in his unbounded, uncircumscribed, individual power, did He honor him merely with the divine name, by saying: "in the image"? This is not the case at all. For the Scripture says: "In the image of God He created him [Gen. 1.27]," and elsewhere says: "God established man in incorruptibility, and in his own image of benevolence He created him [Wis. 2.23]." And another divinely acquainted wisdom said: "Man is the image of God [I Cor. 11.7]." In the very beginning God ordained that man should be close to God and aware of his form, for He was anxious not only to establish him, but rather to make him acquainted with Him.[1] For God appeared in the likeness of a man in creating him as dust from the earth [Gen. 2.7], and He blew into his face living breath, and man came into being as a living spirit. He created man with his own hands and put in him life, by blowing with his mouth the life-giving breath of wise intelligence, rationality, and awareness, that the creature, opening his eyes, might know the Creator and thus become familiar with, and close to, and aware of, and a witness to, the benevolent creative activity of God.[2]

1. See also §264 note 2 and 265 note 1.
2. Man was created to know God; see also §261 where the purpose of man's creation is explained as rather to praise God.

272. And how could all created things receive a command to come into being from immaterial, undifferentiated, formless matter;[1] and as if accustomed to [material] form and the voice of command, without delay all creatures obediently fulfill the commands? The essential Deity in secret, superior to material likenesses or to voicing aloud his warnings, in his own individual being has his own [existence]. But he took a shape for the sake of these visible creatures, to humble Himself for the strengthening of the creatures. For if He had not done so, there would have been no one who

could endure the vision of his nature or the sound of his voice.[2] But that they might be able to see Him, for this reason He took a visible likeness and acted with a voice.

1. Immaterial matter, see Introduction, p. 14. Cf. the ambiguity of Clement of Alexandria on creation *ex nihilo*, *The Cambridge History of Later Greek and Early Medieval Philosophy*, Cambridge 1967, p. 171.
2. See also §356–359.

273. Thus man was created in the image of God, with freedom, wisdom, rationality, and independent honor in accordance with the action of creation, not according to the hypostasis of the nature of God, which only the Only-begotten possesses as the express image of the being of the Father [Heb. 1.3]. Then God led all creatures of his creation to Adam to see what he would call their names [Gen. 2.19], whereby it is clear that Adam knew the name of the Creator first.[1] For this was the first necessity, because the only-begotten Son of God said to the Father: "This is my will, that they should know you only to be the true God [Jn. 6.40; 17.3]." So by necessity Adam first named the Creator, because from whose face he received life, Him he saw before all others; for the creatures were established to make known to him the Creator.

1. Cf. Chrysostom, *In Gen. Sermo*, VI 1, where it is indicated that Adam must have had knowledge before tasting of the tree or he would not have been able to name the animals, and Cyril Alex., *In Jo.*, I 9: ὁ Ἀδὰμ οὐκ ἐν χρόνῳ, καθάπερ ἡμεῖς, τὸ εἶναι σοφὸς ἀποκερδάνας ὁρᾶται, ἀλλ' ἐκ πρώτων εὐθὺς τῶν τῆς γενέσεως χρόνων τέλειος ἐν συνέσει φαίνεται.

274. So he gave names to the [animals] led up before him in the presence of the Creator and became acquainted with them in turn; he had general dominion over them not only by naming them, but also by wisdom and power.[1] As yet he was both first [among men] and the culmination [of creation].[2] Amongst all creatures he was alone by himself, and there was no one as his auxiliary, and no companion and no one similar to him.

1. For Adam's dominion (աիրելլ) over the animals, cf. Chrysostom, *In Gen. Hom.*, XIV 5, where Adam's ἐξουσία and δεσποτεία are elaborated.
2. Սկսա մխնշ չ ոէռ. մխայ սկիզրն եւ կատար է ինքն մխռquwմայն. This phrase is obscure; կատար occurs six times in the Armenian bible, rendering κορυφή or κεφαλή. The meaning is perhaps that Adam was the culmination of God's creatures, in which case սկիզրն (beginning) may mean simply that Adam was the first man to be created. See also ps. Athanasius, *C. Apoll.*, I 8.

275. Then the Father creator took counsel with the Son fellow-creator and Spirit fellow-creator, like the previous counsel at the first creation of man, as He then said: "Come, let us make man in the similitude of the image of our form [Gen. 1.26]," and then He created Adam and established him in

life from non-existence. In similar fashion here also the Father said to the Son and to the Spirit:[1] "Come, let us make for Adam a helpmate similar to him in the similitude of his image and in the similitude of his form [Gen. 2.18]." And then He put a marvelous sleep upon him, and taking a bone from his flank, fashioned it in the image of a woman and set her before him [Gen. 2.21–22]. And then Adam knew with his divinely endowed wisdom that: "This bone now is from my bone, and this flesh from my flesh; she will be called woman, because she was taken from her husband. For this reason a man will leave his father and his mother and will cleave to his wife, and they two will become one flesh [Gen. 2.23–24; Mt. 19.5–6; Mk. 10.7–8]."

1. See also §622. Throughout the *Teaching* there is a strong emphasis on the consubstantiality of the Trinity, though the usual patristic exegesis of "let us make" (either Gen. 1.26, as in §263, or Gen. 2.18 as here) explains the plural as the Father addressing the Son. Cf. the credal δι' οὗ τὰ πάντα ἐγένετο, and Athanasius, *C. Gentes*, 46: ἀφ' ὧν δείκνυται ὁ Θεὸς ὡς πλησίον τινὶ διαλεγόμενος περὶ τούτων· οὐκοῦν ἀνάγκη συνεῖναί τινα τούτῳ, ᾧ καὶ ὁμιλῶν ἐποίει τὰ ὅλα. τίς οὖν ἂν εἴη εἰ μὴ ὁ τούτου Λόγος; τίνι γὰρ ἄν τις φαίη Θεὸν ὁμιλεῖν ἢ τῷ ἑαυτοῦ Λόγῳ; and Basil, *Hex.*, III 2 and IX 6; Chrysostom, *In Gen. Hom.*, VIII, and *In Gen. Sermo*, II. See also R. McL. Wilson, *The Early History of the Exegesis of Gen. 1.26*, *Studia Patristica*, II (1957), pp. 420–437.

276. Would he not then say this in the presence of God, where all the hosts of angels were raising the praises of the Lord, and man also took part? The saying he prophesies with all-understanding knowledge, making explicit the deed performed by the ever-wakeful one while [Adam] slept. For she who was taken from the man knew, and he also knew, that the man is from the earth, and the earth from nothing, and that God alone is really existent. And by saying: "He leaves his father and mother and cleaves to his wife, and the two will become one flesh," he knew all the orders of this world and all its fulfillment.[1]

1. Fulfillment: * կատարած*; cf. Chrysostom, *In Gen. Hom.*, XV 4: τὸ κεφάλαιον ἁπάντων.

277. [*The fall of Adam*] Then God took the man and set him in the delightful garden of Eden [Gen. 2.15]; to him He revealed two trees, one of life and the other of the knowledge of good and evil; He commanded him that he should not taste of the tree under threat of death [Gen. 2.17]. For by keeping the command of God, preserving the enviable God-given wisdom, through the observance of the command he would acquire and enjoy the divine power in the inalienable glory of the existent one. And as we said above, He left the angels and men with independence[1] and imposed appropriate commands on each, that they by the disposition of their will might become obedient to the commands of the Creator and thereby become worthy of attaining greater glory.[2] Then a small command was placed on man—

not to taste of the tree, that by this he might attain greater honor, as we said above.[3] But a command was laid upon the multitude of hosts of angels to remain in their unceasing praising of the Creator, who had placed them in great honor and glory, in the invisible magnitude of the upper heavenly eternal light.

1. Independence: *անձնիշխանութիւն*, lit. αὐτεξουσία.
2. See also §270 note 1.
3. The *Teaching* here differs from Chrysostom, *In Gen. Hom.*, XIV 3, who explains that God's command indicated that Adam's duty was obedience to God.

278. But one from the celestial hosts of powers of angels, when he saw the promise of good things made by the benevolence of the Creator to man, and that man was standing in the word of his Creator, and that he was firmly keeping the commandment, by his own will the evil one worked evil, and was named evil; whence he inherited the name of Follower behind,[1] Adversary,[2] Satan.[3] Then the evil one in his jealousy threw man from glory into death by deceit.[4] For the sage says: "By jealousy of the devil death came into the world [Wis. 2.24]," bringing corruption by deceit.

1. Follower behind: *զկնի երթալոյ (անուն)*; cf. Mt. 4.10: *երթ զկնի իմ, Սատանայ*—ὕπαγε ὀπίσω μου.
2. Adversary: *հակառակորդն* (lit. loving opposition), not a biblical term, but it may render ὁ ἀντικείμενος, a frequent epithet of the devil; cf. Lampe, *Lexicon*, p. 154.
3. For an explanation of the devil's names, cf. Cyril Jer., *Cat.*, II 4. For a different explanation in Armenian, see Eznik, §51: Satan means *խոտորեալ*, erring.
4. Cf. Chrysostom, *In Gen. Hom.*, XVI 1. For Armenian parallels see Eznik, §51 ff., and Eliše, *History*, p. 37.

279. Then the enemy of man[1] produced deceit of trickery; and you see what he says: "Why, says he, did God command you not to taste of the tree [Gen. 3.1]?" Whereby it is clear that Adam had freedom and free will and wisdom from God, by knowing that God was the command-giver and Adam the commanded.[2] Perhaps indeed this was revealed [to him] by deceit before the command [was given],[3] yet this was not hidden from the Knower of all, for He is the searcher of hearts and reins [Ps. 7.10; Jer. 20.12].

1. Enemy of man: a frequent epithet of the devil; cf. Lampe, *Lexicon*, s.v. ἐχθρός.
2. See also §277 note 3. The *Teaching* here follows Chrysostom, *In Gen. Hom.*, XIV 3: ἵνα εἰδέναι ἔχῃ (viz. Adam) ὅτι ὑπὸ Δεσπότην ἐστιν, ᾧ προσήκει αὐτὸν πείθεσθαι, καὶ τοῖς ὑπ' ἐκείνου προσταττομένοις εἴκειν.
3. The phrase is obscure.

280. And thus you see what he said: "If you will taste, he says, you will become God [Gen. 3.5]." He gave them the excuse and underneath tried to snatch them into his own power; for he misled him away from the promises,

that perchance he might be able to inherit his place.[1] Just as the Apostle of God, wise and versed in the divine mystery, also says: "The lawless prince, as he wished to become God, seized and bound all mankind by sin [III Cor. 11]," that like those who had attained such blessings, he might be able to seize what had been promised. But they, deceived by his excuses, tasted, and transgressing the commandment were stripped of divine glory.[2]

1. Cf. Eznik, §264, Lyonnet, *Diatessaron*, pp. 75–76.
2. Cf. *Apoc. Bar.*, 4: ὁ Ἀδὰμ . . . τῆς δόξης τοῦ Θεοῦ ἐγυμνώθη.

281. But as a father with sons who need punishing,[1] He had mercy and acted benevolently, as the Scripture says: "They heard the voice of the Lord God descending and walking in the garden in the evening of the day [Gen. 3.8]." And they fled and hid and covered themselves with leaves from the trees—but it was impossible to escape the notice of the all-knowing by a deception. For which reason He says: "As Lord God I am near, says the Lord, and not a distant God. Is it possible for man to flee and hide from me by his covering, that I may not see him? Are not the heavens and earth filled by me [Jer. 23.23–24]?" And another of the holy prophets, knowing greatness says: "Where shall I go from your spirit, or where shall I flee from your face? If I rise to the heavens you are there; if I descend to hell, there also you are near [Ps. 138.7–8]," having them in mind, although they intended to hide.

1. The simile is paralleled in Chrysostom, *In Gen. Hom.*, XVII 1. Cf. Ps. 102.13.

282. But the Benevolent raised his voice: "Where are you Adam?" And he said: "I heard your voice, and I was afraid as you were walking in the garden, because I was naked, and I hid [Gen. 3.9–10]." Do you see how aware and acquainted with God they were, even to being not unaware of the sound of his footsteps? Because the Benevolent gave an occasion [for repentance] to the ignorant, first making a sound with his feet, that the man approaching the propitious feet, by being himself narrator of his faults, might find salvation.[1]

1. Cf. the role of conscience in Chrysostom, *In Gen. Hom.*, XVII 1–2 and of confession, ibid., 5.

283. But that did not occur; yet He was unwilling to be the accuser or to attack him frightfully, so He was merciful and condescending[1] and said: "Who said to you that you are naked [Gen. 3.11]?" For He wished by being somewhat indulgent to capture him, that the gentleness of God might lead them to penitence. But since thereby they did not turn from their error but

were ungrateful, giving excuses for each other,[2] then He set judgment, passed sentence, which they paid and returned to dust [Gen. 3.19]; for the judgment of God is true over those who work evil.

1. Cf. Chrysostom, *In Gen. Hom.*, XVII 4: σκόπει τῆς ἀγαθότητος τοῦ Θεοῦ τὴν ὑπερβολήν, ὅπως καθάπερ φίλος φίλῳ διαλεγόμενος καὶ ἐγκαλῶν ὡς παραβάντι τὰ παρ' αὐτοῦ ἐνταλθέντα.
2. Ibid.: ἀπολογίαν Ἀδὰμ συντιθείς.

284. After this He mentioned the revolt, saying: "Behold, Adam became as one of us, to know good and evil. Let us remove him from the tree of life, lest by eating he live for ever [Gen. 3.22]." But "like as one of us" is not that he became God, for he is not the true being in his existence, but it means supposed existence.[1] Just as false gods are supposed by men, which were fashioned in the irrationality, foolishness, and foulness of mankind, so I saw among you your errors of worshipping stones and wood [Deut. 28.64; 29.17; Wis. 14.21; Jer. 3.9; Ez. 20.32], which were fashioned by you in ignorance, which neither hear nor speak, neither understand nor move, have neither breath nor mouth. And you left the living God, the Creator of heaven and earth, and offered worship to breathless, voiceless stones [I Cor. 12.2], which are nothing.[2]

1. The *Teaching* here differs from Chrysostom, who explains the quotation differently, *In Gen. Hom.*, XVIII 2: βούλεται γὰρ ἐνταῦθα διὰ τῶν ῥημάτων τούτων τῆς ἀπάτης ἡμᾶς ὑπομνῆσαι ἣν ἠπατήθησαν ὑπὸ τοῦ διαβόλου.
2. See also §522 ff.

285. For which reason the God-seeing, holy prophets took care, like wise doctors,[1] to prepare the medicine of cure for the pain of the illness, to remove and extirpate the scandal and destroy it completely. As one of them, filled with the power of the divine Spirit, cried out, saying: "The gods who did not create the heavens and earth will vanish from the earth under heaven. But the Lord made the earth by his own power and extended the heavens by his own marvelous counsel, and prepared the universe by all his own wisdom; and He thunders with his voice, and fills the heavens with a multitude of waters, and gathers the clouds from the ends of the earth, and made his lightning in the rain, and draws the winds from their caverns [Jer. 10.11–13]."

1. Prophets as doctors; cf. Origen, *In Jer. Hom.*, XIV 2. (To the references s.v. ἰατρός in Lampe, *Lexicon*, p. 662, the following could be added: Chrysostom, *In Gen. Hom.*, XXVII 1: τοὺς πατριάρχας . . . διδασκάλους καὶ καθάπερ ἰατρούς, idem, *Huit Catéchèses baptismales*, VII 5: [μαρτύρας] ἰατροὺς τοίνυν πνευματικούς.)

286. All men turned to foolishness from knowledge, bringing misery upon themselves. Then by themselves they make their faces shameful [Ps. 82.17–18]

and prepare themselves for the great anger of God. But now let this suffice to reprimand your error, for it fits suitably in its place. And now what we have begun to relate to you, we shall expound in order.[1]

1. The author of the *Teaching* makes Gregory address his audience at frequent intervals in order to preserve the fiction of a sermon, especially from §520 to the end where the main emphasis is on personal repentance. The systematic nature of the *Teaching* is brought out by the references to each section being expounded in order, e.g., §376 and the paragraphs in the *History* just before and after the *Teaching* (§258, 716).

287. So ejecting man from the delightful garden of repose, He settled him outside the garden and closed for him the road to the tree of life [Gen. 3.23–24], that he might not see again the delightfulness of the garden. Then were cursed the earth and thorns and thistles and the bread of pain and the death of mortal Adam [Gen. 3.17–19]. And this is a sign of benevolence, as God says by the mouth of the prophet: "Your rebellion will correct you, and your wickedness will reproach you. Then you will know that it is evil and bitter for you to abandon me, says the Lord your God [Jer. 2.19]." And another says for God: "When you return and lament, then you will live and know where you are [Is. 30.15]." For when he is in the midst of the bitter taste and uncertainty of death, there will gradually come to his mind the memory of the tree of life, and with groaning he will seek the approach to the garden of delight. For his being settled opposite the garden bears witness to these sayings.[1]

1. Cf. Chrysostom, *In Gen. Hom.*, XVIII 3: ὥστε καὶ τὸ πλησίον καὶ ἀπέναντι τοῦ παραδείσου προστάξαι κατοικεῖν τὸν ἐκεῖθεν ἐκπεπτωκότα μεγίστης κηδεμονίας σημεῖον ἦν, ἵνα καὶ τὴν ἐκ τῆς θέας ὑπόμνησιν ἔχῃ, καὶ τοῦ ἐντεῦθεν κέρδους ἀπολαύῃ, καὶ μηδὲ ἐπιθυμίαν τῆς φιλοζωίας ἔχων, καὶ ἔξω τυγχάνων, κατατολμήσῃ τῆς τοῦ ξύλου βρώσεως.

288. [*The sons of Adam*] But the benevolent one, not only in the garden but also outside of it, did not remove Himself from them when He settled them opposite the garden. And because of his benevolence He ordered them to multiply on earth, where by the command of the attentive Creator they brought forth on earth and began to increase according to the saying: "Grow and multiply, and fill the earth [Gen. 1.28]."

289. Of the sons of Adam the elder was called Cain and the other Abel [Gen. 4.1–12]. They then showed the wisdom of the giver, by his wisdom to know the same to be Creator. Cain, the elder son, took his offering of roots, binding a sheaf of wheat, and offered it as sacrifice to Him. When Abel saw this, he gave offspring from the lambs of his flocks and offered from his sheep. And God in his kindness condescended to the gifts of the sons of Adam and was known as being near. For then He makes a choice: knowing

the one to be sincere He accepts his sacrifice, knowing the other to be malicious towards his brother He condemns and rejects him because of his malice.[1] Then he for this reason meditated death and killed his brother. Then the earth was cursed on his account, and he himself cursed with his seed.

1. Cf. Chrysostom, *In Gen. Hom.*, XVIII 5. "Sincere" (ⲓⲗⲱⲓⲏⲟⲡⲓ.ⲓ ⲫⲓⲥ) and "malicious' (ⲓⲣⲓⲙⲓⲏⲟⲡⲓ.ⲓ ⲫⲓⲥ) have parallels in the προαίρεσις and ἀγνωμοσύνη of Chrysostom.

290. Then another son was established for Adam by God instead of the murdered Abel, who was named Seth [Gen. 4.25]. But the murdered one, because of his righteousness, is living in the presence of God.[1] For He who created him from nothing, the same gives him life whenever He wills—as is very easy to relate to you. When we see you fervent in the faith, we mention him whose righteousness is preserved for ever and ever. So the treacherous and murderous Cain was cursed. Therefore he was cut off by the command of God, for God blessed Seth and gave him a command, that his blessed seed should not mingle with the cursed seed of the murderer Cain.[2] Then mankind increased generally over both families' regions of the earth [Gen. 6.1].

1. Living in the presence of God, a phrase usually applied to martyrs in the *Teaching*, e.g., §563. According to the *Ascension of Isaiah* Abel was in heaven with Adam and Enoch; cf. Daniélou, *Theology*, p. 253.

2. Cf. Chrysostom's explanation of Gen. 6.2, the sons of God and the sons of men, *In Gen. Hom.*, XXII 3: ἐξ ἐκείνου (viz. Seth) λοιπὸν οἱ ἑξῆς τικτόμενοι υἱοὶ Θεοῦ προσηγορεύθησαν παρὰ τῆς θείας γραφῆς ... υἱοὺς δὲ ἀνθρώπων ἐκάλεσε τοὺς πρὸ τοῦ Σὴθ γεγονότας, τοὺς ἀπὸ τοῦ Κάϊν.

291. The patriarchs of the tribe of Seth were righteous men until the eighth generation;[1] the kindness of God was near them, and He was continuously close to all men lest they should be forgetful of his confidence. So He made the fathers long-lived and granted them long-lived children, that at least on account of their desire for sons they might seek God,[2] especially because the begetting of offspring is most important in the life of earthly creatures.

1. In Genesis 5 (and Luke 3) nine generations are enumerated before the just Noah. But if the *Teaching* does not include Adam or Seth but only their descendants, then the number eight (which includes Noah) is in accordance with the tradition of II Peter 2.5 (cf. also *Clementine Recognitions*, I 29, Justin, *Dialogue*, CXXXVIII 1–2). On the significance of the number eight see Daniélou, *Shadows*, pp. 81–82. See also §295 note 1.

2. See also §293.

292. [*The first patriarchs*] The patriarchs[1] [Gen. 5.1–24] in order are: the first Adam created by God, that is Adam; and Seth, and from him Enos, and from him Cainan, and from him Malaliel and from him Yared, and from

him Enoch; and Enoch lived a hundred and sixty-five years and begat Mathousala, and Enoch was pleasing to the Lord.

1. See §295 note 1.

293. He was the longest-lived of all the patriarchs. As they were begotten and increased by God's benevolence, so also after their births they were made for long life, in order that those who were created by God, as fathers might relate to their sons. For as the commands are warnings to make them aware of God, so also it was said: "Ask your fathers, and they will relate to you, and your old men, and they will tell you [Deut. 32.7]." Whereby it is clear that for this reason they were long-lived and not for the sake of a multitude of offspring.[1]

1. Cf. the ἀκρασία mentioned by Chrysostom, *In Gen. Hom.*, XXIV 1–2, and the remarks of Łazar, *Letter*, p. 190.

294. For although God said to Adam: "Increase and multiply and fill the earth [Gen. 1.28]," as He said in his knowledge of the future concerning the material blessings to be, God wished not only for the increase, but also for this, that they would pass into eternal immortality. So we see Enoch after a long life, after marrying and begetting sons in a life of rectitude, raised up while still alive to a destiny of immortality [Gen. 5.24]. Which was not for that man only, but that his path might make a road for others;[1] and he was not taken forcibly into life, but he paid the debt of a pleasing life. In the same way God wished to change all to immortality, after all had been pleasing here.

1. Cf. Chrysostom, *In Gen. Hom.*, XXIV 4: βουλόμενος (viz. God) τοὺς ἐξῆς ζηλωτὰς ἐκείνου καταστῆσαι καὶ τὴν αὐτὴν ἐκείνῳ βαδίσαι ὁδόν.

295. All men of the eighth generation[1] were subject to death, being servants of sin [Rom. 6.17], and they forgot the Creator, losing hope in the life of God and destroying their own straight road. God handed them over to their own will, taking the spirit of the grace of his love for man from them; and the taking of it is mentioned as contrition. The repentance of God [Gen. 6.6] is a sign of his awesome solicitude,[2] that perhaps thereby He may be able to care for those who forgot the power of the Creator, who mingled with the cursed seed of Cain[3] in fornication and dissolute lives, to eat carrion [Lev. 15.17]. The earth was totally polluted and made horrible by the lives of men [Gen. 6.11–13], as [the scripture] says: "All were completely overthrown into impiety, and every man fouled his path upon the earth [Jer. 3.2; Ez. 36.17]."

1. In contrast to §291 the *Teaching* here implies that there were eight generations before (not including) the just Noah. In §292 eight patriarchs are enumerated, but Lamech (Gen. 5.28) has been omitted. So the significance of the number eight has been lost. See §291 note 1. For a different enumeration making Noah eleventh from Adam, see Cyril Alex. *Glaph in Gen.*, 2.

2. Cf. Chrysostom, *In Gen. Hom.*, XXIII 1.

3. See also §290.

296. [*Noah and the flood*] But then was found one just man from the justified family, who was called Noah [Gen. 6.9]; being pleasing to God, he was loved by Him. He received a command from God to make an ark [Gen. 6.14–22], a chest of wood, a task of many years, for the punishment of the miserable race. He promised consequently to take Noah with his family and all the living creatures into the ark and to close up the ark with his all-saving hand. And then bringing back the sandy chaos over the dry land [Gen. 7.11 ff] with the torrents let loose from the heavens, in his anger with a punishing flood He purified what was below the heavens and inundated everything and washed it clean.[1] Then after his castigation had passed, He established the just man as father of the world[2] and lord of the earth with an eternal covenant [Gen. 9.9 ff]; He made him long-lived to inform the coming generations of the universal contract of his anger.

1. Cf. Chrysostom, *In Gen. Hom.*, XXV 6, and *Hom.*, XXVI 5.

2. Noah as father of the world (աշխարհածնաւր): this is not a biblical expression, though Abraham is called πατὴρ πλήθους ἐθνῶν (Gen. 17.4, 5). The *Teaching* here follows Chrysostom, *In Gen. Hom.*, XXVI 5: ὁ δίκαιος οὗτος ζύμη τις καὶ ἀρχὴ καὶ ῥίζα γίνεται πάντων τῶν μετὰ τὸν κατακλυσμόν.

297. [*The tower of Babel*] But then the race which was one family and of one language [Gen. 11.1–9] multiplied, and they took counsel to build a round tower reaching to the heavens, celebrated to eternal memory, in place of the eternal God, whose "name is told from age to age and whose memory from people to people [Ps. 134.13]." Who as a warning from on high showed his divine knowledge in mixing, confusing, and dividing the race which had been brought up as one into many races, speaking tongues unknown to each other, and scattered them over the face of the earth, that they might not fix a self-willed limit for themselves, but might walk in obedience to the eternally ordained limits of God; who in dividing the races and confusing the tongues and scattering the sons of Adam set limits to all races according to the number of the angels of God [Deut. 32.8].[1]

1. The Hebrew and Syriac of Deut. 32.8 say that God set the bounds of the people according to the number of the sons of Israel, but the LXX and Armenian read "angels" for "sons of Israel." The identity of the number of men and of angels is repeated later in §321, where their role as protecting spirits is elaborated (a theme discussed in Eznik §141

based on Mt. 18.10), and §640. On the other hand, Cyril Jer., *Cat.*, XV 24, reckons that the number of angels exceeds that of men by 99 to one, basing his argument on Mt. 18.12.

298. [*The call of Abraham*] And because the scattered races, in the knowledge which forgets God, had separated into each one's worship of material creatures and had gone astray into the abyss of error, then a certain man, aroused by the divine warning, blessed over all, whose name was Abraham, being a follower of the true God, followed his commandments and obeyed them.[1] To him God sent word that he should leave his fatherland [Gen. 12.1], for God is peremptory in his requests.

1. Cf. Chrysostom, *In Gen. Hom.*, XXXI 5.

299. Then Abraham went from his native land [Gen. 12.4] following the commands of God and walked by faith; he was made worthy to receive the great gospel, and he fulfilled the will of his Creator. He emigrated[1] to the midst of foreign heathen races; he bore upon himself patience[2] for many years, according to the requirements of piety.

1. Emigrated: *ելեալ պանզ խափեզաւ* (κατώκησεν); cf. Gen. 13.12, 20.1 etc., and Chrysostom, *In Gen. Hom.*, XXXI 6.
2. Patience: *համբերութիւն*, not used of Abraham in Genesis, but Chrysostom, *In Gen. Hom.*, XXXIX 2, explains the ὑπομονή of Abraham as his long wait for children (παιδοποιία); cf. Łazar, *Letter*, p. 190.

300. Then when his ninety-nine years were completed, God appeared to Abraham, made a covenant,[1] spoke with him, and left him [Gen. 17.1–22]. Again through the angels coming from Mambre [Gen. 18.1–15] He promised the gift of seed, and that his Son would come in the flesh, taking flesh from the seed of Abraham, and would become a son of Abraham [Lk. 19.9], and that he would be the father of righteousness for all believers [Rom. 4.11], and that He would set him up as patriarch of the just.[2]

1. The covenant was circumcision (Gen. 17.10), but this ritual act is never discussed in the *Teaching*. Christ's circumcision on the eighth day is briefly referred to in §401.
2. Patriarch of the just: *նահապետ արդարոց*, not a biblical phrase, but cf. Irenaeus, *Adv. Haer.*, III 11.8.

301. He received also the bodily promise of unlimited seed [Gen. 22.17]. In similar fashion also He warned the evil-working land of the Sodomites through the men made blind [Gen. 19.4–11]; then, when they were not persuaded, He sent down fiery rain [Gen. 19.24] as a general judgment in his divine anger.

302. And after this He fulfilled for him the promise of seed, for a son, Isaac, was given to him [Gen. 21.1–5]. And God appeared again to Abraham that he might offer Isaac as a testing sacrifice[1] [Gen. 22.1–19], whereby he received the gospel of the future.[2] In the same way also God appeared to Isaac the son of Abraham, informing him of his native land [Gen. 26.2–5].

1. Testing sacrifice: *փորձական զոհ*; cf. Gen. 22.1: *փորձեաց Աստուած զԱբրահամ* and Heb. 11.17.
2. Gospel of the future: *աւետիք հանդերձելոցն*; cf. Gal. 4.28: κατὰ Ἰσαὰκ ἐπαγγελίας τέκνα ἐσμέν (*աւետեացն որդիք եմք*). There is also the idea of the sacrifice of Isaac prefiguring the crucifixion of Christ; cf. Irenaeus, *Adv. Haer.*, IV 5.4 and Origen, *In Gen. Hom.*, VIII 6. Chrysostom comments on this passage from Genesis: ταῦτα δὲ πάντα τύπος ἐγένετο τοῦ σταυροῦ (*In Gen. Hom.*, XLVII 3), but his idea is not elaborated in the *Teaching* despite its emphasis on typology; see Introduction, p. 16.

303. The Lord became known and appeared also to Jacob, the son of Isaac, in a most wondrous vision, that of a ladder reaching to heaven with all the angels [Gen. 28.10–22];[1] and He once appeared like an ordinary man, fighting in single combat with him by night. But the prophet says an angel [Gen. 32.24–30; Hos. 12.4]. He made him lame and signed him with the name "who has seen God";[2] and this is a continuous reminder of the appearance of the Lord, which will make glorious the seed of Jacob.

1. The ladder was frequently likened to the cross; cf. Aphraates, IV 4, Irenaeus, *Dem.*, 45. The connection is not explicitly made here, but see also §629 (the cross links heaven and earth) and Daniélou, *Theology*, pp. 287–288.
2. The etymology of Gen. 32.28 is rejected in favor of the more usual patristic one. The *Teaching* is again following Chrysostom, *In Gen. Hom.*, LVIII 2: Ἰσραὴλ δὲ ἑρμηνεύεται, ὁρῶν Θεόν.

304. And thus He increases his appearances, familiar and very close, even to the heathen kings in a vision for the safekeeping of those who knew Him. Concerning them [the scripture] relates: "He reproached the kings on their account not to approach the anointed of the Lord [Ps. 104.14–15; I Chron. 16.21–22]," making it clear that: "Truly Jacob is the portion of the Lord, and Israel the lot of his inheritance [Deut. 32.9]."

305. He followed them at all times, giving help to bless, increase and multiply their seed in their pilgrimage. He brought them down to the land of the Egyptians for bread in their mouth for the same reason [Gen. 42.2]; and they were [there] for the time of five patriarchs from the age of Abraham—about four hundred and thirty years [Ex. 12.40; Gal. 3.17]. Then one could see the great abundance of grace of the benevolent God in the land of the Egyptians, for one man held a captive in prison He released and

raised up [Gen. 41.14], making him famous by the art of prophecy, and setting him up as lord of the Egyptians [Gen. 41.40].

306. [*God's revelation to Moses*] After this He increased his people in the land of the Egyptians and saw them being oppressed by them [Ex. 1.7, 11–14]. Then the Lord came and appeared to a certain man from among the people of the Hebrews, with whom He was very pleased, and whom He found worthy of the divine mysteries, whose name was Moses. He appeared to him on the hill of Horeb as a burning flame in the bramble [Ex. 3.1–14]. He informed Moses of his native land and showed him his name—"the one who is"[1]—and sent him to Egypt. At whose going down He inflicted various plagues on the Egyptians as a warning [Ex. 7–10].[2]

1. On this phrase see Introduction, p. 11.
2. Warning: խրատ. On this term see R. W. Thomson, *"Vardapet" in the Early Armenian Church*, *Le Muséon*, 75 (1962), p. 383 note 51.

307. And bringing forth the Israelites, He shepherded them with the cloud and the light in the form of a pillar and menaces of flaming fire [Ex. 13.21], dividing the abyss of the deep sea and drowning the Egyptians [Ex. 14.21–30]; He made the people pass over and brought them to the desert, as is wonderfully described. He led them to Horeb, [Ex. 17.6] and brought them to the mountain of Sinai [Ex. 19.1], and there over the mountain of Sinai He pitched a tabernacle of divine clouds [Ex. 19.16 ff], in which was a radiant globe like a pillar; and a mist like a curtain of cloud enveloped the mountain, and myriad hosts of angels were there.

308. He then called Moses there to experience the divine vision, who observed clearly the footstool [Ex. 24.10] like a plinth of precious blue stones, pure and clear azure[1]—in order to recall the work of clay and water,[2] and the impure heart of the impetuous people—and from the glory of the throne and round about it shone awesome splendor like blazing fire.

1. Though based on Ex. 24.10, the terminology of this passage does not correspond very closely to that of the Armenian O.T.
2. Clay: կաւ. The only biblical use of this term in Genesis or Exodus is Ex. 1.14, where it refers to the tasks set the Israelites by the Egyptians. Water: lit. sea. This rather obscure phrase seems to mean that God's footstool (plinth: աղիւսանման, like brick) was intended to remind Moses of the πλινθεία, աղ աղիւսոյ, the Israelites had to perform in Egypt (as Ex. 5.14).

309. God, who is absolute light, absolute fame, absolute sight, absolute word, absolute power, absolute wisdom, living spirit, burning fire, immutable

light, ineffable glory, inscrutable vision, infinite greatness, was revealed to them so far as they could support the intensity of his appearance.[1] Then He appeared visibly to the priests with the elders and appeared in the presence of all the people in a vision of blazing fire and a sound as a trumpet to give them words of command [Ex. 19.18–19]; the hand of God wrote on stone tablets that they should revere justice and keep his commandments [Ex. 24.12]; and He said to him: "I come in clouds to meet the Israelites, to speak with you, that they may believe you [Ex. 19.9]." And He appeared with chariots and cherubim [Ps. 67.18], and as a pillar with clouds and misty fire.

1. The inability of men to endure the full vision of God is frequently stressed in the *Teaching*, as §272, 310, 354, 356 etc. Cf. Chrysostom, *De Incomprehensibili*, III, defining the condescension of God: τί δέ ἐστι συγκατάβασις; ὅταν μὴ ὡς ἔστιν ὁ Θεὸς φαίνηται, ἀλλ' ὡς ὁ δυνάμενος αὐτὸν θεωρεῖν οἷός τέ ἐστιν, οὕτως ἑαυτὸν δεικνύῃ, ἐπιμετρῶν τῇ τῶν ὁρώντων ἀσθενείᾳ τῆς ὄψεως τὴν ἐπίδειξιν.

310. When he came the second time to stand before the Lord, he said: "If I have found compassion from you, reveal yourself to me that I may know your name, for I have found mercy from you [Ex. 33.13]." The Lord said to him: "You are not able to see my face, for there is no man who will see me and live. But behold, I place you in a cave of the rock and cause my glory to pass by you [Ex. 33.20–22]." And He showed him that He is merciful and compassionate, and He appeared to him in humility, that he might not die, but be saved and live. He also came before the whole people and appeared, whose voice was heard by all while He was conversing with Moses.

311. And thus after making vigils for many days on the mountain, and becoming an eyewitness, and receiving the code of inspired law on the mountain, he taught the sons of Israel. [God][1] gave them commandments drawn up by Himself, and He also gave Moses the description of the creation of the world.[2] He showed also in similitude an immaterial tabernacle [Ex. 25.9 ff]; when Moses saw it, with the sons of Israel he then fashioned a material tabernacle according to the example shown, whereby God might dwell in their midst.[3] He continually spoke with Moses and related to him the multiple laws He ordained; He was with them all the time in their sojourn in the desert, and He led them with awesome signs and brought them to the promised land.

1. There is no indication in the Armenian that the subject of this phrase is different from that of the previous phrases, but as nowhere else in the *Teaching* is it suggested that Moses composed the laws (as Origen suggests, *C. Celsum*, II 54), it seems probable that God is the subject, as He must be also of the following sentence.

2. This idea is expressed more elaborately by Ełišē, *History*, p. 35, but he links it to God's talking with Moses from the bramble. The description of the world is suggested by the tabernacle which represented the universe; cf. Goodenough, *By Light Light*, p. 56.

3. It is surprising that the author of the *Teaching* limits himself to noting the literal meaning of Ex. 25.22 when he is generally interested in typology and does not mention the mystical significance in Christian exegesis of the tabernacle (e.g., Origen, *In Ex. Hom.*, IX, thinks of the tabernacle as the church, or Gregory of Nyssa, *De Vita Moysis*, as Christ).

312. And He was with them in the desert and made them wander for forty years [Ex. 16.35] that He might cause them to forget their custom of worshipping spirits and stones, that perhaps they might be able to free themselves from their vain pagan teachings, which ensnared them in their folly. For He decided thus, that after He had brought them from the land of the Egyptians, since, by their being accustomed to evil, perhaps where they were led, seeing the people there still more full of evil, they might burn yet more for evil—just as wind, seeing fire, makes it flame all the more—He would first purify them from the old stain and then lead them to destroy the impure tribes of Canaanites, and that He would settle them there [Ex. 6.4].

313. For this reason he made them wander through the desert, being seen Himself on the mountain; and He instructed the seed of Abraham by various signs and miracles through Moses. He gave them as food heavenly bread of the sweetness of manna [Ex. 16.14–31]. Water gushing from a rock He made to flow in rivers for the thirsty [Ex. 17.1–7], and He satisfied their desire with quail found around the camps [Ex. 16.13].

314. Yet there they offended the Creator and angered Him by their habitual nurturing of evil. Setting up a calf instead of the benevolent God, they gave it the name of God and called it "redeemer" [Ex. 32.4].[1] Therefore the anger of God came upon them and caused countless numbers from the people to perish [Ex. 32.10]; so a command came that they would not reach the promised land. And then they perished and were destroyed in the desert, all the lawless race of the perverse sons of Israel [Ps. 77.8].

1. Redeemer: *փրկիչ*, a term not used in Ex. 32.

315. And the great prophet Moses by the command of God came to the mountain and there died, whose[1] tomb to this day no one has been able to know [Deut. 34.1–6]. And they increased and multiplied in the desert, those who did not know at all the nurturing of evil or anything of sin.

1. Whose: *որ ... նորա* instead of *որոյ*. It seems a Syriacism; see §269 note 1.

316. [*Joshua, the judges and kings*] Then over them by the hand of Moses at the command of God a chosen man was set up as commander and leader, whose name was Joshua [Deut. 34.9], who took the seed of Abraham, the sons of Israel, out of the desert and brought them to the promised land. He extirpated and destroyed seven nations of the impious [Josh. 18] and led them and settled them. Where he revealed a place, there first they built a temple[1] to the name of the Lord [Josh. 8.30]; and it was clear from the command of God that there only they had power to offer to Him holocausts of sacrifices, where God was dwelling in the midst of men. And then He raised up for them judges [Judg. 2.16], who according to the will of God judged them, who were also full of the spirit of prophecy.[2] And they made intervals when the judges died, when they were again impious towards God and rendered worship to demons and worshipped images [Judg. 2.19]. Therefore He then brought them back into the hands of foreign races and warned them by heathen kings.

1. Temple: *տաճար*, the term in Joshua is "altar," *սեղան*. Origen compares the altar to a building which is the church, *In Jes. Hom.*, IX 1.

2. The spirit of prophecy is not attributed to the judges in the book of Judges.

317. After this they themselves sought kings from God [I Sam. 8.6], and He gave to them. Among these He raised up David [I Sam. 16.13], who was full of the Holy Spirit, to whom He bore witness: "I found David the son of Jesse a man according to my heart, who will do and fulfill all my wishes [Ps. 88.21; Acts 13.22]." And He set up his throne and the throne of his seed.

318. [*God's appearances to the prophets*] Then again one could see in the promised land numerous prophets, who were also called seers [I Sam. 9.9] because of the divine revelations which they enjoyed. They spoke with loud voice to the tribe of Israel in the order of each, as King David sang of his universal lordship: "Lord, our Lord, how wonderful is your name in all the earth [Ps. 8.2, 10]."

319. For he appeared to one with a chariot as a shining warrior; and another saw the Ancient of Days [Dan. 7.9] like a judge on the judgment seat [Ps. 9.5], or like the Son of Man coming on the clouds of heaven [Dan. 7.13]; and another [saw Him] like a man upon the altar, according to the saying: "I have seen the Lord standing upon the altar [Amos. 9.1]." Do you see that although He is seen as a man, He is known as Lord?

320. And another saw a still more wonderful appearance: "I have seen the Lord upon a high throne and six-winged cherubim around the Lord [Is. 6.1–2]." One must understand all this in a divine way, just as God made to Abraham countless visions and to all his seed. As the prophet says for the Lord: "I have multiplied visions and through the prophets made similitudes [Hos. 12.10]."[1]

1. Cf. Eznik §118 for the various appearances of God to men in different forms.

321. Who in dividing the races and confusing the tongues and scattering the sons of Adam set their limits according to the number of God's angels [Deut. 32.8];[1] just as the angels themselves related to the gracious Daniel [Dan. 10.11] concerning the individual limits,[2] whom the benevolent God punished but in his anger remembered his mercy. For from the foul army of devils, from the warlike demons, the divinely ordered sweet-smelling[3] spirits will keep the races of mankind unafraid, in order to prepare them for the knowledge of God; as blessed David proves, relating: "Armies of angels of the Lord surround those who fear Him, and He guards them [Ps. 33.8]." And the great Jacob: "The angel which guarded me from my childhood [Gen. 48.16]"; and the Lord of all: "My angel will go before to prepare your journey [Gen. 24.40]." His safekeeping is in order to make known the divine knowledge to the nations of like nature but divided, those fallen from the face of God, that perchance through his visible creatures they may know the invisible God.[4]

1. See §297 note 1.
2. I.e., the seventy weeks. Does the author of the *Teaching* here have in mind the common idea that each of the seventy nations since their scattering at Babel has its guardian angel (though he always refers to seventy-two nations)?
3. Sweet-smelling: there may be here a reminiscence of the role of the angels in offering the ὀσμὴ εὐωδίας; cf. Daniélou, *Theology*, p. 183.
4. Cf. Eznik, §141, quoting Heb. 1.14.

322. For "He created from one man all the races of mankind to dwell on the face of the earth; and He established and ordered the seasons and bounds of their dwelling for them to seek God, that perhaps they might search for Him and find Him [Acts 17.26–27]," "for his invisible [creatures] from the beginning of the world are understood and seen by the created things [Rom. 1.20]." For the Lord is known to those worthy of Him. In the same way also from the Lord is all protection, for where the Lord is, there are the hosts of fiery[1] angels—just as the patriarch Jacob, according to the revelations made to him, was directly in the midst of hosts of angels [Gen. 32.1–2]. For the angels were arranged according to their likenesses to be messengers

to mankind by the benevolent will of God, which is to be understood as referring to the six-winged seraphim.

1. See also §262 note 2.

323. Although they are not physically winged but only winged in appearance, yet the angels sometimes really appeared like men. For they were entertained in human fashion by Abraham and Lot [Gen. 18.1–16; Gen. 19.1–22]; and one appeared as a man to Daniel [Dan. 10.5], likewise in a profound vision to Gideon [Judg. 6.12]. Zecharia mourning in the hills saw one [Zech. 1.9], and Joshua really like a man unexpectedly [saw one] and asked him unafraid: "Are you from us or from our enemies [Josh. 5.13]?" And when he discovered that he was a commander of God's hosts, he fell down and worshipped. And similarly with all who saw angels.

324. In truth then, we consider that all the appearances in human form of the spiritual race to men took place in order to relate the duty of the commands of God and for service at different times; and they did not always conserve the same form. Whose immaterial persons the prophet predicted: "Who made his angels spirits, and his servants a flame of fire [Ps. 103.4; Heb. 1.7]," because "they are ministering spirits, who are sent to the service of the heirs of salvation [Heb. 1.14]."

325. Concerning this Moses did not relate anything, that the intelligent and rational spirits be not considered with the insensible creatures, but that in obedient service they themselves might carry the commands of the greatness of God's glory. But concerning their created nature from above the prophets loudly announced: "He made his angels spirits [Ps. 103.4]," and another: "I am the Lord God, who established the heavens and the earth, whose hands established all the armies of heaven [Hosea 3.14]." But if they were material, then they would be visible and not invisible, and they would not have been revealed to any one. But if this is so for created beings, how much more so will the invisible nature of the truly existent God be understood as uncreated and inaccessible.

326. To all the perfect who see God He appeared in the likeness of a man at each time. He is known from his voice and commands to have appeared in human form, because He spoke with mankind concerning the invitation[1] to the vision of the promised blessings and did not always conserve the same form. He is able to show the truth by similitudes in which all difficulties are made easy and the incomprehensible comprehensible; He is powerful over all, and nothing is impossible for Him [Gen. 18.14; Lk. 1.37]. Of Him the

seers loudly cried, that from limited revelations they knew the unlimited and invisible and knew in a momentary vision the truly existent hypostasis according to their ability.[2]

1. The invitation (*Հրաւիրել*) is a common theme in the *Teaching*, developed fully later; see §484 note 1. Cf. Zeph. 1.7.
2. See also §309 note 1.

327.   Him also the patriarch Abraham called Lord [Gen. 14.22] and judge of all the earth [Gen. 18.25]; and the great Moses [called Him] God who is [Ex. 3.14] and creator of all, who also desired to see his glory, for all the prophets were seers.[1] One said "The Lord, the Lord has sent me and his Spirit [Is. 48.16]," and: "The mouth of the Lord spoke this [Is. 1.20; 58.14]." Certainly whoever heard from his mouth also saw his form. And another made supplication, saying: "Lord, Lord, behold I know not how to speak, for I am a child [Jer. 1.6]." You see "behold" shows his presence. And all the commandment-bearers, when they came from the face of the Lord, all cried with a loud voice, one: "The Lord of hosts has spoken [Is. 53.13; Jer. 8.3; Amos 4.13]," and another: "The Lord omnipotent has commanded [Amos 3.13; Zech. 3.9; Mal. 1.9]." By the voice of Amos He is certainly known, by his saying: "God will not do anything without revealing his plan to his servants his prophets [Amos 3.7]."

1. Seers: *տեսանողք*; cf. I Kings 9.9: ὅτι τὸν προφήτην ἐκάλει ὁ λαὸς ἔμπροσθεν ὁ βλέπων (*յառաջ տեսանող*).

328.   And so it is clear consequently by these sayings that He revealed the same likeness to the first-created man in the beginning, just as afterwards for all the perfect who see God He kept the same, lest He might terrify the seers with very strange and unknown forms. Especially as it is better that the son, informed by his father who saw God, be more easily prepared as for something familiar and observe what he had heard with his ear also with his eye.[1] Just as the blessed Job, beloved of God, the just, said to God: "With the hearing of my ears I heard you at first, but now my eye also has seen you [Job 42.5]." To whom also God said: "Strengthen like a man your loins and do not consider that something strange has been revealed to you [Job 40.2–3]."

1. See also §293.

329.   Because in the beginning God appeared according to the declaration, as [the scripture] says: "According to the image of God He created man [Gen. 1.27]," so for all eternity in the same likeness the God of glory appears,

as the martyr Stephen said: "The God of glory appeared to our father Abraham [Acts 7.2]." And they all called Him Lord Sabaoth and God omnipotent.

330.   So one must understand that the revelation of God in the likeness of man was according to the weakness of the seers and not that the immeasurable nature of God is limited or circumscribed or that He, by whom all is filled, sometimes appears altering his own limits to other limits. But by condescension and expediency He made Himself familiar by means of likenesses that He might make them familiar with Him, aware of God and witnesses of the true forms. Because undoubtedly the truth is to be sought from the likeness.

331.   Him the great Moses also desired and beheld; for although Moses knew and spoke with God hand in hand and face to face, yet he was anxious to grasp the true beauty, saying to God: "Show me yourself [Ex. 33.13]." Note then the answer: "There is no man who will see God and live [Ex. 33.20]." So by a lesser symbol He restrains him who solicits, and He preserves his natural invisibility because He is incomprehensible.

332.   Do you see that He is invisible to those who seek Him and inscrutable to those who search for Him in his particular form? For his likenesses are not material forms at all, but passing visions, and the truth is his essential nature. A likeness was shown to Moses as the model[1] of the material tabernacle, according to which he fashioned a material tabernacle [Ex. 25.9]; and to Ezechiel a temple [was revealed] as the type[1] of the temple [Ez. 40]. Even so to the first man God revealed his immaterial likeness in the form of a man that He might make man through material matter aware of the truth. For God with his impenitent benevolence [Rom. 11.29] ordained the first man to be near Him, familiar with God and the divine joy.

1. Model, type: *տիպ/տաւակ* (τύπος as I Cor. 10.6). On types in the *Teaching* see Introduction, pp. 15–16.

333.   And on one after the other God poured his Spirit abundantly, on the ranks and companies of the prophets in the race of Israel; who following the will of God ordered their people to keep carefully the commandments of God. They were the chosen people [Ps. 33.12; Is. 43.20] and received the command not to approach other peoples and not to mingle with the races of the heathen [Josh. 23.12], lest they learn their sins.

334.   But they mixed with them and became involved in marriage alliances; they took and learnt their idolatry and mingled with kings and princes.

Therefore the prophet complained and cried: "They have mingled with the heathen and have learnt their deeds; they have served their idols, and they were for them a snare [Ps. 105.35–36]," and: "They sacrificed their sons and daughters to their demons and shed innocent blood, the blood of their sons and daughters whom they sacrificed to the idols of Canaan [37–38]."

335.   But the Lord God at the time that He oppressed the land of the Egyptians, in order to bring them [the Israelites] out from there destroyed all the firstborn of the Egyptians [Ex. 12.29–33], and delivered them from there. For which reason He made a covenant with their fathers that they should consecrate their firstborn sons to the Lord their God [Ex. 13.12]. But instead of this, they took their sons and daughters and sacrificed them to the demons of the heathens, building altars on the land which the Lord God had called his own and named as the lot of his inheritance. They set up images instead of Him and worshiped stones and wood; and soiling the earth with the blood which they prostituted to the demons, they increased the fornications of the flesh. And so they were impure in their paths.

336.   For when they entered the land which He had given them, He ordered them to exterminate the lawless races who were in the land. But they did not destroy them but became their allies, making covenants with the lawless races with whom they united and inherited impiety. For God, because of their evil deeds, had removed the real inhabitants of the earth from their habitation. But they entered [the land] and began to work the same deed of unity with their kings and princes and priests.

337.   Therefore the Lord God in his great compassion and love for man sent to them the prophets and warned them with messages that they might turn away from their works of lawlessness and serve God the Creator of all, who on account of his love for mankind had pity and compassion on their wickedness. Who through the prophets complained about them: "They said to the wood, 'you are my father,' and to the stone, 'you begat me,' and they have turned their backs to me, and not their faces [Jer. 2.27]."

338.   [*The persecutions of the prophets*] Then the wicked and thoughtless race in their blindness rose up against the prophets, stoned them and killed them [Heb. 11.37], and they so destroyed them that at last one prophet cried: "I alone have remained [Is. 49.21; III Kings 19.10; I Mac. 13.4]." And they took the holy name prophet and applied it to the false and vile heathen priests.

339.   Likewise, the perverse race would not listen to the God-seeing true prophets who related truthfully to them the coming of the true Son of God to the world with his incarnation.[1] So they imposed death upon them all the more, so that no one was left whom they did not kill with various torments.

1. For the prophets foretelling the Incarnation, see also §341, 344, 346, Eznik, §345. A major theme in the *Teaching* is the realization of the Old Testament in the New; see also §415, 423.

340.   Therefore the Lord God was angry at that people and made their inheritance detestable [Ps. 105.40], delivering them into the hands of the heathen. For He delivered them into the hands of those whose gods they loved to worship and with whom they had fornicated, and these He raised up over them as tormentors and offenders and captors. As He said: "I shall deliver them into the hands of their heathen paramours, for those they hate to rule over them and their enemies to oppress them, humbling them beneath their hands [Ps. 105.41; Ezek. 23.9, 22]." For although He saved them many times from the hands of their oppressors, yet after their escape from oppression they increased in the same [Ps. 105.43]; they angered God in their counsels and were crooked in their lawlessness.

341.   But the Lord looked upon their oppression on hearing the voice of their prayers; remembering the covenant which had been made with their fathers, He had compassion according to his great mercy and afforded them mercy in the face of all their captors [Ps. 105.44–46]. The Lord God saved them and gathered them from among the heathen [Ps. 105.47], bringing them out from imprisonment after seventy years from the land of Babylon, from the region of Assyria. He rebuilt the ruins and renewed the temple of his name; He gave them prophecy [Ezra. 5.2] and restored the priesthood [Neh. 13.30], making everything new again; and then revealed his word, which after the passing of the ages He has fulfilled through his Only-begotten.

342.   [*Prophecies foreshadowing Christ*] For not after the Omniscient had taken thought did the Son come and appear to the world and elevate mankind to the glory of honor, but according to his resolution in the beginning He accomplished it in the end.[1] For the mystery which was hidden with God from the nations for ever [Eph. 3.3, 11] now has been revealed to his saints because the likenesses revealed temporarily to the just were auguries[2] of the eternal truth which was to come.

1. This idea is elaborated in Eznik, §346–349. See also below, §352–353.
2. Auguries: գուշակք; see Introduction, p. 16.

343. For "in many modes and in many ways God spoke previously with our fathers through the prophets; in the end of these days He has spoken with us through the Son, whom He set as heir of all things, by whom also He created the ages, who is the light of his glory and the image of his being, who upholds all things by his word and his power [Heb. 1.1–3]."

344. Do you see the modes and ways and prophets in great numbers and God singly, who spoke concerning his one Only-begotten? The prophet said on behalf of God: "I am God, and there is no other except me who would foretell the last things before they come about, and all of them will be completed [Is. 46.9–10]." For he knew the mystery concerning the only wise God, which was hidden from time and was revealed through the prophetic writings.

345. Then when the Savior Himself came, the Son of God, He revealed to the disciples: "Blessed are your eyes for what you see, and your ears for what you hear;[1] for many prophets and just men and kings desired to see what you see and have not seen, and to hear what you hear and have not heard [Mt. 13.16–17; Lk. 10.23–24]."

1. For what you see . . . for what you hear: զոր տեսանէք . . . զոր լսէք. This reflects neither the Armenian nor the Greek text of Matthew, but is explicable as a mistranslation of the Syriac dᵉḥāzyān . . . dᵉšāmᵉān.

346. Do you see that the warning [prophets] were likenesses of the true form of Christ, and through these temporary likenesses they foreshadowed the eternal forms? And so also the laws of Moses indicated and illuminated the future in all its details.[1]

1. Cf. Irenaeus, *Adv. Haer.*, IV 15.1: Itaque lex et disciplina erat illis et prophetia futurorum (further references in Lampe, *Lexicon*, s.v. νόμος).

347. For when God saw that sin was universal throughout the world, and that by it death was reigning and had swallowed up everything from Adam to Moses [Rom. 5.14] and had turned to oblivion the life-giving promise formerly written, as a raging fire burns which will destroy the hills and the plains, then He introduced the law like a fierce torrent to extinguish that universal [sin]. Therefore He says: "Whoever will do this will live in the same [Lev. 18.5; Rom. 10.5; Gal. 3.12]." For just as death was threatened to Adam if he should taste of the tree—whence death began to reign [I Cor. 15.21]—so also He said concerning the laws: "Who will do this will live in the same," whereby death was extinguished [I Cor. 15.54].

348. For the law, which is a foreshadowing[1] of Christ the fulfillment[2] of the law, destroyed death, whereby it also made clear the extent of sin and assessed it, and according to the faults of each, threatened them with death. And it weakened everyone and put them under a curse and judgment, that when He came, the Savior of all, Christ, might remove the sins which brought malediction and death, and the freed might say: "Thanks be to Him who has saved us from such death [II Cor. 1.10]."

1. Foreshadowing: ստուերագիր; cf. Col. 2.17: ἅ ἐστιν σκιὰ τῶν μελλόντων.
2. Fulfillment: արբիանակատար; cf. Rom. 10.4: τέλος γὰρ νόμου Χριστός. See also §423 below, and Irenaeus, *Adv. Haer.*, IV 4.2: Adimpletio enim eius (viz. legis) Christus.

349. The last makes it clear that the law remained until Christ by saying: "The law was added because of transgression until the seed should come to whom it was promised; it was ordained by angels through a mediator [Gal. 3.19]." For "under the law, he says, we were shut up and guarded, looking to the future [Gal. 3.23]," to which not only the races born from heaven, but also the invisible armies of angels with all insensible creatures remained in bondage,[1] according to the saying: "The expectation of the creatures waits for the manifestation of the Son of God. For the creatures were made subject to vanity, not by their own will, but because of him who subjected them in hope, because the creatures themselves will be made free from the slavery of corruption into the freedom of the glory of the Son of God [Rom. 8.19–21]."

1. The angels too had freewill (§277) which Satan abused (§278), and as created beings the *Teaching* includes them with all creatures enslaved to sin since the transgression of Adam, and hence in bondage to the law.

350. When Adam, who was created according to the image of God, and all his seed, who were called the "sons of God [Gen. 6.2]," by their own will inherited corruption, with them all creatures also became subject and were corrupted, not by their own will, but on account of the foreordained will of God to set them free in Christ [Rom. 6.18, 22]. For those who once were formed for the delight and glory of man became corrupted and dishonored on account of his anger. And the earth was cursed and made to produce thorns [Gen. 3.17–18], flooded and consumed by fire [II Pet. 3.6], shaken to its foundations and disturbed; and the winds were corrupted according to the seasons, the luminaries were darkened and became signs of blood [Joel 2.31], and the heavens lost their color, just as is indicated concerning what was to come to pass by the prophetic writings. The same the prophets endured from their fellow countrymen; for although the honored ones were sent by God, yet they were hated [II Chron. 36.16] and stoned [Heb. 11.37] by those who would not receive them; just as the Lord of all

says: "On your account I have destroyed the prophets by the word of my mouth [Hos. 6.5]."

351. Likewise also the angels, messengers to the races of men, dishonored and saddened by those who did not receive them, returned, as it is possible to understand concerning the others from the angels who came to Lot [Gen. 19]. For if the return of one sinner brings rejoicing to all the angels [Lk. 15.10], how much more will the revolt of all work sadness, whereby the name of God is blasphemed and the Holy Spirit saddened? But although in this way all creatures bore tribulation and were subject to vanity, yet all served the liberating hope which was set before them, angels and prophets and all creatures. For one said: "I shall stand on my guard and shall be on the rock and shall hope [Hab. 2.1]," and another: "I shall hope in the Lord and shall serve God my Savior [Micah 7.7]," and another: "Who out of Sion will give salvation to Israel [Ps. 13.7]?"

352. Why then did the Only-begotten prolong his bringing such tribulations on the creatures, unless it was first to give warning and make them previously accustomed to Him, lest when He appeared unexpectedly and unknown, He might not be received? Rather it was that He might come and give knowledge to people who as it were had seen and served Him. For if He came to his creatures and was not received after such opportunities, how much less [would He have been received] by those who had not been warned or informed.[1] But by forewarning mystery He informed all races and ages to come [Eph. 1.9].

1. Identical arguments in Eznik, §118. Cf. *Teaching*, §342.

353. Just as one of the Messengers of God says: "To me this grace was given to announce to the Gentiles the inscrutable greatness of Christ and to illuminate all concerning the providence of the mystery which was hidden from all ages with God, who created all things, that He might reveal now to principalities and powers who are on earth, through the church, the multiple wisdom of God, according to his plan for ever, which He effected by our Lord Jesus Christ [Eph. 3.8–11]." Who also concerning the same, revealed "when the fullness of time had come [Gal. 4.4]."

354. But who would this be from among men who would be able to know and speak such teaching about the Godhead? But He Himself so wished to make Himself known that they might know Him and live. But we creatures are not able to speak of God, we who are nailed to types of this image[1] according to the Maker's creating; but as much as our weakness can bear[2]

He wished to inform us. For no one knows about God save the Spirit of God and the Son, who came and told us and revealed and showed that "who has seen me, has seen my Father [Jn. 14.9]."

1. Types of this image: տիպք պատկերիս. Տիպ does not occur in the Armenian bible; the usual rendering of τύπος is պատկեր or աւրինակ; cf. Introduction, p. 16.
2. See also §330, 356, and note 2.

355. But God is a living Spirit [Jn. 4.24], burning fire, immeasurable and unchangeable, glory inexpressable, power infinite, beauty unparalleled and amazing, incomprehensible to mind or thought, inexpressable to the tongue, not contained in thought, outside all speech, unseen by the eye and unheard by the ear; nor can the reflection of the heart grasp Him.[1] The heavens altogether, the world altogether, and the universe altogether are not able to contain Him. His word raises up and supports everything, and at the power of his command the universe is suspended[2] without wings in flight over the winds, as if flying. He Himself envelops everything, is within all, above all [Eph. 4.6], outside of all; everything is from Him [Rom. 11.36], everything is in Him, and everything is for his glory [Ps. 18.2].

1. See also §263, 309, 362, 366; Eznik, §1; Ełišē, *History*, p. 30; *Yačaxapatum*, I.
2. See also §259.

356. And in many signs and in many wonders[1] He spoke with our fathers through the prophets at various times [Heb. 1.1], in unrelatable visions, in different transformations, in wonderful sounds, in praiseworthy beauty, in divine forms; sometimes in the likeness of light, in the form of a man, sometimes like blazing fire, in the form of a man. He appeared to many just men according to the ability of those who beheld Him, and according to the endurance of those listening He spoke with them.[2] For man is incapable of seeing God in his essence [Jn. 1.18; I Jn. 4.12],[3] as wax cannot bear fire; for the hills are not able to see Him, since when they see Him among them they will melt [Ps. 96.5].

1. Ի բազում նշանս եւ ի բազում արուեստս, not the biblical բազում մասամբք եւ բազում աւրինաւք, as in §343. Cf. the variation in Łazar, *History*, p. 179: բազում կերպարանաւք եւ այլ այլ գուգակութեամբք.
2. See also §330, 354 etc. Cf. Cyril Jer, *Cat.*, VI 2.
3. In his essence: զոյն; see also §382 note 1 and Introduction, p. 12.

357. But when of his own will and benevolence He revealed Himself, He appeared in the form of man, sometimes light, sometimes fire, and sometimes wind, and in cloud and in mist and in the tempest.

358. But if we say that He is fire [Deut. 4.24; Ez. 1.4], we say what we see; if we say He is light [I Jn. 1.5], we take our idea of his likeness from our own nature, we give a form to the invisible in a visible way because of our incapacity. But He was revealed according to our littleness, lest the material creatures be burnt up by the awe of his glory. And no one knew his name, for there was not yet any one there except Himself who could give Him a name.[1]

1. On the name of God, cf. Chrysostom, *In Heb. Hom.*, II 2, Gregory of Nyssa, *Quod non sint tres Dii.*

359. And in his appearing to the just men, He restricted[1] his awesomeness and appeared in the form of men and angels, intelligible according to the capacity of their eyes. Creatures are unable to examine their Creator, nor does matter know its Fashioner.

1. Restricted: *ամփոփէր*; see §363 note 1.

360. But the Creator has compassion on his creatures, for God made all creatures and decked them in praiseworthy beauty and majestic glory. From the earth He created earthly flesh [Gen. 2.7], and from light the angels [II Cor. 11.14],[1] adorning them in glorious light, and covering and arranging the throne of glory where rise the blessings of the angels, the voices of the Seraphim, and the praises of the watchers [Is. 6.1–3],[2] the hosts of the armies and troops of saints and ranks of praisers, and the blessings of those in heaven, and the prayers of the just, and the worship of the saints, Seraphim and Cherubim and the united hosts of light.

1. See also §262 note 2, but here the angels are made of light; see the luminous hosts in §365.
2. Watchers: *զուարթունք*; cf. Dan. 4.10. The word is a common synonym for angels in Armenian and is frequent in the *Teaching*. It is a parallel to the Syriac ʿīrā, on which see W. Cramer, *Die Engelvorstellungen bei Ephräm dem Syrer, Orientalia Christiana Analecta*, 173 (Rome 1965), pp. 11 ff.

361. [*Exposition of the faith: the Trinity*] In mentioning this witness, we have set out in your hearing the true holy faith, which the Holy Scriptures[1] have clearly taught us by the Holy Spirit, concerning the eternal kingdom of the Godhead, which was revealed by a mystery to our just fathers [Rom. 16.26; Eph.3. 5], and was preached among us by the Son and the Holy Spirit, and was announced by the holy prophets and apostles;[2] and confirmation of the faith was given to us.

1. For faith as taught by the scriptures see §389, 699; also Cyril Jer., *Cat.*, IV 17.
2. The apostles and prophets are frequently associated in preaching the gospel; cf. Polycarp, *Epistle*, VI 3 (and other references in Lampe, *Lexicon*, s.v. ἀπόστολος); also Athanasius, *Ad Adelphium*, 6.

362. That through faith we might aver in one God, Father and Lord and Creator of all; and in the only-begotten Son, who is from the Father and beside the Father and with the Father; and in the Holy Spirit, who is from the being of the same,[1] by whom He created all the creatures. Who is one Lordship, one power, one authority, one greatness, one knowledge, one mystery, one government, one hypostasis without beginning, three perfect Persons, one perfect will, the ineffable and inscrutable unity of the Trinity. One essence, one being, one Godhead, Father, Son, and Holy Spirit; three Persons, one hypostasis of the Godhead. The Father from Himself, the Son from the Father, the Spirit from Them both and in Them both. In essence, being and deity equal, the same; alike in depth, height, length, and width [Eph. 3.18]. One being in nature, one crown of the Trinity, and the heavens and earth are full of his glory [Is. 6.3].[2]

1. For the ideas in the *Teaching* on the procession of the Spirit see Introduction, p. 130.
2. For similar credal statements about the Trinity see §259, 383–384, 705. Cf. *Yačaxapatum*, I and II. For the technical terms involved see Introduction, pp. 11–13.

363. So King Solomon, son of the prophet, said in his inspired prayers: "The heavens and the earth are not sufficient for you [III Kg. 8.27 = II Ch. 6.18]." And the prophet said on behalf of the Lord: "The heavens are my throne, and the earth a stool for my feet. What sort of house will you build for me, says the Lord, or what place will you prepare for me as a dwelling? Did not my hand create this universe? And to whom shall I grant rest and respite, except to the gentle and humble and to those who have trembled at my words [Is. 66.1–2]?" And: "I shall be their God, and they will be my people [Jer. 24.7; Ez. 36.28; 37.23, 27; Zech. 8.8]." But Him for whom the heavens and earth are not sufficient, how will the heart of man grasp Him, unless man be somewhat greater than the heavens and the earth? But whatever is willed by the Godhead occurs, whatever He desired He created, whatever He desired it was done, whatever He wishes He does not neglect; yet He was restricted, made small [Philipp. 2.7],[1] and became what He also willed.[2]

1. *Ամփոփեցաւ, փոքրկացաւ.* For these and other technical terms used in the *Teaching* to describe the Incarnation see especially §377–379, 587–596, and Introduction, pp. 18–20.
2. It is remarkable that the *Teaching* does not always distinguish carefully between the Trinity, the God of the Old Testament, and the Incarnate Son. Indeed the author speaks of the "Ancient of Days," the "Lord of Hosts," and "He who is" becoming man (§381, 431, 588, 680). In the later Moses Dasxuranc'i this last expression is also used of the Incarnate Son (II 7). In Łazar, *History*, p. 61, the Incarnation of "one of the Trinity" (*մի ի սրբոյ երրորդութեանց Շաւր*) is mentioned, but there is no confusion of Persons. In P'awstos, however, Is. 40.12 is referred to the Son (V 4). There are parallels in Justin, who refers to the God who appeared in the O.T. theophanies as the Son or the Logos (*Cambridge History of Later Greek and Early Medieval Philosophy*, p. 163 note 1). In

ps. Athanasius, *De Inc. c. Ar.*, 10, the Lord Sabaoth is Jesus. Cf. Grillmeier, *Christ*, p. 65, for the confusion in the early church concerning Christology and the Trinitarian faith.

364. [*The birth of Christ*] God sent his own Son into the world, who came and was born of a woman and was enveloped in our human flesh;[1] He gave life to all flesh by his own flesh. By Him also the Creator of the world succeeded in renewing the just[2] and in liberating them from births involved in sin,[3] and in making them like the angels,[4] and in calling them sons of God [I Jn. 3.1], and in rendering mortals immortal by the immortal Spirit, and in giving them honor by the divine glory. They are arrayed in majestic light and pass from earthliness to heavenliness, from mortality to immortal life [I Cor. 15.54]; they are robed in light which passes not away and in incorruptible beauty of form.

1. Enveloped in our human flesh: *ի մարմնեղէն մարմին պատեցաւ.* There is only one word in Armenian for "flesh" or "body": *մարմին,* though very occasionally *մս* is used in the context of communion. The verb *պատել* is used twice in the Armenian N.T., Luke 2.12 to render ἐσπαργανωμένον, and Heb. 9.4 περικεκαλυμμένην. This is not the usual expression in the *Teaching* to describe the mode of the Incarnation; "joined" (*խառնեալ*) is the most common (see Introduction, pp. 18–19), but a wide variety of other terms is used. See especially §377–379 and notes.
2. A conflate of Rom. 1.17 with II Cor. 5.17, Eph. 2.15.
3. Jn. 9.2; I Jn. 3.9, 5.18. See also §412 note 2, and Introduction, p. 17.
4. Cf. Origen, *In Lev. Hom.*, IX 11: Eligamus ergo vitam, eligamus lucem, ut in die honeste ambulemus, ut et nos sequentes Iesum intra velamen tabernaculi interioris, iam non simus ut homines mortales, sed ut angeli immortales, cum novissimum inimicum destruxerit mortem ipse Dominus Iesus Christus.

365. How much more ineffable is the Deity, whose will is the source of all blessings and who is Lord of all deeds, by the word of whose mouth all creatures are established, from whom all luminaries take their light,[1] and in whose power stand firm all creatures, the upper stage of the heavens and all the world and what is in them! "And by the spirit of his mouth [were established] all their powers [Ps. 32.6]." And the terrestrial ministers and the luminous hosts of the saints stand dependent on his hope and aspire to his mercies, and at his glance all creatures' needs are provided. In his power lives everyone, and "the eyes of all hope in Him [Ps. 144.15]."

1. See also §267 note 2. But here, as in §566, it is not so much implied that the luminaries shine with a borrowed light as they that produce their light by imitating the divine light, as Aristotle's subsidiary movers move by imitating the unmoved mover.

366. He is the Creator and establisher and leader of all by the nature of his essence;[1] the infinite power which is from Him stretches out and surrounds all things; from Him come the life-giving powers; He passes among all things; from Him

creatures, heavenly and terrestrial, through wind and air, fire and water, through light and shadow, abyss and height; He goes forth with his invisible hosts in his piercing light; the power of his spirit is unlimited, it reaches everywhere and extends everywhere; the rays go forth by his power and incomprehensible nature. He has no limit in height above nor in the abyss below; He comes to a finite end neither to right nor left, neither in front nor behind. Six rays in power;[2] six ages of a thousand years; the seventh age is rest for the just.

1. By the nature of his essence: *խելութեան բնութեամբն.* On these terms see Introduction, pp. 12, 19.
2. Sargisean, *Agat͑angelos*, p. 374, thinks that the "six rays in power" refer to the six days of creation rather than the six ages. He points out that the *զարդ* of Gen. 2.1 ("the heavens and all the earth were finished and all their κόσμος") is changed to *զաւրութիւնք* (powers) in the Armenian version of Ephrem's *Commentary on Genesis, Ep͑remi Matenagrut͑iwnkʿ*, I, p. 9. For the doctrine of the six ages see the more extended development in §668–671 and notes ad loc.

367. In what respect do we preach God to be similar to us who are composed of jointed members from earth? Each member carries its own function in itself and is not competent at the function of its companion: the eye does not hear, nor the ear see, the tongue does not smell, nor the hands walk, nor do the feet cry out [I Cor. 12.14 ff]. The mouth is for eating, the nose for smelling, the palate for tasting; each one is bound to its own nature.[1]

1. Cf. Athanasius, *C. Gentes*, 38.

368. But He Himself by his own will made his all-saving advent and fulfilled the will of the Father. God the holy Son was sent by God; He took flesh from the virgin, perfect man, perfect in his divinity.[1] He revealed the power of the Deity and showed the weakness of the flesh; He became a fellow servant [Philipp. 2.7] in the flesh of our humanity and freed the flesh of mankind from sin. In it [his flesh] He descended into Hell and brought out from there those who had been shut up in Hell [I Pet. 3.19]. He was persecuted in the flesh and cast out Satan and enchained sin.

1. Perfect man, perfect in his divinity: *մարդ կատարեալ, կատարեալ Աստուածութեամբն;* see also §377, true man: *ճշմարիտ մարդ.* The expression "perfect man" ἄνθρωπος τέλειος, only became frequent in the anti-Apollinarian controversy in the second half of the fourth century, but it is occasionally found much earlier; see Grillmeier, *Christ*, p. 113. It is frequent in the works of Theodore of Mopsuestia which circulated in Armenia in the 430's, causing complaints from Acacius of Melitene (*Girkʿ T͑ltʿocʿ*, pp. 14–15, 19–21; Tallon, pp. 21–28). The expression "true man" is common in the works of Athanasius; cf. also the phrase κατ᾽ ἀλήθειαν γέγονεν ἄνθρωπος in Proclus's *Tome to the Armenians*, 5 (Armenian text in *Girkʿ T͑ltʿocʿ*, pp. 2–8), a work which was highly regarded by Armenian theologians.

369. For to those who believed in his flesh He made known his divinity; and those who were scandalized by his flesh denied his nature.[1] For He was united to the flesh by nature and joined the flesh to his divinity.[2] Those who believed in Him will enjoy ineffable blessings; and those who strayed from this faith walked on unfrequented and hidden paths and erred and completely destroyed the fortune of their souls; and they seduced many from the true faith. When they thought they had found something, they found nothing, as it is written: "They went after nothing and found nothing [Jer. 2.5]." For the search after gain is labor, but labor without discovery leads to idolatry by false teaching.[3]

1. The emphasis throughout the *Teaching* is on the divinity of the Son; see Introduction, pp. 20. Although the *Teaching* is not explicitly a polemical treatise (though see §389 note 3), Sargisean, *Agat'angełos*, p. 375, is probably right to see in the frequent stress on Christ's divinity an attack on Arian ideas. (One may add in connection with this suggestion the fact that P'awstos Buzandac'i, writing probably in the early fifth century, also places great emphasis on anti-Arian teaching, and not only in the sermon supposedly delivered by Nerses to the Arian Valens, IV 5. Cf. N. G. Garsoian, *Politique ou orthodoxie? L'Arménie au quatrième siècle*, Revue des études arméniennes, n.s. 4 (1967), pp. 297-320.) More important confirmation of Sargisean's suggestion comes from the emphasis in the *Teaching* on the two births of Christ (§382, 391), a doctrine denied by the Arians and upheld against them by the orthodox; see Lampe, *Lexicon*, s.v. γέννησις.

2. Խառնեաց զխառնիին բնդ իւր ԱստուածուԹիւն. Խառնել is the most important of the terms used in the *Teaching* to define the mode of union in Christ of the human and divine. It corresponds to the Greek συγκεράννυμι; cf. I Cor. 12.24 συνεκέρασεν, or μίγνυμι, Lk. 13.1 ἔμιξεν, both of which were used quite early, e.g., Hippolytus, *Antichr.*, 4: ὁ λόγος ... συγκεράσας τὸ θνητὸν ἡμῶν σῶμα τῇ ἑαυτοῦ δυνάμει, καὶ μίξας τὸ φθαρτὸν τῷ ἀφθάρτῳ. The expression κρᾶσις was taken over from Stoic conceptions; see Grillmeier, *Christ*, pp. 155, 336. It figures most predominantly in the writings of Gregory Nazianzenus (e.g., *Or.*, XXXVIII 13: ὢ τῆς καινῆς μίξεως, ὢ τῆς παραδόξου κράσεως), whose works were popular in Armenia; see Zarp'analean, *Matenadaran*, pp. 346-358. This quotation is also found in a catena composed by a Chalcedonian Armenian probably in the seventh century; see G. Garitte, *Un Petit Florilège diphysite grec traduit de l'arménien*, Analecta Biblica, 12 (1959), pp. 102-112. It is most likely that the use of the term խառնել in Armenia is to be derived from Gregory Nazianzenus, though it was also common in the Syrian fathers; cf. Ephrem, *De Nat.*, 6, *De Fide*, 77. The same verb is also used with reference to the redemption; see Introduction, p. 19.

3. This sentence is obscure, but may be a confusion of Wisdom 14.12.

370. For from above through all the prophets He informed those to come about the future ages. And by the previous examples[1] He often taught those who came later, sometimes speaking with terrible threats, by mention of first seeking revenge in order to terrify the unbelievers and exhort them to orthodoxy—like the various plagues of Egypt, and the bitter retribution of revenge on them—or He mentions those who fell into unbelief in the desert and all those who experienced the anger of God.

1. Examples: աւրինակաւք; see Introduction, pp. 15-16.

371. Similarly He made the land of Sodom and Gomorrah an example of Christ,[1] lest, some of them not believing, they suffer even worse than this. Or He calls to mind the various glorious wonders and the benefits to the just of the gifts of God. He recalls at the same time the order of the firmament of creation, often saying: "I raised the heavens and established the earth [Zech. 12.1]," and: "I enclosed the sea within limits [Job. 38.3]," in order that by all this He might strengthen the belief of his hearers in the promises.

1. This sentence is ambiguous; it could mean: similarly Christ made the land of Sodom and Gomorrah an example.

372. [*Christ as the fulfillment of the promises in the Old Testament*] Then when He came, the Savior of all fulfilled what had once been promised concerning Him. And by witness we can verify the coming of the Son, by the predictions of the prophets concerning the birth in the flesh of the Son of God, by the inspired saying concerning the divine flesh;[1] as God previously showed the coming of his Son by the voices of his worthy prophets.[2]

1. Divine flesh: աստուածախառն մարմին (lit. flesh joined to God); see §369 note 2.
2. See also §339 note 1.

373. For "God sent his own Son, who came, was born of a virgin and entered under the law, that He might ransom those who were under the law, in order that we might receive adoption [Gal. 4.4-5]." In like fashion John the Baptist said: "Repent, for the kingdom of heaven is near [Mt. 3.2]." This also the Lord of ages mentioned as a parable[1] of the kingdom, saying: "The time is fulfilled and the kingdom of God has arrived [Mk. 1.15]."

1. Parable: առակ; cf. Introduction, p. 16.

374. Then came the wondrous Son of God, sharer of his council,[1] to fulfill the mystery[2] which had been established before all ages [Col. 1.26]; as the prophet says: "He established the words of his servants and justifies the councils of his angels [Is. 44.26]." The angel also has to prepare the way for Him, who greeted the virgin in order to fulfill the prophecy: "A virgin will conceive and bear a son, and they will call his name Emmanuel [Is. 7.14; Mt. 1.23]"; and he says: "Rejoice, be joyful, the Lord is with you [Lk. 1.28]."

1. Sharer of his council: խորհրդակից; see also §260 where the following terms are applied to the Son: արարչակից, խորհրդակցալ, խորհրդակատար, հաւասարծն, and §420 note 4.
2. Mystery: խորհուրդ, as Col. 1.26, μυστήριον; see also §393. The Armenian word also means "thought, counsel, plan"; see also note 1.

375.   And then he shows in what fashion the Lord would be with her, saying: "The Holy Spirit will come upon you, and the power of the Highest will be a shadow over you; for he who will be born is holy and will be called the Son of the Highest [Lk. 1.35]." And also looking to the prophecies, he says: "The Lord God will give him the throne of David his father, and he will reign over the house of Jacob for ever, and there will be no end to his kingdom [Lk. 1.32–33]." Concerning Him the patriarch Jacob, filled with the Spirit, also spoke, and recognizing Juda as glorious said in prophecy: "There will not lack a prince of Juda, nor a leader from his loins, until there comes he to whom belongs the kingdom, for he is the hope of the nations [Gen. 49.10]."

376.   So we see all prophecy completely fulfilled and perfected; behold, we see all nations serving Him willingly or unwillingly. He says: "He will bind his ass to the vine and his donkey to bunches of grapes [Gen. 49.11]," that is his coming in humility to the laborers of the vineyard, who did not desire the Lord of the vineyard. He suffered by his own will and endured it. This in its own time we shall narrate; about his birth[1] we still have words to say to you, the prediction of the prophecies, the preaching of the apostles, the witness of the martyrs.[2]

   1. About his birth: *որ...վասն ծննդեան,*, a Syriacism; see §269 note 1.
   2. The audience is frequently addressed in the *Teaching*, in keeping with its character as an oral catechism. Several times reference is made to the order of the exposition; see §286, 391, 497, 601, 658.

377.   [*Exposition of the faith: Christology and prophecies concerning Christ*] He is Himself in his being, as indeed He is [Ex. 3.14].[1] But when He wished, He took human form and put on flesh[2] and descended to our likeness; He who was infinite and inconceivable in all the fullness of the Godhead for our sake came down into bounded form[3] and was restricted to flesh;[4] He was contained truly in the flesh and became a true man[5] and descended to humility that He might raise us up. But in his own Godhead He is in heaven and on earth, beside the Father and with the Father. And all creatures move at his command in the way each one has been ordered and arranged.

   1. A difficult sentence: *որ նա ինքն է յէութեանն, որպէս եւ էն իսկ.* The expression *որ է* (Ex. 3.14) is not normally applied to the Son, but see §363 note 2.
   2. Put on flesh: *զգեցաւ մարմին.* For the ambiguity of the Armenian *մարմին,* see §364 note 1.
   3. Bounded form: *չափաւորութիւն,* an expression similar to the μέτρον ἀνθρώπινον common in Cyril of Alexandria.
   4. Restricted to flesh: *ամփոփեցաւ ի մարմին*; see also §359 note 1, 363 note 1.
   5. True man: *ճշմարիտ մարդ*; see also §368 note 1.

378.   But although it was for our sake that He came down to humility, yet He remains in his own nature.[1] As He Himself says: "I am the same and have not changed [Mal. 3.6]." For although He took the form and flesh of mankind, yet He mingled[2] and united and submerged[3] the flesh in his divinity. And again [the scripture] says: "He is God, our God for ever and ever [Ps. 47.15]," and again: "You are the same, and your years do not pass [Ps. 101.28]." A similar saying came also to the greatest of the prophets: Moses: "I am He who was from the beginning; thus you will say: 'God who is from the beginning sent me to you [Ex. 3.14]'". John also said this in his letter: "Who was from the beginning, of whom we have heard, of whom we were eyewitnesses, at whom we looked, and our hands touched the word of life; and life was made manifest, and we have seen and bear witness [I Jn. 1.1–2]." For He Himself is the true God and everlasting life.

   1. See also §369 note 1.
   2. Mingled: *խառնեաց,* on which see §369 note 2.
   3. Submerged: *ընկղմեաց.* Sargisean, *Agat°angelos*, p. 377, notes that this expression is found in the Armenian version of Ephrem's commentary on the gospel, ch. 2. But there the phrase "humanity submerged into divinity" (*մարդկութիւն ընկղմեալ յաստուածութիւն*) refers more specifically to Christ's ascension to sit at the right hand of the Father; Leloir, *S. Ephrem, Commentaire, Version arménienne*, p. 30. This section is missing from the Syriac, Leloir, *Ephrem, Commentaire, Texte syriaque*. The expression as it stands tends to Eutychianism, and such extreme tendencies are usually avoided in the *Teaching*. The same word is used in a redemptive context at §595.

379.   The unknowable took flesh and was touched and known[1] in the flesh; and all the circumstances[2] of the flesh He took upon Himself of his own will and suffered in humility, being among strangers; and not by anyone's constraint, but by his own independent will He bore this, as He Himself said: "I have power to lay aside my life at my own will, in order to take it up again [Jn. 10.18]."

   1. The unknowable was known: *անըմբռնելին...ըմբռնեցաւ* (lit. the ungraspable was grasped); cf. Ephrem, *De Fide*, 17.
   2. Circumstances: *անցք,* equivalent to the Greek πάθη. The willingness of Christ to undergo all the sufferings (in the wide sense of πάθη) necessarily attendant on human existence is often stressed in the *Teaching*, but there is no reflection of the theological and philosophical difficulties concerning the πάθη of Christ which caused such controversy between Apollinarians and more orthodox theologians.

380.   And He Himself was born of a virgin and by his own will fulfilled the will of Him who had sent Him. He says: "I came to fulfill the will of my Father [Jn. 6.38]," that He might show the single, indissoluble, indivisible unity of their essence. By the Father's will He entered the virgin's womb and abhorred it not, for He makes all things holy. By his own will

He was wrapped in swaddling clothes and placed in a beast's stable [Lk. 2.7], for He is the Lord and Creator of all greatness and the source of all blessings.

381.   The Ancient of Days became a child for us[1] and took the form of the flesh of the weakness of our humanity that He might change us to his immortality.[2] But although He put on flesh and came down into our likeness, yet He remains in the glory of his divinity of the Father's nature.[3] Just as He was, He is, and remains for ever with his Father on high in his own nature, with the flesh of ours which He put on, glorified continuously by the angels of spirit and fire.

1. See also §363 note 2.
2. See also §679 note 1.
3. See also §369 note 1, §378 note 1, and Elišē, *History*, pp. 38, 87.

382.   He came and became a man that mortals might be able to see [the Father]. Nobody has seen God in his essence [Jn. 1.18; I Jn. 4.12],[1] neither angels nor archangels, neither Seraphim nor Cherubim, nor the myriad hosts of heavenly angels. But the Son, hidden in the flesh, showed and revealed Him to the perfect in mind and understanding that they might be filled with the wonder of his light. "Who has seen me, has seen my Father [Jn. 14.9]," And He came and fulfilled the promises, from the holy virgin. And the first birth is from the Father before unbounded ages, an eternal and everlasting birth, from an eternal and everlasting Father before all.[2]

1. In his essence: զηյիւ; see also §356 note 3 and Introduction, p. 12.
2. The two births; see also §388, 391. The emphasis on the eternal birth of the Son from the Father in anti-Arian (see §369 note 1), but the juxtaposition of the eternal birth with the birth from the virgin is more typical of later opposition to Nestorius or Eutyches; see also §388 note 1.

383.   Thus much only can we, who have been created by Him, know in our weakness—that He and the heavenly Father are one, whence all paternity is named of heavenly and earthly [creatures]. One sole Lord, three Persons in one hypostasis, three Persons, one hypostasis, one unity of knowledge, one hypostasis consubstantial in glory, one only in illumination, one only in essence;[1] for no one can examine how or why He came about.

1. For similar statements about the Trinity, see §359, 362, 665, 705. For the technical terminology see Introduction, pp. 11–12.

384.   Believe in the Trinity, aver in the unity with profound silence, silent in faith. But we earthbound creatures formed from dust, how can we examine

the unfathomable and inscrutable, or know the All-Highest? And we who had a beginning, how can we examine the eternal and incomprehensible?[1]

1. The incomprehensibility of God is frequently stressed in the *Teaching*; see §309 note 1.

385.   The true faith is this: He humbled Himself and joined his divinity to our humanity and the immortal to the mortal to link[1] all mankind to the immortality of his own divinity. When in the flesh He entered the presence of the Father on his right hand, the only-begotten Son of God, companion in power of the Father, joined us to his divinity.[2] By Him [the Father] established the foundations of the earth and bestowed extension on the heavens [Prov. 8.29; Is. 40.21–22]. Of Him the prophet says: "The Lord revealed his right hand and his arm to all nations, and all races of the earth saw the salvation of our God [Ps. 97.1–3]."

1. Link: ωὕρωկ ωրωug; see also §706 note 1.
2. The purpose of the Incarnation is variously explained in the *Teaching*. For a recapitulation of the main points see Introduction, pp. 17–18.

386.   The right hand of the Father[1] and his arm[2] indeed are the only-begotten Christ; and by Him have all creatures been illuminated. Who "in the beginning was the Word, and the Word was with God, and the Word was God, by whom[3] all things were made [Jn. 1.1–3]," and by Him all things in heaven and in earth have been established. It was necessary that they should be hallowed by Him by whom they were created and established,[4] and that by Him they should be illuminated; for God willed that the creatures should live and not perish.

1. Christ the right hand of the Father, one of the most common Christian interpretations of the O.T. δεξιά (for references see Lampe, *Lexicon*, s.v. δεξιός). It is noteworthy that Athanasius contrasts the χείρ of God, viz. Christ, with the δάκτυλος of God which was Moses, *Ad Serapionem*, IV 22.
2. An interpretation based on Jn. 12.38 quoting Is. 53.1. For patristic references see Lampe, *Lexicon*, s.v. βραχίων; see also *Teaching*, §444.
3. By whom: որ...ὕnιῼωι, a Syriacism; see §269 note 1.
4. Cf. Athanasius, *De Incarnatione*, 1: οὐδὲ γὰρ ἐναντίον φανήσεται, εἰ δι' οὗ ταύτην (viz. τὴν κτίσιν) ἐδημιούργησεν ὁ Πατήρ, ἐν αὐτῷ καὶ τὴν ταύτης σωτηρίαν εἰργάσατο.

387.   So God sent his Holy Spirit to the virgin Mary [Mt. 1.20; Lk. 1.35], and the Son of God took flesh from the virgin, by which He destroyed evil,[1] and by the same flesh paid the debt for sins, by the flesh joined to the Deity. By his humility united to his majesty He joined the invisible to the visible. The report of the angels to the shepherds [Lk. 2.8–14] presaged the divine glory; the stable and swathing bands [Lk. 2.7] indicated the humble poverty

of the flesh; by the guiding star and gifts of the magi [Mt. 2.1–11] the lordship of the Lord of all was revealed, [that] by the earthly [signs] we might know the flesh and by the heavenly recognize the divinity.[2]

1. Evil: զչարէն, either "evil" or "the evil one."
2. The distinction between the earthly signs showing Christ's humanity and the heavenly his divinity is brought out by Athanasius, *De Incarnatione*, 18.

388.   But see what the grace of the spirit of prophecy in Micah says to us: "And you, Bethlehem, he says, have attained no less a destiny; from you will rise up for me a leader and prince of the house of Israel, whose goings forth [have been] from the beginning of the days of the world [Micah 5.2; Mt. 2.6]." "From the beginning" shows the divinity, "Bethlehem" means the flesh. The archangel says: "She will give birth to a son, and they will call his name Jesus [Mt. 1.21; Lk. 1.31]." And the Psalmist sang "before the sun his name [Ps. 71.17]." One refers to his birth in the flesh, the other shows his divinity born from the Father before the morning star.[1]

1. See also §382 and note 2, 391. The juxtaposition of the birth from Mary in time and the eternal birth from the Father is found frequently in Cyril of Alexandria and later Greek writers (for references see Lampe, *Lexicon*, s.v. γέννησις). For the Syrian tradition see Ephrem, *De Nat.*, XI; but in Ephrem there is also the idea that the baptism of Christ is another birth; cf. Beck, *Le Baptême chez saint Ephrem*, *L'Orient syrien*, I (1956), p. 116.

389.   We have this true faith from the Scriptures and the canons of the church[1]—a guide of life for the journey to God—and by faith in the teaching in the Holy Scriptures. And do not deviate from the rules of wisdom, neither to the right nor the left, for these are not indeed seeds sterile and spoilt, dried up and atrophied, plants which we sow in the desert of the hearts that hear them, but they are from the divine Scriptures, the inspired[2] books; and if any one will sow any such seeds in addition to this in the hearing of his audience, such are anathema. Even if he be an angel from heaven [Gal. 1.8–9], he is cursed like the earth-eating serpent, who by lying and deceitful words wished to alter the command of the Creator.[3]

1. Faith is taught by the scriptures (see §361 note 1) and by the canons (here աւրէնք, at §700 կանոնք) of the church; see also §699.
2. Inspired: հոգեպատում (lit. spoken by the Spirit). This word does not occur in the Armenian bible; θεόπνευστος, II Tim. 3.16, is rendered literally by աստուածաշունչ (which is now used as a title for the Bible).
3. Sargisean, *Agatᶜangelos*, p. 379, thinks that the Sabellians may be in the mind of the author of the *Teaching*. But it is more likely, since the anathema is aimed strictly at those who distort the scriptures rather than the faith, that the Marcionites are here being attacked (but cf. Gal. 1.8–9). Eznik also directed part of his treatise *De Deo* against the Marcionites, who had adherents in Armenia; cf. R. P. Casey, *The Armenian Marcionites*.

390.   But we do not offer you such deceit. And to this we bear witness before God, for He alone knows the secrets of hearts [Ps. 43.22], and all hidden things are revealed to Him, for we are before Him at all times. And now we speak before Him his words, encouraging, succulent, fruitful, meritorious, profitable, decorous, fulsome,[1] which are able to fatten you here with fleshy fruit, and there in the kingdom to give you joy in unsurpassable and heavenly delight. To Him, the Lord of all, be glory [Rom. 11.36; Gal. 1.5], who for our salvation was incarnate and moved in human form; He ate like us and drank, was tortured, suffered, was crucified, was nailed, died, buried, and resurrected; He rose up, ascended, and went and sat at the right hand of his begetter God. And the Father has given life to all who have believed in Him.[2]

1. The author of the *Teaching* is not infrequently carried away by lists of synonyms; see the elaborate lists in §644 etc.
2. The passage is cast in credal form and corresponds most closely with the Constantinopolitan creed, notably in having no mention of the descent into hell (but see §368) as the standard Armenian creed; cf. J. Catergian, *De fidei symbolo quo Armenii utuntur Observationes*, Vienna 1893, pp. 1–2.

391.   But we still have to relate to you the birth from the virgin of the Son of God; the details of how it occurred we shall relate in order.[1] For not indeed from after the birth from the virgin took place was the beginning of the existence of the uncreated Word, but before all ages He was born from the Father and then for our sake came down and was born in the flesh from the virgin. But of the birth from the Father who begat Him, He only knows. The second birth [occurred] by his grace among mankind in order that He might give life to mankind, and save the earth from the first malediction [Gal. 3.13], and renew it by coming with blessing in his footsteps. Because he saw men being destroyed, He gathered the scattered and found the lost.

1. See §376 note 2.

392.   And so the blessed virgin conceived by the Holy Spirit [Mt. 1.20; Lk. 1.35] the son of God in her chaste and pure womb in a manner that passes comprehension. And in the usual fashion of childbirth she brought forth her firstborn [Mt. 1.25; Lk. 2.7] son in the city of David, in Bethlehem, for the fulfillment of the prophecy: "You, Bethlehem, house of Ephrat, the least, will become among the powers of Juda. From you will come for me a leader and prince of Israel, and his goings forth are from the beginning of the days of the ages of the world [Micah 5.2]."

393.   Do you see his predicted goings forth? Do you see also the message of the angels in the dwellings of the shepherds? "Today is born to you a

Savior, who is anointed Lord in the city of David [Lk. 2.11]." Do you see that He whose goings forth are from the beginning of the world is said "to be born today"? They speak of the anointed to indicate the prophecy: "Who speaks among men of his anointed [Ps. 104.15]." And he gave a sign about the anointed: "You will find the child wrapped in swathing bands and placed in a manger [Lk. 2.12]." This was the eternal mystery hidden with God [Rom. 16.25; I Cor. 2.7; Col. 1.26], which was revealed to the heavenly powers.

394. In his divine honor the heavenly host raised anthems of praise and taught the shepherds [Lk. 2.13-14], lest He should be despised by the shepherds because of the manger and swathing bands. So the shepherds made haste and came and found the child as the angel had indicated [Lk. 2.16]; who was made known not only to those nearby, but also by a divine star to the distant East [Mt. 2.2]. So were to be understood the inspired prophetic books: "A child was born to us and a son was given to us, whose power is on his shoulders. And his name was called angel of mighty counsel, wonderful counselor, powerful God, prince, and Father of the world to come [Is. 9.6-7]."

395. Do you see that "son and prince and angel and counselor and mighty God and Father of the world to come" indicate the child who "is born today"? For He is indeed Son because He is the power of God, counselor and mighty God, by whom the ages were established. And "child" because today He was born from the holy virgin in Bethlehem, as also the prophecy said: "The Lord said to me, you are my son, and today I have begotten you [Ps. 2.7]." And "Father of the world to come" because the second man [I Cor. 15.47], born of a virgin and coming from heaven, will renew this world which had become old and mortal because of the first man born from dust. And "prince" because "a branch springs from the root of Jesse, says Isaiah, and a flower from his branches [Is. 11.1]," that is, the birth of the daughter of David. Then He will sit on the throne of David and will bring his kingdom to success.

396. So the days have arrived which the prophet previously defined. "Behold the days come, says the Lord, that I shall establish my words as good, which I spoke over the house of Israel and over the house of Juda. In that day and in that hour I shall raise up for David a shoot of righteousness, who will work justice and righteousness on the earth [Jer. 23.5]." Concerning this [the scripture] also says: "Turn, Jacob, and take hold of it, at the first appearance of its light; give not your glory to another, nor your profit to a foreign race [Baruch 4.2-3]."

397. Another prophet declares most clearly: "On that day I shall raise up the altar of David, and shall raise up what has fallen, and shall set up again his breaches and ruins, and shall build it for eternity, that the rest of mankind may seek me, and all the heathen, over whom my name is called, says the Lord [Amos. 9.11-12]." Who does this is revealed from the beginning of ages, because in a former promise to David He said: "Of the fruit of your womb I shall set on your throne [Ps. 131.11], higher than all kings of the earth, establishing his throne according to the days of heaven, like the sun before me, like the moon, for it is established in the air [Ps. 88.37-38; 28, 30]."

398. He came "whose is the kingdom, and He is the hope of the Gentiles [Gen. 49.10]," just as Moses related; and the universal king was raised up, bringing all races into obedience, and not transferring his kingdom to another race, according to the saying of Daniel [Baruch!]. Similarly David, whose son Christ was called, speaks from his heart in the word of the inspired prophet, revealing the epithets of the king. First: "He is more beautiful than all the sons of men and drops grace from his lips [Ps. 44.3]," and beautiful not of form, but of incomparable glory. And again: "Take your sword with you, mighty one, for it adorns your truth [Ps. 44.4]." After this he immediately declares: "Your throne, O God, is from ages to ages a rod of equity, a rod of your kingdom [Ps. 44.7]." And he indicates that He is anointed, of whose coming as anointed the prophet himself sang, saying "For this reason God anointed you, your God with oil of joy more than your companions [Ps. 44.8]."

399. Do you see that the prophet first made known by the Holy Spirit that the only begotten Son of God, the beloved who shares the Father's throne,[1] became a son of David [Mt. 22.42] and elevated his throne for ever? As he says: "Previously I saw the Lord before me at all times and on my right hand [Ps. 15.8]," as he also knows that God swore an oath to him to set on his throne from the fruit of his womb [II Kg. 7.12]; to which also the examples bore witness: "From the race of David and from the village of Bethlehem comes the Christ [Jn. 7.42]."

1. Cf. Athanasius, *Or. c. Arianos*, I 61: τήν τε γὰρ τοῦ Πατρὸς βασιλείαν βασιλεύων ὁ Υἱὸς ἐπὶ τὸν αὐτὸν θρόνον τῷ Πατρὶ κάθηται.

400. And He was declared king not only by the previous indications, but also by a sign at the time itself by the magi who came and said: "Where is he who was born king of the Jews [Mt. 2.2]?" And they inquired from the scribes and arrived where the child was; there they worshipped and paid Him obeisance, and straightway, being informed by the Lord and an angel, they returned.

401. "And when eight days were accomplished for his circumcising, his name was called Jesus, which was named by the angel before he was conceived in the womb [Lk. 2.21]." As also the prophet says: "Before he created you in the womb, I knew you, and before you came forth from the womb, I made you holy [Jer. 1.5]." And this is explained with reference to the Lord "whom the Father hallowed and sent into the world [Jn. 10.36]." And another prophet: "From the womb the Lord called me and called my name from the womb of my mother [Is. 49.1]."

402. And so see that He took a true form from the holy virgin, and not a phantom[1] or an appearance. For He takes a beginning, who is without beginning. And reckoning by days, the Son was circumcised on the eighth day [Lk. 1.59] before the morning star [Ps. 109.3], the seed of Abraham [Heb. 2.16] promised by the gospel, by whom all nations of the earth are blessed [Gen. 18.18]. So the circumcising of Jesus Christ was to fulfill the gospel to the fathers: "Who came, he says, under the law to save the lawful, and that we might receive adoption [Gal. 4.5]."

 1. Phantom: *ապաշար*, the φάντασμα of Mk. 6.49.

403. But He was not received, and so the Son of David was pursued to Egypt [Mt. 2.13–15], to fulfill the saying: "From the land of Egypt have I called my son [Hos. 11.1]," because omniscient God had previously defined by his inspired prophets what sorts of endurance his only-begotten Son would suffer from the Jews. As Peter in the book of the Acts of the Apostles says: "God, as he previously spoke through the mouth of all the prophets of the sufferings of his Christ, even so accomplished them [Acts 3.18]." As also the Lord Himself said: "I have come to fulfill the law and the prophets [Mt. 5.17]."

404. Being called from Egypt, He passed to Nazareth [Mt. 2.23] to his supposed fatherland according to the flesh; the Son of Man grew up and increased in stature [Lk. 2.52] according to the law of mankind. He submitted to the race of Israel, that they might of their own will have recourse to the opened source of life. For the Psalmist indicated of Him that: "From you is the source of life [Ps. 35.10]." This also the Savior revealed to the Samaritan woman, saying: "If you knew the gifts of God, and who it is who says to you 'give me to drink,' you would indeed have asked of him, and he would have given you the living water [Jn. 4.10]."

405. He then, when his twelve years were completed, came to Jerusalem and exchanged words with the teachers of the law and amazed them all

[Lk. 2.42–51], for the fulfillment of the prophecy: "Behold my child will understand, and will be raised and elevated and greatly glorified [Is. 52.13]." For although the Deity from heaven was humbled, yet He is known as elevated [Heb. 7.26] by the inhabitants of earth below. They understood that although He descended in humility, yet He is raised by the power of his own natural glory, according to the presaging vision of the prophet: "He will be raised and elevated and glorified [Is. 52.13]." Because He is in no way lacking in glory, after completing of his own will his desires in his patient power, elevated by nothing extrinsic but by his own natural glory, He was known to the heavenly host [I Tim. 3.16], according to the saying: "God is gone up by grace, and our Lord by the sound of a trumpet [Ps. 46.6]."

406. But the trumpet, would it not call out like a horn [blown] by a mouth full of breath, with cheeks bulging with air by the blowing of trumpets, to cry and fill the universe with the wonderful gospel:[1] "Behold God, behold the Lord [Is. 25.9]"? For they will make the journey of the preaching of his life-giving teaching, and will understand and know Him. "Behold the Lord for whom we were waiting; let us rejoice and be glad at our salvation [Is. 25.9]." By Him[2] the paths of preaching are opened to their life of light, blessings and rest; and understanding, they will know that being raised with Him to the kingdom, they will become dwellers in the mansions of light. They will consent to listen and understand, that is, for the world to know Him. As the Psalmist said: "All races of the earth will remember and turn to the Lord [Ps. 21.28]."

 1. Cf. Clement, *Protrept.*, XI 116: σάλπιγξ ἐστὶ Χριστοῦ τὸ εὐαγγέλιον αὐτοῦ. See also §638–641, 659 below.
 2. By him: *որ նովիմբ*, a Syriacism; see §269 note 1.

407. And "to be raised and elevated [Is. 52.13]," because He descended to humility in the humble flesh; for that reason He is elevated in the form of the same humility in the flesh. He appeared humble as a man, more gentle and humble than all men, and showed patience in bearing the afflictions which He assumed in the flesh [II Cor. 10.1; Heb. 12.3]. For this reason He is raised in the same flesh from the humilities, raised in his manhood, elevated and glorified. Because He raised up the form of a man which He took [Philipp. 2.7], He imprinted the character of humility as a model[1] in Himself.

 1. Imprinted as a model: *արիւնակալալ սպասուրկը*; see Introduction, pp. 15–16.

408. [*The baptism of Christ*] Then after refraining for thirty years from revealing Himself [Lk. 3.23], growing in stature of the body according to the

nature of the increase of the flesh, He submitted also to baptism [Mt. 3.13; Mk. 1.5; Lk. 3.21]. And He sent first John the Baptist, the greatest of the prophets, to prepare a way for Him and straighten the paths of his revelation [Mt. 3.3; Mk. 1.2–3; Lk. 3.4; Is. 40.3]. He submitted to give the baptism of repentance [Mt. 3.11; Mk. 1.4; Lk. 3.3], not the baptism of the divine mark[1] of illumination of eternal life, but to give the baptism of the holiness of repentance; as in the age of Moses, when God wished to appear to them, He ordered them to wash and purify themselves [Ex. 19.10],[2] that they might become worthy of the revelation of the divine glory.

1. Divine mark: սատուծաշտ[րու]զմ. Ꝗրու]զմ renders χαρακτήρ in Lev. 13.28, and χαρακτήρ was a frequent synonym for the seal of baptism; cf. Lampe, *Seal*, p. 7 and §410 note 1 below.
2. Cf. I Cor. 10.2, and the commentary thereon of Gregory Naz., *Or.*, XXXIX 17: ἐβάπτισε Μωύσης, ἀλλ' ἐν ὕδατι· καὶ πρὸ τοῦτο ἐν νεφέλῃ καὶ ἐν θαλάσσῃ. τυπικῶς δὲ τοῦτο ἦν, ὡς καὶ Παύλῳ δοκεῖ.

409.   So also John came and washed the people with repentance, in order that when the Son of God should appear they might be ready to approach with worthiness and hear the teaching of the same, to build a road in their hearts, that they might be able to receive the Lord of all in gentle and humble lodging.

410.   Then He came and was Himself baptized by John; undertaking to write an eternal covenant and sealing it with his own blood [Heb. 13.20], to give life to all by the illuminating and life-giving baptism, He ordered all born from the earth, all humans, to imitate the divine image of salvation. Then He came to the seal-giver[1] John to be baptized by him, who, seized with awe, refused: "I must be baptized by you [Mt. 3.14]." He heard and answered and boldly commanded him to baptize Him: "Suffer it now, for thus it is fitting to occur, that we fulfill all righteousness [Mt. 3.15]."

1. The seal-giver: ｢ｨ.ｐｗｍｐｉｴ, a surprising epithet for John, as "seal" is usually reserved for Christian baptism.

411.   And what is the righteousness except what the father of the same John, Zecharia, cried by the Holy Spirit: "He remembered, he said, the oath which He swore to our father Abraham, that He would give us without fear salvation from our enemies and from the hands of all who hate us, to serve Him with holiness and righteousness [Lk. 1.71–75]." In the same way the Psalmist also says: "He remembered his covenant with Abraham and his oath with Isaac, and He established for Jacob his commandment, and for Israel his covenant for ever [Ps. 104.9–10]." By the faith of the fathers He blessed the whole earth, He blessed and fulfilled the promises, and for

the same reason He Himself came down upon the waters, and made the waters at once purifying and renovating.[1]

1. See below, §413–414.

412.   And because He made the first earth emerge from the waters [Gen. 1.9] by his command, and by water were fattened all plants and reptiles and wild animals and beasts and birds, and by the freshness of the waters they sprang from the earth; in the same way by baptism[1] He made verdant the womb of generation of the waters, purifying by the waters and renewing the old deteriorated earthy matter, which sin had weakened and enfeebled and deprived of the grace of the Spirit.[2] Then the invisible Spirit opened again the womb by visible water, preparing the newly born fledglings for the regeneration of the font [Titus 3.5], to clothe all with robes of light[3] who would be born once more.

1. For the waters of baptism as a womb see also §679. Cf. Cyril Jer., *Cat.*, XX 4: τὸ σωτήριον ἐκεῖνο ὕδωρ καὶ τάφος ὑμῖν ἐγίνετο καὶ μήτηρ, and Daniélou, *Bible*, pp. 47–49.
2. See also §364 note 3 and "the mortality of creation" in §516.
3. See also §672 note 3, and Gregory Naz., *Or.*, XL 25: ἡ ἐμφώτειος ἐσθὴς ᾗ λαμπρυνθήσομαι; cf. Col. 1.12.

413.   For in the beginning of the creation of time, the Spirit of the Deity moved over the waters [Gen. 1.2], and thence set out the order of the creatures, and commanded the coming into being and establishing of the creatures. He also ordered to be established the firmament of heaven [Gen. 1.8], the dwelling of the fiery angels, which appears to us as water.[1] In the same way He came and completed the covenant which He made with our fathers [Gen. 17.7; Lk. 1.72]. He came down to the waters and sanctified the lower waters of this earth,[2] which had been fouled by the sins of mankind.

1. See also §260, 262, 277, 414.
2. Cf. Ignatius, *Eph.*, XVIII 2: (Christ) ἐβαπτίσθη ἵνα τῷ πάθει τὸ ὕδωρ καθαρίσῃ, Clement, *Eclogae*, 7: ὁ Σωτὴρ ἐβαπτίσατο... ἵνα τοῖς ἀναγεννωμένοις τὸ ὕδωρ ἁγιάσῃ, and Daniélou, *Bible*, p. 75.

414.   Treading the waters with his own footsteps, He sanctified them and made them purifying. And just as formerly the Spirit moved over the waters, in the same way He will dwell in the waters and will receive all who are born by it. And the waters massed together above are the dwelling of the angels. But He made these waters just as those, because He Himself came down to the waters, that all might be renewed through the Spirit by the waters and become angels,[1] and the same Spirit might bring all to adoption [Rom. 8.15, 23; 9.4; Gal. 4.5; Eph. 1.5] by the waters for ever. For He opened

the gates of the waters below, that the gates of the upper waters of heaven might be opened, and that He might elevate all men in glory to adoption.

1. See also §640, 674, 679. Cf. also Origen, *In Lev. Hom.*, IX 11: (commenting on Lev. 16.17) qui potuerit sequi Christum et penetrare cum eo interius tabernaculum et coelum excelsa conscendere, iam non erit homo, sed secundum verbum ipsius erit tanquam angelus Dei . . . (quoting Ps. 82.6) . . . sive per resurrectionis gloriam in angelorum ordinem transeat, recte iam non erit homo. See also §364 note 4.

415. The true Son of God humbled Himself and descended to the waters of baptism, that He might fulfill the promises of the fathers and the gospel.[1] Before this He also took upon Himself circumcision [Lk. 2.21], that He might bestow grace and blessings on both parties; that by his own circumcision He might complete the basis of the promises, and for the encouragement of the invitations[2] of those worthy of the inheritance of adoption. And at his baptism He vivifies all baptized by having Himself received baptism, and He made baptism honorable by his own descent to baptism.[3]

1. A major theme in the *Teaching* is the fulfillment of the prophecies; see also §339 note 1, 423.
2. Invitations: Հրաւիրմանք (used to render πρόθεσις in Rom. 8.28). The theme of invitation is extensively developed later in the Teaching in connection with the preaching of the gospel, §508 ff.
3. Cf. Cyril Jer., *Cat.*, XII 15: παρεγένετο ὁ Χριστὸς ἵνα βαπτισθῇ καὶ ἁγιάσῃ τὸ βάπτισμα.

416. And He was first understood and known as the true Son of God by the voice of his Father and the descent of the Spirit over Him [Mt. 3.17; Mk. 1.11; Lk. 3.22; Jn. 1.34].[1] For thereby He is understood and known, for the fulfillment of the prophecy of the Father: "Behold my child will deal prudently, he will be raised up and exalted and glorified exceedingly [Is. 52.13]."

1. Epiphany homilies in Armenian usually represent the baptism as the occasion of the spiritual rebirth of Jesus, Conybeare, *Rituale*, p. 188; cf. the Greek Epiphany rite of the blessing of the waters, ibid., pp. 415–436. The Armenians have kept the early custom of celebrating the baptism of Christ on the same day as the Epiphany and Nativity. Although the *Teaching* stresses the baptism as the moment of Christ's revelation, there is no trace of the extreme ideas of Theodotus, for example, as reported by Hippolytus, *Ref. omn. Haer.*, VII 35: φάσκων . . . τὸν Ἰησοῦν εἶναι ἄνθρωπον . . . ὕστερον ἐπὶ τοῦ βαπτίσματος ἐπὶ τῷ Ἰορδάνῃ κεχωρηκέναι τὸν Χριστὸν ἄνωθεν κατεληλυθότα; cf. ibid., X 23. For the history of Adoptionist ideas in Armenia, see N. G. Garsoian, *The Paulician Heresy*, The Hague/Paris 1967, esp. pp. 220 ff.

417. For thirty years He moved silently and unseen among them [Lk. 3.23]; then He came to baptism, and at the baptism was made known to all. John

bore witness and said: "This is He of whom I said 'who comes after me was before me, for He was first'; for from his fullness we have received grace [Jn. 1.15–16, 30]."

418. And the Spirit came down over Him in the likeness of a dove [Mt. 3.16; Mk. 1.10; Lk. 3.22; Jn. 1.32]. Why then should the Holy Spirit of God appear in the likeness of a dove? To teach those watching that in no other respect can one approach the Son of God, except in sinlessness and righteousness and holiness;[1] that taking from the likeness of a dove, they might bear in themselves that form.

1. For the dove signifying sinlessness and purity, cf. Song 1.15, 2.14, and §603 note 2 below.

419. For He is the searcher of hearts [Ps. 43.22; Heb. 4.12], knower of secrets, and revealer of all hidden things; for He knows everything, and everything He says He can bring to fulfillment, and nothing is impossible for Him. As Gabriel said to the holy virgin: "For God nothing will be impossible [Lk. 1.37]." He exposes the secrets of the hearts of men and reproaches them, "who created each one of their hearts, who understands all their works [Ps. 32.15]," of those who were to approach Him.

420. For this reason the Spirit came down in the form of a dove, to teach those watching to approach the Son of God with pure minds, and to receive the grace of the blessing of the Spirit, and to become pleasing to the Father. For this reason the Son of God came and fulfilled the covenant of the fathers, since they had called Him "son." The Son of God, therefore, came and was baptized, to establish the baptism of all who would be baptized, that handing on this tradition[1] He might reveal salvation to all, and be understood and known, and that by this He might open his life-giving teaching of truth to be revealed to the world.[2] As the prophet says in the name of the Lord's Son: "Come near to me and hear this: not from the beginning did I speak anything in secret, nor anything in a place of darkness in the earth. For when he was, then was I. And the Lord has sent me and his Spirit [Is. 48.16]." Do you see the unity of being? "When he was, I then was," he says, demonstrating the consubstantial hypostasis[3] of the Trinity, acting together[4] in establishing and united in renewing.

1. The handing on of the tradition of the O.T. which Christ received at his baptism from John is a major theme in the *Teaching*; see §429–435, 468.
2. I.e., the baptism marks the beginning of Christ's public ministry.
3. Consubstantial hypostasis: մարմին զաւրութիւն; see Introduction, pp. 12, 13.
4. Acting together: համագործ; see also §260 note 2, 374 note 1.

421. Then the heavens opened and the Father cried: "This is my beloved Son [Mt. 3.17; Mk. 1.11; Lk. 3.22; Jn. 1.32]." And the Spirit descended in the likeness of a dove that the consubstantial mystery of the power[1] of the coming of the Son might be revealed.

1. Power: զաւրութիւն. It is not always clear when this word means "power" and when "hypostasis" (see Introduction, p. 12), but here the former meaning is clearly intended.

422. And what is the saying "from the beginning I spoke [Is. 48.16]" except the auguries of the holy prophets, in which He spoke about Himself? And consubstantial in mystery with the Father and the Spirit, He came and was revealed at the end of these times, "who was from the beginning the Word, and the Word was with God, and the Word was God. He was from the beginning with God. Everything was made by Him, and without Him nothing was made that was made. In Him was life, and the life was the light of men. And the light shone in the darkness, and the darkness overcame it not. There was a man sent from God, his name was John; he came for a witness, to bear witness about the light, that through him all might believe [Jn. 1.1–7]."

423. Then fulfilling and completing all things, the light of the Son of God came to our midst to illuminate all men who would come into the world, and darkness cannot confront or overcome Him. By this light was the world made, but it knew Him not. So for this reason He came, that they might understand his light and become sons of God [Jn. 1.12]. He came to confirm the law and the prophets [Mt. 5.17][1]; He surpassed the types[2] and established the truth .

1. See also §339 note 1, 348 note 2.
2. Types: աւրինակ, see Introduction, pp. 15–16.

424. And what is meant by "the Word," surely not a simple sound, a blow of the tongue with breath, which before the speaker has pronounced is not distinct and after disappears without a trace? But for this reason He was called "Word," for as a word in the mouth of the speaker, so all the commands of God's will come from the mouth of the Son.[1] For He knows the Father and fulfills his will, just as He Himself says: "No one knows the Father except the Son, just as no one knows the Son, except the Father [Mt. 11.27; Lk. 10.22]." And again: "I came to fulfill the will of Him who sent me [Jn. 4.34]." And, furthermore, John says: "No one has ever seen God; but the only-begotten Son who is in the bosom of the Father has declared Him [Jn. 1.18]."

1. Cf. Origen, *In Gen. Hom.*, III 2: Nam si vox humana aer ictus, id est lingua repercussus definitur, potest et vox Dei dici aer ictus, vel vi, vel voluntate divina. But the opposite

interpretation to that of Origen was usually taken: Athanasius, *C. Gentes*, 40: Λόγον δέ φημι . . . οὐδὲ οἷον ἔχει τὸ λογικὸν γένος λόγον τὸν ἐκ συλλαβῶν συγκείμενον καὶ ἐν ἀέρι σημαινόμενον, or Basil, *Hex.*, II 7 (Giet, p. 172): ὅταν δὲ φωνὴν ἐπὶ Θεοῦ καὶ ῥῆμα καὶ πρόσταγμα λέγωμεν, οὐ διὰ φωνητικῶν ὀργάνων ἐκπεμπόμενον ψόφον, οὐδὲ ἀέρα διὰ γλώσσης τυπούμενον, τὸν θεῖον λόγον νοοῦμεν, ἀλλὰ τὴν ἐν τῷ θελήματι, ῥοπὴν διὰ τὸ τοῖς διδασκομένοις εὐσύνοπτον ἡγούμεθα ἐν εἴδει προστάγματος σχηματίζεσθαι, or Gregory of Nyssa, *Or. cat.*, 1: οὐκοῦν κἂν λόγος Θεοῦ λέγηται, οὐκ ἐν τῇ ὁρμῇ τοῦ φθεγγομένου καὶ τὴν ὑπόστασιν ἔχειν νομισθήσεται, καθ' ὁμοιότητα τοῦ ἡμετέρου μεταχωρῶν εἰς ἀνύπαρκτον. The *Teaching* follows Gregory; cf. also his *Or. cat.*, 2. The same idea is found in Ephrem, *Commentary on Diatessaron*, I 3 (Syriac and Armenian): Non autem verbum vile audias, neque demittas ad vocem; vox enim non est in initio, quia antequam pronuntiaretur, non erat, et postquam pronuntiatur, iterum non est. But Ephrem continues in a different vein from the *Teaching*: Non igitur vox fuit ille qui erat similitudo Patris sui, nec est vox Patris, sed imago eius.

For the Logos as the expression of the will of God, cf. Justin, *I Apol.*, XIV 5, Clement, *Str.*, I 9.

425. And He Himself said to the Father: "The hour has come, Father; glorify your Son [Jn. 17.1]." And there came a voice from heaven: "I have glorified, and I shall glorify again [Jn. 12.28]." This was not to seek a refuge, or because He is lacking at all of the Father's glory,[1] but in order that the creatures might hear and be confirmed in the Son. In the same way the Son, standing in our midst, shows the Father and the Holy Spirit to the world, as the Father cried concerning the Only-begotten: "This is my only-begotten Son; He is pleasing to myself. I shall set my Spirit over Him [Mt. 12.18]," who was revealed at his descending and resting on Him; just as He Himself said of the Holy Spirit: "He glorifies me [Jn. 16.14]."

1. Cf. Ps-Athanasius, *Expositio Fidei*, 2: συναπεγεννήθη ἐκ τοῦ πατρὸς ἀϊδίως ἡ ὁμοία δόξα καὶ δύναμις (Casey, *Armenian Version*, p. 75: որ բղխ ՛ի նմա ծնաւ ՛ի հաւրէ մշտն կայ ՛ի նմ ՛ի փառաւոր, եւ զաւրութեամբ).

426. And He came and fulfilled all the wishes of his Creator; He also cried, saying: "Who believes in me, believes in Him who sent me [Jn. 12.44–45]." And in this way He shows to all by his revealing teaching the glory of the Father in Himself.

427. And the Father sent the forerunner, a messenger; he came first and cried: "He is the Son of God, He is the lamb of God, He it is who comes to take away the sins of the world [Jn. 1.29]." And he ascended a high mountain,[1] to the majesty of the power of the Godhead, as the foreseeing prophet said on behalf of the Lord: "On the holy mountain, on the high mountain there all races of the earth will serve me [Ez. 20.40]." And again another seer cried: "Go onto this high mountain, bringer of good tidings to Sion; raise your voice, bringer of good tidings to Jerusalem. Go up, raise your voice and be not afraid. Say to the city of Juda: Behold our God, behold the Lord

comes in his power, and his arm is mighty in his rule; behold the reward of his compensation is with Him, and each of his deeds before Him. Like a shepherd He will pasture his flocks, and gather his lambs into his arms, and will receive them to his bosom, and will be merciful to those who are heavy with young. Who has measured all the waters with his palm, or who has measured the heaven with his hand and all the earth with his span? Who has placed the hills in a balance and weighed the plains with scales? Who has known the mind of the Lord, or who has been counselor to Him [Is. 40.9–14]?"

1. See §428 note 1.

428.   And what is this saying "go onto this high mountain, bringer of good tidings to Sion," except like the saying: "The Lord gave a command [Jonah 2.1]?" For the Lord's commands are above all, and the commands of the All Highest are from on high. And what could be higher and more imposing than the commands of the Deity? The heralds of the Godhead went up to the same high hill of commands to preach boldly before all without fear or trembling.[1]

1. There is a parallel to the association of prophets with mountains in Origen, *In Jer. Hom.*, XVI 1.

429.   [*John the Baptist passes on to Christ the Old Testament traditions*] Then came the great John, son of the high priest Zacharia. Here came the companion of the temple,[1] not a stranger. Here was the heir and inhabitant of Sion, of the same ephod-wearing priesthood, wearing a tiara of the honor of the robes of holiness, bearer of the tradition of the commandments, not a foreigner but suitably girded, the descendant[2] of Moses and the branch of Aaron and the evangelist of Sion, worthy of anointing;[3] he received the honor of the priesthood of his forefathers. And completing the prophecy of the prophets, going out into the desert because of the divine commands to those dwelling on mountains,[4] the evangelist of Jerusalem, going up, raised his voice, for he was the sound of a voice in the wilderness [Is. 40.3; Mt. 3.3; Jn. 1.23], and said: "Behold our God, behold the Lord [Is. 25.9; 40.9]," and the same is king of Israel.

1. Companion of the temple: *ասպարիկից*, as III Macc. 2.13.
2. Descendent: *շառաւիղ*, lit. branch.
3. Worthy of anointing: *աւծութեան անկլու*. Norayr Buzandacʻi suggested *աւծութիւն րնկալաւ* "he received unction" (apparatus of critical text, ad loc.), but this emendation has neither manuscript authority nor biblical parallel.
4. *լեռնագելոց*, the idea of §428 note 1.

430.   So all the grace of the tradition of the prophecy of the race of Israel, which the keeper of the tradition of the blessing of the covenants and the

anointing bore, the priesthood, with the kingship, was entrusted [to him] through the tribe of Levi.[1]

1. A major theme of the *Teaching* (§429–437, 468) is the link between the two testaments effected by Christ who received the tradition of the O.T. from John. Cf. Cyril Jer., *Cat.* X 19: Ἰωάννης ὁ βαπτιστής, ὁ μέγιστος μὲν ἐν προφήταις, ἀρχηγὸς δὲ τῆς καινῆς διαθήκης, καὶ τρόπον τινὰ συνάπτων ἀμφοτέρας ἐν αὐτῷ τὰς διαθήκας. The three important facets of the tradition are the priesthood, the kingship, and the prophecy (§431, 433), only the last of which is specifically associated with John in the N.T. (cf. Mt. 11.13, Lk. 16.16). Ephrem, *Diatessaron*, IV 3, says that at his baptism Jesus received from John the priesthood and prophecy; see also §433 note 1.

431.   For at the time when the Lord called Moses in the midst of the fire and cloud to the top of the mountain of Sinai, and the vision of the glory of the Lord was burning like fire, when Moses took the commandments of the laws from the hands of God [Ex. 19], and saw God was beneficent from his answer to him: "I am merciful and compassionate [Ex. 34.6]," then he received the tradition of the authority of the priesthood,[1] kingship,[2] and prophecy[3] from God. Then He gave him a type of the anointing of Christ, that first might occur examples and then the truth might come—He who is [Ex. 3.14].[4] Then He ordered him to make the horn[5] of anointing and the thurible of incense [Ex. 31.11].

1. The priesthood was instituted by Moses on the direct command of God (Ex. 28.1).
2. In the *Oracula Sibyllina*, XI 38, Moses is called μέγας βασιλεύς, but the kingship is connected with the priesthood through the common feature of anointing.
3. For Moses as prophet, cf. I Clement 43, Chrysostom, *In Gen. Hom.*, II 2.
4. See §363 note 2.
5. Although Moses anointed Aaron priest, the horn is associated with the anointing of kings. It was first used by Samuel, I Kings 16.1, in anointing David; Saul was anointed from a vial, *սրուակ*, I Kings 10.1.

432.   The horn was the type of the anointing of Christ,[1] and the thurible the type of the holy virgin Mary. For as the former was full of the odor of sanctity, so also the virgin was full of the Holy Spirit and the power of the Highest [Lk. 1.35].[2] The horn of oil was the type of the anointing of Christ, for who were anointed once in his example were anointed from it. Thence also Aaron was anointed to the priesthood of the Lord [Ex. 40.13], and he took the crown of priesthood, to anoint according to the same type, to place on them the veil, to serve the holiness of the Lord, and to order the daily bread on the table [Lev. 24.5–9], which bore the type of the flesh of the Son of God.[3]

1. See §431 note 5. But although the horn was used for the royal anointing, the priestly anointing was also considered in Christian exegesis to be a figure of Christ—the anointed one; cf. Daniélou, *Bible*, pp. 115–117.

2. Cf. Proclus, *Or.*, VI 17, the virgin as θυμίαμα. The figure is common in the later Byzantine theologians; cf. Ps-Basil, *Historia mystagogica*, 42: ἡ γαστὴρ τοῦ θυμιατηρίου νοηθείη ἂν ἡ μήτρα τῆς ἁγίας παρθένου φοροῦσα τὸν θεῖον ἄνθρακα Χριστόν.

3. Origen, *In Lev. Hom.*, XIII 3, calls the showbread an "imago" of the bread which came from heaven. Cf. Cyril Jer., *Cat.*, XXII 5: ἦσαν καὶ ἐν παλαίᾳ διαθήκῃ ἄρτοι προθέσεως, ἀλλ᾽ ἐκεῖνοι παλαίας ὄντες διαθήκης τέλος εἰλήφασιν. ἐν δὲ τῇ καινῇ διαθήκῃ ἄρτος ἐπουράνιος καὶ ποτήριον σωτηρίον. The *Teaching* does not often refer to the eucharist, but see §690. At §464 and 491 Christ's giving of his body and blood to the disciples is interpreted as showing that He went willingly to death.

433. Then Moses made the silver horn of his anointing from which were anointed the priests, prophets, and kings. Thence proceeded in order the unction in succession according to the command of the authority of the commandment, which proceeded in order by seniority. The mystery was preserved in the seed of Abraham, because they passed on the tradition to each other until John, priest, prophet, and baptist. And coming to him, it remained on him as on an heir. For it came to him from the first forefathers, the kings, prophets, and anointed priests, as to a keeper of tradition. And he gave the priesthood, the anointing, the prophecy, and the kingship to our Lord Jesus Christ.[1]

1. See §430 note 1. But Cyril of Jerusalem declares that Christ did not receive his priesthood from any man but from the Father, nor did He deliver it to a successor (*Cat.*, I 14). Cf. Ps-Athanasius, *Dialogue between Athanasius and Zacchaeus*, 86: ἔλαβε σάρκα ἐκ Μαρίας, ἵνα γενόμενος ἄνθρωπος . . . γένηται ἱερεὺς κατὰ τὴν τάξιν Μελχισεδέκ, ὃς οὐ κατὰ νόμον ἐντολῆς σαρκίνης ἐγένετο ἱερεύς, ἀλλὰ πνεύματι ἁγίῳ χρισθεὶς ἐστιν ἱερεὺς εἰς τὸν αἰῶνα; cf. Heb. 11. But the *Teaching* is following the tradition of Ephrem, who frequently speaks of the priesthood, kingship, and prophecy coming to Christ; cf. his *Commentary on Diatessaron*, III 9, IV 3.

434. And the prophecy of Jacob was fulfilled in the saying to the sons of his race: "There will not lack leadership of authority until he shall come, whose is the kingdom; for he is the hope of the Gentiles [Gen. 49.10]."

435. The first fathers were his type, in whom the forms of God were represented, for all creatures obeyed them because they saw the forms of the Creator in them. But how did irrational, voiceless, mute creatures obey mortal men, unless they saw the signs of God in them and the forms of the Creator?[1] And thus in succession the traditions were handed down to John, and John gave the tradition of his trust to his Lord.

1. See also §263 note 1, Adam rules over the creatures by virtue of being in the image of God.

436. And then the Lord Himself came forward, and John bore witness: "I am not the Christ, but I am sent before Him. He who has the bride is the bridegroom, and he who is the friend of the bridegroom stands with him

and obeys him; he also has great joy in his rejoicing for he hears the bridegroom's voice. This joy of mine is fulfilled and completed; he must increase and I must decrease. He who comes from above is over all. Who is from the earth, speaks of the earth; he who comes from heaven, bears witness to what he has heard and seen, and his witness no one receives. But who receives his witness has secured and sealed that indeed God is true. For he who has been sent by God speaks the words of God; for the Spirit was not given him by measure. The Father loves the Son and has given all things into his hand. Who believes in the Son receives everlasting life; and who believes not in the Son does not see eternal life, but the wrath of God dwells on him [Jn. 3.28–36]."

437. Behold, the messenger John came to prepare the ways for his Lord. For as Gabriel was the harbinger of his birth, so he was of his revelation, and coming first said: "I am sent before Him, but whose the bride is, he is the groom [Jn. 3.28–29]."

438. But who is the bride, or who is the bridegroom, except he of whom the prophet said: "Thus says the Lord, 'I shall betroth you to me for ever, and I shall betroth you to me in righteousness and justice and mercy and compassion. And you will know that I am the Lord your God, and you will abandon your beloved of wood and stone and will say, I shall return to my first husband? [Hos. 2.19–20; 7].'"

439. For men abandoned the worship of their Creator, and all obeyed wood and stone; and they abandoned the first man[1] who made them from nothing, and committed adultery with all the material things which met their eyes, and they went awhoring after the vain worship of creatures. Therefore the Son of God came down to abolish from earth the vanity of whoring and adultery with stone lovers, and to bring [men] back to the worship of the Father, and to give his man the name of first man. And [He is called] "first" on account of his primordial nature,[2] as Paul the Apostle explains to the Gentiles: "I established and betrothed you in marriage like a holy virgin to present to Christ [II Cor. 11.2]." And the prophet says: "The queen will stand on your right hand [Ps. 44.10]." He brings back the whole world like a bride to a groom. Thus he indicates the man who came from heaven, the Son of God, as John says: "Whose is the bride, he is the groom. And we, friends and servants, run at his command; our wills are towards him, and we obey him and rejoice in his gladness, and hear the voice of the bridegroom [Jn. 3.29]."

1. See note 2 below.

2. Primordial nature: ԶՈՒ... The divine "first man" is a Gnostic concept, basic to the Apocryphon of John and other writings, and it is surprising to find it echoed here. (Cf. H.-M. Schenke, *Der Gott "Mensch,"* Göttingen, 1962.) But see also ps. Athanasius, *C. Apoll.*, I 8.

440. This is he whom the prophet mentioned: "Hear, daughter, and see, incline your ear, forget your people and the house of your father. For the king has desired your beauty. For he is your lord; you will worship him [Ps. 44.11–12]." He is the same who says: "My cousin, you will arise, you will awake, my near one, my beloved. You will open for me the doors of the house, and give me a kiss from the kisses of your mouth. For your breasts are more abundant than wine, and the odor of your perfume more than all the incense of sweetness. Your name is perfume poured out, therefore the young men have loved you. We shall follow the sweetness of your perfume. The king led me to his chamber [Song 1.1–3]."

441. Who is the bride except the church of the Gentiles,[1] or who the groom except Jesus Christ the Son of God,[2] who descended from heaven and subdued everything to the worship of the Father? And what are the two abundant breasts except the testaments of God, which give drink to all the ignorant with the spiritual milk of knowledge?[3] And what is the saying "the odor of your perfume more than all incense of sweetness," and "your name is perfume poured out"—it reveals the anointing of Christ and his name.[4] And the kiss is the sign of love, because the church is Christ's, and Christ is the Son of God.

1. The church as the bride is a familiar figure, but it is usually the whole church that is intended (cf. Lampe, *Lexicon*, s.v. νύμφη). At §672 the bride is interpreted as the "just among men," i.e., those saved. The emphasis on the gentiles in the *Teaching* may be a reflection of its emphasis on missionary preaching. The apostles are mentioned by Aphraates as the suitors (makore⁾) when he refers to Christ as the groom and the believers as the bride, XIV 39.
2. The universal tradition of patristic exegesis; cf. Lampe, *Lexicon*, s.v. νύμφιος. There is little trace in the *Teaching* of the spiritual interpretation which is the main feature of Gregory of Nyssa's commentary; see also §672 note 4.
3. The spiritual milk (I Cor. 32, Heb. 5.12, I Pet. 2.2) usually refers to Christian teaching rather than specifically the two testaments. But Origen, interpreting this passage, *In Cant.*, I, draws a distinction between the wine in the breasts which is the "dogmata et doctrinae quae per legem et prophetas ante adventum sponsi" and the wine revealed at the advent of the Word. Origen does not distinguish between the two breasts, but his interpretation is closer to the *Teaching* than that of Gregory of Nyssa, *In Cant.*, I: μαζοὺς δὲ τὰς ἀγαθὰς τῆς θείας δυνάμεως ὑπὲρ ἡμῶν ἐνεργείας εἰκότως ἄν τις ὑπονοήσειε. But Gregory also contrasts the milk of human breasts, the ἔξω σοφία, to the wine of the θεῖοι μασθοί (ibid.). Cf. also Victorinus of Petau, *Comm.* on Apoc. 1.13: mammae duo sunt testamenta.
4. For the name of Christ as perfume (խունկ, μύρον), cf. Eusebius, *Dem. ev.*, IV 16, and also Daniélou, *Bible*, pp. 122–126.

442. "He must increase and I decrease [Jn. 3.30]," that is, he means the time of decrease. For the baptism which he gave to the crowd was the baptism of repentance. "Who has come from above, he said, is above all [Jn. 3.31]," indicating his coming from the bosom of the Father to us. "But I, he said, spoke from earth, taking my knowledge from heaven [Jn. 3.31]." But He who came from heaven speaks the Father's [words] and works the Father's works. As the Lord Himself said to the Jews: "I am in the Father and the Father in me. Whatever I see that the Father does, the same I do also. For this very reason I have come, to do the will of my Father, and to complete his works [Jn. 5.19; 10.38; 14.10]."

443. He said also concerning the Jews: "You do not receive his witness; but who receives his witness has wrapped and sealed that his justice will be imperishable, and [established] by an oath that certainly God is true [Jn. 3.32–33]," in order that the righteousness of the faith might be assured and immovable and imperishable; and the oath is the seal, as with Abraham [Gen. 22.16–18; Lk. 1.73]. For He who came from the bosom of the Father is versed in the mysteries of his begetter. For there is no lack with Him of the grace of the Spirit, but He Himself is one with the Father and the Spirit in will, in mind and purpose;[1] for He Himself is the distributor of the grace of the Holy Spirit.[2] For the Father loves his Son, and all things established by the Father are through the Son. And what is of the Father, the same is also of the Son; and as is the Father, so also is the Son; and all the grace of the Spirit is distributed by the Son. And "who believes in the Son has everlasting life; who does not believe in the Son, does not see everlasting life [Jn. 3.36]."

1. For the consubstantial nature of the Trinity, see also §362, 383, 705.
2. On the procession of the Holy Spirit see Introduction, p. 13. The verb բաշխել (distribute) renders the ἐπιχορηγεῖν of Gal. 3.5, which is used frequently in patristic exegesis of God giving the gifts of the Holy Spirit. For Christ as giver of the Spirit, cf. Ephrem, *Commentary on Diatessaron*, I 31.

444. John bears witness, saying: "Of whom I spoke, He is the only-begotten Son of God. I saw and bear witness that He it is who takes away the sins of the world [Jn. 1.29]." He is the heir of the vineyard. The Lord walks with power, and his arm is strong through his lordship. For He is the strong arm of the Father,[1] and keeps his lordship, although He appeared willingly in humility.

1. See §386 note 2.

445. "Behold, [the prophet] says, the reward of his retribution is with him [Is. 40.10]," and He is the establisher of all, "and the works of each one

are before him." And similarly: "He considered all their works [Ps. 32.15]."
"Like a shepherd he will shepherd his flocks [Is. 40.11]." Who also as
Savior coming among us says: "I am the good shepherd; the good shepherd
lays down his life for his flock [Jn. 10.11]." And in his arms he will gather
his lambs and will receive them into his bosom.

446. He, the Savior, came and was revealed in taking and gathering the
children in his divine arms [Mk. 9.36; 10.15]. And as an example to all [He
said]: "Unless you are converted and become like this child, you are not
able to enter the kingdom of God [Mt. 18.3]." He orders [us] to renew ourselves [Tit. 3.5] and to strip off the old manhood [Col. 3.9] through the bath
of baptism. For although one may be greatly oppressed and laboring, bearing a heavy weight of sins according to the saying: "Behold he was in labor
for injustice, conceived pains and gave birth to unrighteousness [Ps. 7.15],"
yet opening the doors to repentance, coming into our midst, stands the Savior
crying out: "Come to me all who are laden and in travail, and whoever have
heavy loads, and I shall give you rest. And take my yoke upon you and learn
from me; for I am gentle, calm, and humble in heart, and you will find rest
for yourselves. For my yoke is gentle and my load is light [Mt. 11.28–30]."

447. But if anyone should ask who it is who will be so compassionate to
those in travail, let him hear the prophecy of Isaiah who this may be; he
says: "Who has measured all the waters with his fist, and all the earth with
his span? Who has placed the hills in the balance, and weighed the plains
with scales? Who has known the mind of the Lord, or who has been companion of his counsel [Is. 40.12–13]?" He who learnt from the Father the
sentence of judgment, the same came, was made man and preached to the
world, joining[1] in his love all men to the Deity. And therefore came the light,
coming to our midst "to illuminate every man who was to come into the
world [Jn. 1.9]." He preached and said: "Repent, for the kingdom of God
is nigh. The times are fulfilled; believe in the gospel [Mt. 4.17; Mk. 1.15]."

1. Joining: խառնեալ, on this important technical expression see §369 note 2.

448. [*The calling of the disciples*] When He passed along the seashore, He
saw Peter and Andrew and James and John. And He called them from
fishing. They straightway left their father with the ship and followed Him
[Mk. 1.16–20]. And He called many from various other occupations and
named them as the twelve disciples and apostles [Lk. 6.13], whom he taught
to be free from all occupations. They followed Him about and became
worthy of the mystery of the divine tradition.[1]

1. See also §420 note 1, 433 note 1. The theme is developed more fully in §468 below.

449. [*Christ's miracles*] Then the benevolent Christ introduced his all-
powerful healing to cure all diseases and torments. And He fulfilled the prediction of the holy prophets, recalling the saying: "He will remove our ill-
nesses [Mt. 8.17; Is. 53.4]." And He justified their words[1] according to the
saying: "He justifies the words of his servants the prophets [Is. 44.26]."

1. A major theme of the *Teaching*; see also §339 note 1.

450. And then He began to surpass the examples:[1] "In all places through
the Spirit of truth they will worship the Father, for the Father seeks such
worshippers [Jn. 4.23]." And: "I prefer mercy to sacrifices [Hosea 6.6;
Mt. 9.13; 12.7]." And: "I am the Son of the Father, for the Father bears
witness to me by the Spirit with truth [Jn. 5.37]." And: "Moses first wrote
to you about me; and Jacob spoke concerning me to Juda: 'There will not
lack a prince of Juda, nor a leader from his loins, until there comes he whose
is the kingdom. For he is the hope of the nations [Lk. 24.27, 44; Jn. 5.46;
Gen. 49.10].'"

1. Examples: օրինակ; see Introduction, p. 16.

451. And: "All the prophets wrote concerning me; they took knowledge
from Him who sent me, and they revealed that mine is the vineyard, and
you are the laborers. And I came for I am the heir of the vineyard [Mt. 21.38;
Mk. 12.7; Lk. 20.14]. I came to seek the fruit of the vineyard to take it
away. Just as the Father sent me, so I came to fulfill the will of my Father
[Jn. 5.30]." And: "I came to fulfill the gospel promised to Abraham, that by
the promise the seed of Abraham might live, and that the seed of Abraham
might know these things [Jn. 8.37]." Then He straightway expounded the
truth: "Before Abraham was, I am [Jn. 8.58]." Then He raised their minds
to higher things, according to the saying, asking them about the prophecy:
"How do you say Christ is the Son of David, of whom David made mention by the Holy Spirit: 'The Lord said to my Lord, sit on my right hand?'
How then is he the Son of David [Mt. 22.43–45; Mk. 12.35–37; Lk. 20.41–44;
Ps. 109.1]?"

452. Likewise in all his revelations and parables He reproached and exposed their hypocrisy and impiety and lawlessness. But they, being deaf
and blind to the truth, eagerly rushed, in the wickedness of their anger,
to the destruction of their souls. But He came and was a doctor [Mt. 9.12;
Mk. 2.17; Lk. 5.31][1] in his loving kindness, to give sight to the blind, make
the lame to walk, heal the lepers, save all the oppressed from Satan, to raise
the paralyzed, open the ears of the deaf, give speech to the dumb, raise the
dead. He gave his believers power to tread Satan underfoot [Lk. 10.19],

and promised to go and prepare dwelling places in the kingdom of heaven [Jn. 14.2–3]. And He made Himself an example to all, to bear toils with virtue.[2]

1. See also §565 note 1.
2. See also §407, 687; cf. I Clement 16.

453. He turned the water into wine [Jn. 2.1–11], that his divinity might be revealed, [to show] that He who made the water into the nature of water from nothing, the same also turned the water into wine, as He wished. And He who because of sin partook of pain, the same came to distribute well-being. And many believed in his name when they saw Him and the signs which He worked [Jn. 2.23]. But He, because He was the knower of hearts [Ps. 43.22; Acts 15.8], knew all the secrets of men, because He knows what is hidden.

454. Then after this He gave a decree: "If anyone is not born by water and the Spirit, he cannot enter the kingdom of God [Jn. 3.5]." And he will not be renewed a second time.[1] For "that, He says, which is born of flesh, is flesh; but what is of the Spirit, is Spirit. For the Holy Spirit blows where He will; you hear his sound, but you do not know whence He comes or whither he goes [Jn. 3.6–8]." "For there is no one who has ascended to heaven except He who came down from heaven, the Son of man [Jn. 3.13]."

1. Cf. Cyril Jer., *Procat.*, 7: οὐκ ἔνι δὶς καὶ τρὶς λαβεῖν τὸ λουτρόν . . . εἷς γὰρ κύριος, καὶ μία πίστις, καὶ ἓν βάπτισμα (Eph. 4.5).

455. And He said concerning his foreordained passion: "As Moses suspended the serpent in the wilderness so must the Son of man be suspended, that he who once believes in Him may receive everlasting life. For God so loved the world that He gave his only-begotten Son for it, that everyone who believes in Him may not perish but receive everlasting life. For God did not send his Son into the world to punish the world, but that He might save the world. Who believes in Him does not enter the punishment of condemnation; but who does not believe in Him is straightway condemned, because he did not believe in the name of the only-begotten Son of God [Jn. 3.14–18]." "He came to his own and his own received Him not [Jn. 1.11]." Him whose favor and providence and commandments were from the beginning of time they rejected when He appeared in the flesh.

456. "And this is the judgment, that the light came into the world, and men loved the darkness more than the light, for their works were evil. For everyone who works evil will find evil, and he hates the light and comes not

into the light, lest his deeds should be reproved. But whoever does and works the truth, he comes into the light that his works may be manifest that they have been wrought by God [Jn. 3.19–21]." And the Son of God taught all men the paths of righteousness. But the lawless Jews, men accustomed to deeds of darkness, began to plot, and the laborers of the vineyard[1] sought to kill Him, and they did not consider themselves worthy of eternal life. But to such persons He promised hell, saying "woe [Mt. 23.33]" over them.

1. Origen, *In Threnos*, II, interprets the ἀμπελών of Is. 5.1 as Israel. Cf. §451, "I am the heir of the vineyard."

457. Then the good Lord gathered together the twelve disciples, whom He also called apostles [Lk. 6.13], and in addition the seventy-two [Lk. 10.1].[1] He taught and instructed them in the wisdom of God, and testified and spoke to them, and called them his "beloved" and "friends [Lk. 12.4; Jn. 15.15]." "I say to you, my beloved, do not fear those who kill the flesh and are unable to kill the Spirit [Lk. 12.4; Mt. 10.28]." And: "I know you as my friends [Jn. 15.15]," and: "What once my Father said to me and showed me, I have showed you [Jn. 5.20; 10.32]." And He revealed to them his coming from the Father and his return to the same, saying: "I came from the Father and came into the world; and again I leave the world and go to the Father [Jn. 16.28]."

1. On this number see §503 note 1, 686 note 3.

458. He gave them also the good news of the Holy Spirit sent by the Father: "I go and send you the Comforter, who will come and comfort those in sorrow for my sake [Jn. 14.16; 15.26; 16.7]." See the equality, see the unified hypostasis, see the true being,[1] see the single completeness of accord. "He will come and fill my place for you, and guide you in the same truth, and will reprove the world that they did not believe in me; He will judge also the supposed prince of this world. He will again straighten you concerning me, for He is sent by the Father. His coming bears witness of my going to the Father. He, when He has come, will guide you in all truth [Jn. 16.8–13]."

1. True being: ζ‍ա‍կ‍ա‍ն‍ո‍ւ‍թ‍ի‍ւ‍ն; cf. Introduction, p. 11.

459. [*Jesus foretells his passion*] Then Jesus accepted the foreordained mystery of suffering, to fulfill it in Jerusalem, concerning which He had frequently foretold that He would die and rise on the third day [Mt. 16.21; Mk. 8.31; Lk. 9.22].

460. And for whose sake then would He go to death, unless He was in some way guilty[1] of death? But the prophet says: "He worked no injustice, nor was deceit found in his mouth [Is. 53.9]." As He Himself said: "Which of you will reproach me about sin [Jn. 8.46]?" Was He then in any way guilty of death according to the law? But He says: "I came to fulfill the law [Mt. 5.17]," to which the apostle bears witness: "Christ is the fulfillment of the law [Rom. 10.4]." Would He then die by the force of tyrants? But He says: "Of my own will I lay down my life, and no one takes it from me. Willingly, He says, I lay down my life that I may take it up again [Jn. 10.17–18]."

1. Guilty: պարտապան, ἔνοχος in Mt. 5.21 and I Cor. 11.27; ὀφειλέτης in Gal. 5.3.

461. But why should He, being innocent of death, wish to lay down his life? "I am, He says, the good shepherd who die for my sheep [Jn. 10.11]." For which sheep then? For the frightened, the fleeing, those about to be eaten by wild beasts, of whom the prophet foretold: "All went astray like lambs, and every man went astray in his path. And the Lord handed him over for our sins, and he was led to death by the injustices of my people [Is. 53.6, 8]."

462. Concerning this the chief priest of the race who killed their Lord unwittingly prophesied: "It is better for us that one man die for the people, and that the whole race perish not [Jn. 11.50]." But he does not speak on behalf of a single race, but rather that He may gather together all the sons of God, scattered among diverse races. Paul also bears witness: "God revealed his love to us, that while we were still sinners, Christ died for us [Rom. 5.8]." And: "At the [due] time He died for the impious [Rom. 5.6]."

463. And then He came with the disciples to the mount of Olives to fulfill the saying of the prophet: "The Lord my God will come and all the saints with Him. And his feet will stand on that day on the mount of Olives, opposite Jerusalem, on the eastern side [Zech. 14.4]."

464. And on the feast day of the law He came with the disciples to fulfill the law, and to reveal the spiritual mysteries of the feast.[1] And before his sufferings He gave his saving body and blood to the disciples [Mt. 26.26–27; Mk. 14.22–23; Lk. 22.19–20]. So do you see that willingly and not by force the Son of God suffered, who ate before suffering?[2]

1. The death of Christ fulfills the spiritual meaning of the πάσχα; cf. Irenaeus, *Adv. Haer.*, IV 10.1: Passus est Dominus adimplens Pascha. The connection between the two was further strengthened by the popular derivation of πάσχα from πάσχω; cf. Irenaeus, ibid.: (Moses) et diem passionis non ignoravit, sed figuratim praenuntiavit eum, Pascha nominans;

and Gregory Naz., *Or.*, XLV 10: τοῦ γὰρ σωτηρίου πάθους ὄνομα τοῦτο (viz. τὸ πάσχα) εἶναί τινες νομίσαντες ... πάσχα τὴν ἡμέραν προσηγορεύκασιν.

2. The idea that Christ indicated his willingness to suffer by eating the Pascha just before his death is repeated in §491 below. Cf. Cyril Jer., *Cat.*, XIII 6, where also the patience (ὑπομονή) is mentioned, as *Teaching*, §407, 452. For the references in the *Teaching* to communion see §432 note 3; in the *History*, §8, 84, 834.

465. After this He prayed in secret on the mountain to the Father—not because of any ignorance on his part,[1] but to show that in union with the Father He would effect what had been previously laid down. So He had said frequently before: "I say nothing by myself and do nothing of myself, but the Father who dwells in me, He works [these things] [Jn. 5.30; 8.28; 14.10]." He especially fulfills the prophecy: "In return for my love they betrayed me, but I was at prayer [Ps. 108.4]."

1. The *Teaching* emphasizes the knowledge of Christ; see §469 note 1, 470. Like Athanasius, Cyril of Alexandria, and Chrysostom, our author sees no limit to Christ's human knowledge lest this detract from his divinity.

466. He revealed to the disciples his unity of will with the Father, and then came down from the mountain, hastening to lay down his life for the unbelievers, especially when the Gentiles who had come to the feast begged the disciples to go with them to Jesus [Jn. 12.20–21]. By them was fulfilled also the prophecy: "Thus says the Lord omnipotent: 'In those days ten men from all the races will take hold of the skirt of a man who is a Jew, and will say: Let us go with you, for we have heard that God is with you [Zech. 8.23].'" And Jesus listened and said: "The hour has come that the Son of man should be glorified [Jn. 12.23]." Do you see that He calls the sufferings glory?

467. Then when the true disciples were gathered around the true teacher, the Lord Jesus, Savior and Benefactor, and Son of God and Anointed,[1] He asked them: "Whom do men say the Son of man is?" They answered and said: "Some John the Baptist; others Elias or one of the prophets." And Jesus said: "Whom do you say that I am?" Their leader[2] Peter said: "You are Christ, Son of the living God [Mt. 16.13–16; Mk. 8.27–29; Lk. 9.18–20]." For this reason he received the blessing: "Blessed are you Peter, son of Jona, because not from your earthly relations, from the flesh and blood of your race, from mankind, did you receive this knowledge, but the Father gave it into your heart from heaven and revealed it to you [Mt. 16.17–18]." And He made him the rock of establishment of all the churches [Mt. 16.18; Jn. 1.42].

1. Anointed: աւծեալ, not used in Armenian as a translation of Χριστός, which is transliterated Քրիստոս.

2. Their leader: ատաջինն, lit. the first. Eznik, §384, calls Peter "chief" (գլուխ) of the apostles. Cf. Cyril Jer., *Cat.*, XI 3: Πέτρος ὁ πρωτοστάτης τῶν ἀποστόλων καὶ τῆς ἐκκλησίας κορυφαῖος κήρυξ.

468. And the apostles became the foundations [Eph. 2.20], and received the grace of priesthood and prophecy and apostleship and knowledge of the heavenly mystery which came in the seed of Abraham, which John, the keeper of the tradition of the inheritance, gave to the Lord, and the Lord gave to the apostles.[1] And He gave the keys of the kingdom[2] into their hands [Mt. 16.19],[3] for the Son of God Himself was the gate for those who enter [Jn. 10.7, 9]; concerning which the prophet declared: "This is the gate of the Lord, and the just enter through it [Ps. 117.20]." So John gave the priesthood and the power and the prophecy and the kingship to our Savior Christ: and Christ gave them to the apostles, and the apostles to the children of the church.

1. See also §430, 433.
2. Sargisean, *Agat'angelos*, p. 384, links the kingship with the priesthood for reasons inherent in the development of fourth-century Armenian history. But the kingship of §429–433 above is messianic and religious, and this is the meaning here also. A close parallel is found in Epiphanius, *Adv. Haer.*, I 29.4: Ἱερεὺς . . . ὁ κύριος ἡμῶν Ἰησοῦς Χριστὸς εἰς τὸν αἰῶνα κατὰ τὴν τάξιν Μελχισεδέκ, βασιλεύς τε ὁμοῦ κατὰ τὴν τάξιν τὴν ἄνωθεν, ἵνα μεταγάγῃ τὴν ἱερωσύνην ἅμα τῇ νομοθεσίᾳ . . . ἐχαρίσατο δὲ τοῖς ὑπ' αὐτοῦ καθισταμένοις τὸ βασίλειον . . . τὸ βασίλειον τοῦ Δαβὶδ μεταστήσας, καὶ χαρισάμενος τοῖς ἑαυτοῦ δούλοις ἅμα τῇ ἀρχιερωσύνῃ, τουτέστι τοῖς ἀρχιερεῦσι τῆς καθολικῆς ἐκκλησίας.
3. Origen, *Comm. in Mat.*, XII 11, rejects this interpretation of Mt. 16.19 and insists that only Peter received the keys, but the *Teaching* derives the authority of the church from the apostles as a whole. However Peter is given prominence, cf. §467 note 2.

469. They boldly asked the Lord on the mount of Olives when He gave sentence concerning the destruction of the beautiful temple: "Tell us, they said, when will this be, and what sign will there be of your coming and of the end of this world [Mt. 24.3]?" Then He, although He demurred, said: "Concerning that day no one knows, neither the angels of heaven nor the Son, but only the Father [Mt. 24.36; Lk. 13.32]." And Luke in his book of the Acts of the Apostles explained by a parable: "It is not for you, he says, to inquire the hour and the time which the Father has set in his authority [Acts 1.7]"—but who else is the authority of the Father except the Son Himself?[1] Nonetheless He explained in detail to the disciples concerning his awesome coming in the clouds.

1. The *Teaching* is anxious to disavow any ignorance on the part of Christ (see also §465, 470), even at the cost of contradicting scripture. The Son is not normally identified with the authority of God but is said to share or have the same ἐξουσία as the Father; cf. Lampe, *Lexicon*, s.v. ἐξουσία.

470. Do you see that the Son knew not only the day, but also the hour and the form of his coming, and was in no way ignorant? But for the sake of his weakly believing[1] audience He spoke concerning his descent as was appropriate to the time.[2] But although He decreed the destruction of Jerusalem in a confused manner[3] because of those questioning Him, and also related the end of the whole world, it is not at all difficult to understand the end and destruction of Jerusalem, if any one would care to examine it diligently, distinguishing each detail.

1. Weakly believing: թերահաւատ, the ὀλιγόπιστος of the N.T.
2. See also §696.
3. In a confused manner: խառնակապատումն.

471. He then undertook to narrate the circumstances of great persecutions and false Christs and false prophets who would arise [Mt. 24.24; Mk. 13.22], and about anti-Christ [I Jn. 2.18],[1] giving descriptions of these imposters' signs. Concerning this the apostles also indicated that: "In the latter times such men will arise [I Jn. 2.18; II Thess. 2.8]." Then He indicated his unexpected and sudden coming with Noah and Lot given as examples [Mt. 24.37; Lk. 17.26]. As Paul says: "In the twinkling of an eye, suddenly, after the persecutions of those days, the sun will grow dark and the moon will not give its light, and the stars will fall from heaven and the powers of the heavens will be moved. And then will appear the sign of the Son of man in the heavens [Mt. 24.29–30; I Cor. 15.52]." The cross will shine above[2] and fill the whole world with its light, when it denotes his second coming to make his retribution, a reproach on all the people [Ps. 149.7], to the various races, to judge all races with fire in his anger and his judgment [Is. 66.15]. He gave and revealed all knowledge to his apostles and believing disciples and beloved friends.

1. Anti-Christ: նեռն, the ἀντίχριστος of I John.
2. This section of the *Teaching* resembles the beginning of the Apocalypse of Peter; cf. James, *Apocryphal N.T.*, p. 511. The theme of the second coming is worked out fully by Cyril Jer., *Cat.*, XV, who interprets Mt. 24.30 as the sign of the cross in heaven. On the sign of the cross, see Daniélou, *Theology*, p. 268.

472. [*Jesus is delivered up, crucified, and buried*] Then coming into the midst of the people, He drew attention to his reproving and public teaching and said: "I spoke clearly to the world and taught the people at all times in the temple, where all the Jews were gathered, and I spoke nothing in secret [Jn. 18.20]." He also cried out, saying: "Who believes in me, believes in Him who sent me. And who sees me, sees Him who sent me [Jn. 12.44–45]." And thus he bore witness in truth and vowed; afterwards He went to fall into the hands of rebels. For those who have turned their backs on the illuminating and life-giving teaching and have gone astray, perhaps so far as to

lay hands on the Life-giver with violence, will awake and be undeceived of their error.

473. For He was delivered over to the priests and doctors of the law to make them aware through the law of his foretold sufferings; and they took and judged the judge of all [Heb. 12.23] according to all the writings concerning Him. As Paul in Antioch of Pisidia bore witness concerning Him: "The inhabitants of Jerusalem were ignorant of Him, and according to the voice of the prophets which are read every Sabbath they fulfilled them in judging Him; and although they found no cause for death, they sought from Pilate that He should be killed [Acts 13.27–28]." And when they took his life, they hung Him opposite themselves on wood [Deut. 28.66]. And concerning this the Lord had previously indicated from the law: "The Son of man must be raised up [Jn. 3.14]."[1] And then consequently at that time was fulfilled and completed the saying in Job: "Who commands the sun, and it rises not and hides its rays which spread over the world, and who seals each shining star [Job. 9.7]."

1. In John this quotation is connected with the serpent raised by Moses in the desert, Num. 21.8. This serpent was early interpreted as a type of Christ; cf. Barnabas, XII 6: ἵνα τύπον τοῦ Ἰησοῦ δείξῃ, ποιεῖ οὖν Μωυσῆς χαλκοῦν ὄφιν. See also Daniélou, *Theology*, pp. 92, 271.

474. And from the sixth hour, says the evangelist, darkness held the earth until the ninth hour of the day [Mt. 27.45; Mk. 15.33; Lk. 23.44], for the fulfilling of the prophecy of Amos: "It will come to pass on that day, says the Lord of Lords, that the sun will go down at noon, and the light will darken on the earth in the day time [Amos 8.9]." Similarly Zecharias: "It will come to pass on that day that there will be no light, and one day will be cold and clear; and that day is known to the Lord. There will be neither day nor night, and at evening there will be light [Zech. 14.6–7]."

475. And what is "that day is known to the Lord" except that it was previously indicated by the prophets, the day of the Lord whose appointed time has arrived? Just as Daniel, informed by the angel, wrote: "After sixty-two weeks the anointed one will be killed [Dan. 9.26]." But "known to the Lord" means the sign which He shows by the sun, just as in the beginning He brought the luminaries into existence: "Let them be for signs [Gen. 1.14]." For that reason He prolonged his dying with the sign of the dark hour,[1] in order that "they might behold and see whom they had pierced [Jn. 19.37]." But they, more and more blinded, arrived at the extremity of error, and like dogs were silent [Is. 56.10] and made no confession.

1. See also §677 note 1: the sun was dark for it could not endure to see the sufferings of the Lord.

476. And He fulfilled everything, as the Evangelist says: "Then Jesus knew that everything was completed, and He said: 'I am thirsty' [Jn. 19. 28]." In order that the scripture might be fulfilled, they offered Him vinegar mixed with gall [Mt. 27.34, 48; Ps. 68.22] in a cup of derision. For which reason He declared: "All is completed [Jn. 19.30]." Then was fulfilled the word of the prophet: "He himself will accomplish the end [Nahum 1.9]." Paul bears witness that: "When they had completed all that was written concerning Him, they took Him down and placed Him in a tomb [Acts 13.29]."

477. "And at the ninth hour, he says, Jesus cried out with a loud voice and said: 'Eli, Eli, lama sabak't'ani'—which is, my God, my God, why have you abandoned me? [Mt. 27.46; Mk. 15.34; Ps. 21.2]" Do you see that in dying He makes his teaching without rancor, whereby He instructed the thief on the cross beside Him and the centurion and many others? For He came willingly to death, and as All-powerful, was forced by no one. Therefore He cried with a loud voice to fulfill the saying of the prophet: "The sun and the moon will grow dark, and the stars will hide their light" [Joel 2.10; 3.15]; and: "The Lord will cry from Sion and raise his voice from Jerusalem [Amos 1.2; Joel 3.16]."

478. What man, when troubled in mind and near death, would raise a cry or shout? He would rather keep his mouth closed and remain speechless before dying. But the Creator of souls,[1] Christ, willingly in his love coming to death, announced with a loud voice with awesome signs that even in death He was one in will and deed with the Father. And He revealed his undoubted death for the sake of the world by speaking the prophecy: "My God, my God, why have you forsaken me? [Ps. 21.2]" and: "Into your hands I commend my spirit [Lk. 23.46; Ps. 30.6]."

1. Creator of souls: Հաստիչ ոգւոց. Հաստիչ renders κτίστης in I Pet. 4.19. In I Clement LIX 3 Christ is called τὸν παντὸς πνεύματος κτίστην καὶ ἐπίσκοπον (cf. I Pet. 2.25).

479. And lest the deceivers should have any doubt about his prompt and illuminating resurrection, they took Him down from the cross and placed Him in a tomb. About this He Himself had previously indicated, using an example according to the prophet: "Just as Jona was in the belly of the fish for three days and three nights, so the Son of man will be in the heart of the earth [Mt. 12.40; Jona 1.17]." By which He fulfilled the vision of Isaiah: "Behold I place in the foundations of Sion a precious stone [Is. 28.16]."[1]

Similarly the inspired Psalmist: "Into the dust of death they bore me down [Ps. 21.16]." To which Paul bears witness: "He died according to the Scriptures and was buried [I Cor. 15.3–4]."

1. For the frequent use of this quotation and of others likening Christ to a stone, see Lampe, *Lexicon*, s.v. λίθος.

480. Of these sayings the Jews were aware and had been informed. Telling the judge the sayings of Christ: "On the third day I shall rise [Mt. 16.21; 20.19; Mk. 8.31; 9.31; Lk. 9.22; 18.33]," they took a troop of soldiers to keep sleepless vigil with care by night [Mt. 27.62–66]. But the Lord, according to his own saying, rose on the third day so that the sayings of the prophet might be fulfilled, both in death by the will of the Father, and in the glory of the resurrection: "After two days, on the third day we shall rise and stand before him; and we shall follow on to know the Lord, and we shall find him prepared like the dawn [Hosea 6.3]." By this He loosed the pains of death, "because it was not possible for Him to be restrained by it [Acts 2.24]." He was not sold under sin, for although He was wounded [Is. 53.5] and counted among those asleep in the tombs [I Cor. 15.20], yet He was "without support and free among the dead [Ps. 87.6]" for the taking away of sins and the healing of his creatures.

481. For alone and sovereign in his soul and free from sin, He killed "death reigning in power over the world, and wiped all tears from every face [Is. 25.8]." Whereby He fulfilled the saying: "You will not abandon my soul in hell, nor give your holy one to see corruption. You made known to me your paths of life, you filled me with joy from your countenance [Ps. 15.10–11]." He also said: "I am the good shepherd, and for my sheep I lay down my life [Jn. 10.11]." Then He went up from the earth, the shepherd of flocks of rational sheep, and fulfilled the saying of the prophet: "Who brought from the earth the shepherd of the sheep [Is. 63.11]," which the apostle interprets: "He brought from the dead the great shepherd of the sheep, through the blood of the eternal covenant, our Lord Jesus Christ [Heb. 13.20]."

482. [*The resurrection*] And because He had frequently informed those hearing his parables of his sufferings and his resurrection on the third day, not in boasting nor in threatening but in order to bring those in error to the truth of the faith by sweet teaching, He previously set a time for the resurrection so that those to whom He was unknown when He came forth from the virgin [Jn. 1.10], perchance when He came forth from the tomb might hasten to enter the kingdom. For the Life-giver came for the life of the living; and they were given over to death in despair instead of to life.

483. He died then for the dead, and rose that by his resurrection He might be an example. Therefore He made his illuminating[1] resurrection by night, that He might make known the truth of his completed task to those on guard and those on watch. They were exceedingly terrified by the earthquake and splitting of the rocks, and the opening of the graves and the resurrection of the dead [Mt. 27.51–53]. By this the word of the prophet was fulfilled: "The mountains will be moved by him, and the earth was shaken at his face, and the rocks were split [Nahum 1.5]." Whereby "the guards did shake and became like corpses [Mt. 28.4]."

1. Illuminating: *լուսաւոր*; see also §484, where the resurrection is "light-bringing," *լուսաբեր*. But the latter refers to the benefits brought by the resurrection, whereas here the mode of resurrection is intended; cf. Cyril Jer., *Cat.*, XIV 22, who notes that the resurrection took place in the light of the full moon.

484. But the Living-one rose, and with the witness of the angels informed those who had come and were serving Him, as also the prophet indicated: "The Lord is kind to those who serve Him in the day of tribulation, and He knows those who fear Him [Nahum 1.7]." For He first invited[1] them to the expectation of the light-bringing resurrection, by which the saying of the prophet was brought to fulfillment: "Therefore wait for me, says the Lord, until the day of my resurrection for a witness [Zeph. 3.8]."

1. Invited: *հրաւիրեաց*, an important expression in the *Teaching*; see also §326, 573, 630, and especially 617 note 3.

485. Then the guards hastened to the city, and thus noised abroad and declared the divine resurrection [Mt. 28.11], until the same night the women came from the tomb to announce to the disciples the wonders they had seen [Mt. 28.8]. So also the guards came stricken and dejected into the city, and related to the priests and disciples, especially to the excited crowd which had gathered, revealing it to many in the city.

486. Thereby was brought to fulfillment the promised word of the prophet: "I shall open your tombs, says the Lord, and shall raise you from your tombs [Ez. 37.12]." Again Isaiah says: "The dead will rise and will stand up, whoever are in tombs, for this dew from you is their healing [Is. 26.19.]"[1] Perhaps he meant the life-giving blood of Christ which was shed on the cross for all.[2] And to make it clear that it was there prophesied, he referred the saying to the persons of the disciples: "Come, my people, enter your chambers and close your doors, and hide for a time [Is. 26.20]."

1. These quotations from Ezechiel and Isaiah are combined frequently; e.g., I Clement I 4, Cyril Jer., *Cat.*, XVIII 15. Cf. Daniélou, *Theology*, pp. 95–96.

2. See also §554, and the "divine dew" in §648. The source of the explanation in the *Teaching* is Eusebius, *Comm. in Is.* XXVI v.19: οὐκ ἂν δὲ ἁμάρτοις αὐτὸν εἶναι δρόσον λέγων τὸν μονογενῆ τοῦ Θεοῦ Λόγον, ὃς ἐπιστάξας τὰς ἑαυτοῦ ζωοποιοὺς σταγόνας τοῖς αὐτοῦ νεκροῖς, ὁμοῦ καὶ ἴασιν ἁμαρτημάτων . . . παρέξει ὁμοῦ καὶ ἀνάστασιν καὶ σωτηρίαν, καὶ ζωὴν αἰώνιον αὐτοῖς δωρήσεται. Other patristic commentators on Isaiah do not follow this line; cf. Cyril Alex., *In Is.*, III 1 v.19: δρόσος οὖν ἄρα ζωοποιὸς τὸ Πνεῦμα παρα Πατρὸς δι' Υἱοῦ. The author of the *Teaching* introduces his remarks with "perhaps." Had he merely heard of this explanation without reading Eusebius, or did he regard Eusebius' authority insufficient?

487.   But the obstinate race of crucifiers, deaf and blind to the truth, gained no profit at all from the story of the revived or the appearance of the dead or the frightening signs of the divine and victorious resurrection. For concerning them the Omniscient spoke in a parable, recounting the things to come for the rich: "If they did not listen to Moses and the prophets, even if someone were to come to them from the dead, they would not listen [Lk. 16.31]." To them also applies the word of the prophet: "On that day I shall raise over you a parable, and they will make lament and say: 'We have become utterly miserable [Micah 2.4].'" This lament indeed their fellow-kinsman Paul raised: "With lament I speak of the enemies of the cross of Christ, whose end is destruction [Philipp. 3.18–19]."[1]

1. Despite the anti-Jewish polemic of this paragraph (but see §499 note 1 below), Judaizing tendencies were common in early Armenian writers; cf. L. Leloir, *Divergences, Mélanges Eugène Tisserant*, II, p. 307.

488.   [*Christ appears to the disciples*] Christ came therefore in the evening of the first day of the week and appeared to the disciples, although the doors were closed, as the Evangelist says [Jn. 20.19]. And He gave them the life-giving greeting, and brought much joy to the disciples. Then He fulfilled the song of the Psalmist: "The Lord our God appeared to us; make festivals of joy right early unto the corners of the altar [Ps. 117.27]." And what are the corners of the altar except an indication of the cross which shows four corners?[1]

1. The horns of the altar were identified with the points of the cross by early Christian writers; cf. Lampe, *Lexicon*, s.v. κέρας.

489.   He planted one [corner] in the earth to show the placing of the Lord's feet on the earth, in order that on the firm rock He might build and place the depth of the foundations of the church. As the prophet foretold: "On the rock the Lord placed me, to make me immovable [Ps. 26.5; 39.3; 117.22]." Then He set up the principal corner, the top pointing upwards, that that corner which is set upwards, like a counterweight might elevate the nature of Him who rested on it, and thus make the onlookers see the Father, the head of Christ, and reveal his nature. The right corner shows the power of

the right arm; by the right hand He shows the joy of the rejoicing of the just, the adornment of the crowns and blessings prepared for them. But the left corner indicates the torments of sinners.[1]

1. See also §629. The wording of this paragraph is obscure in places, but the theme is familiar from Andrew's address to the cross in the *Acts of Andrew*; cf. also Irenaeus, *Dem.*, 34. Andrew agrees with the *Teaching* in interpreting the cross, its base set in the earth, as supporting the world; the upper part signifies the heavenly word (Andrew) or Christ (*Teaching*). But the interpretation of the side-arms varies: for Andrew the right hand puts the demons to flight and the other gathers the scattered; among other patristic writers, for Athanasius, *De Incarnatione* (Long Recension only), XXV, the two arms gather the Jews and the Gentiles, following Irenaeus, *Adv. Haer.*, V 17.4; for Cyril Jer., *Cat.*, XIII 28, and Gregory of Nyssa, *Or cat.*, 32, and *In Christi Res. Hom.*, I, the emphasis is on the inclusion of the whole world. The *Teaching* has followed a different line and incorporated the idea of Mt. 25.33, the sheep and the goats. On the figure of the cross see Daniélou, *Theology*, pp. 287–288, H. Rahner, *The Christian Mystery and the Pagan Mysteries*, pp. 372 ff., and G. Q. Reijners, *The Terminology of The Holy Cross in Early Christian Literature*, Nijmegen 1965.

490.   Because the altar has four corners, which is the cross, this is in truth an altar, because it received the true sacrifice of the Lord's body which was offered to the Father. Rightly also he mentions the four corners, that it might be set up throughout the four corners of the whole world and make the whole world rejoice at this altar, those in heaven and earth and those in hell [Philipp. 2.10], and the founded [Eph. 2.10], who are the apostles and prophets.[1] And the heavenly beings are the angels, the spiritual hosts, who had and have great joy at the certain return of life. And men are the earthly beings, who lived and returned to the Lord. And you indeed wish to live by the visitation of Christ. And those in hell are those asleep, whom He has saved by his coming. For the cross which is raised up shows the Victor, and the bottom corner shows the victory.

1. The *Teaching* is here closer to Gregory of Nyssa's explanation of the mystery of the cross (references in §489 note 1 above).

491.   At that altar rejoiced first the apostles, for they had seen his resurrection and were glad.[1] And the saying was fulfilled: "Make festival of joy right early unto the corners of the altar [Ps. 117.27]." Then was fulfilled also the song of the Psalmist: "You have freed me from my sack-cloth, and have clothed me with joy [Ps. 29.12]." These show the signs of the sufferings of the Risen one, to whom Paul bears witness: "So He did not die, and death reigns no more over Him [Rom. 6.9]." And because He works wonders and is incomprehensible to scrutiny and is able to work all impossible things, as before his suffering He had given his life-giving body and blood to the disciples to show that He was suffering willingly,[2] so also after the resurrection

He shows in Himself the sign of the nails [Jn. 20.25–27], revealing that the wounds were not able to restrain in the tomb the Healer of the wounded.

1. The altar being the cross, this reflects Gal. 6.14.
2. See §464 note 2.

492.   Likewise He ate with the disciples in the new kingdom [Jn. 21.12], to show that He who could eat in the abundant and delightful kingdom, the same also before his suffering moved in the hungry and care-needing world, lacking nothing Himself, and completely satisfying others. But just as He ate in the former to confirm the disciples, so also in the latter He hungered to convince the world that the real Son of God truly was born in time as a son of man that He might give life to the world. Concerning this the prophet predicted: "God eternal, God who established the extremities of the earth, will not hunger and will not toil, and there is no searching of his wisdom [Is. 40.28]." He appeared to a certain Cleopas and his companion on the way to Emmaus, and put before them the traditions of the prophets who had borne witness to Him [Lk. 24.13–35].

493.   Then He appeared to the disciples by the lake of Tiberias [Jn. 21.1–14], and made signs to confirm them, and revealed to them that the tomb had not in the slightest restrained the divine power, but just as at his birth and before his suffering and during his suffering, He was with the same power also after the resurrection. To this the blessed Paul also bore witness: "Jesus Christ, yesterday and today, the same also for ever [Heb. 13.8]."

494.   He recalls then to the disciples and brings as witness his former sayings: "These are the words which I spoke with you while I was still with you, that it is necessary for all the writings in the law of Moses and in the prophets and in the psalms concerning me to be fulfilled [Lk. 24.44]." And Jesus breathed on them and said: "Receive the Holy Spirit [Jn. 20.22]." And then He opened their minds to understand the scriptures, and said to them: "Thus had Christ to suffer and to rise from the dead on the third day [Lk. 24.46]."

495.   And when He fulfilled the covenant of God concerning the Jewish race, whom He had denounced by saying earlier: "If I had not come and spoken with them, they would have had no sin; but now there is no excuse for their sins for they have seen my works, which no one else did, and they have hated me and my Father [Jn. 15.24]," He then turned his illuminating teaching to the gentiles, whereby He brought to fulfillment the prophecy of Isaiah: "I gave you for a covenant to the people and a light to the gentiles, to be salvation to the ends of the earth [Is. 42.6; 49.6, 8]."

496.   [*The ascension*] And He brought the disciples out to the Mount of Olives, and confirmed them in unity of truth, saying: "Go then and make disciples of all the gentiles, and baptize them in the name of the Father and the Son and the Holy Spirit [Mt. 28.19]." "And raising his hands He blessed them, and as He blessed them He was taken up into heaven [Lk. 24.50–51]," says the Evangelist, that the song of the psalter might be fulfilled: "God was raised up in blessing [Ps. 46.6]." He commanded them: "Stay in Jerusalem, and I shall send the promise of my Father to you [Lk. 24.49; Acts 1.4]," by which the saying of Amos came to fulfillment: "Who builds his elevation in the heavens, and sets his promise on the earth [Amos 9.6]."

497.   We now cast a glance at the fulfillment of these sayings, making a discourse[1] on the good news spoken by Christ and the promises concerning the comforter the Holy Ghost; especially as we shall still have at hand the easy to understand and encouraging blessed Luke,[2] who is knowledgeable and versed in the things done by Christ, concerning whom he loudly cries at the beginning of his gospel which speaks to the world: "I desired also to write to you in order, what from the beginning I have followed in all truth, worthy Theophilus, that you might know the truth of the words in which you have been instructed [Lk. 1.3–4]."

1. See §376 note 2.
2. See Introduction, p. 30.

498.   And because at the end of his gospel he delineated only briefly Christ's journey to heaven, he took up again in his second book of the Apostles to set out the course of events; and immediately recalling the formerly written gospel, he began the Acts of the Apostles by mentioning the same Theophilus: "The former treatise which I made concerning everything, O Theophilus, which Jesus began to do and to teach [Acts 1.1]." Therefore he set it down briefly and hastened to the Ascension, and clearly related the details of the Ascension, the commands of Christ to the disciples, and his journey on the clouds, and the witness of the angels who descended concerning the Ascension of Christ, and the mode of his second coming.

499.   [*The coming of the Spirit*] After this he describes the glorious and most wonderful descent of the Holy Spirit from heaven: "At the completion of the days of Pentecost[1] they were all with one accord together. And there was a sudden sound from heaven coming like a mighty wind, and it filled all the house in which they were sitting. And there appeared to them divided tongues as of fire, and it sat on each one of them. And they were all filled with the Holy Spirit and began to speak different tongues as the Spirit gave them to speak [Acts 2.1–4]."

1. John Awjnec‘i, *Opera*, p. 214, refers to Pentecost as Jubilee (*յոբելեան*), an interesting indication of the general Armenian sympathy for Jewish titles; cf. §487 note 1 and Gelzer, *Anfänge*, p. 140. But Ἰωβηλαῖος was used by Hippolytus, *Fr. 9 in Psalmos*, and later writers as a figure for Pentecost; cf. Gregory Naz., *Or.*, XLI 2.

500. Do you see the coming of the Holy Spirit, amazing, remarkable, and incomprehensible? "And there was, he says, a sudden sound from heaven coming as a mighty wind? [Acts 2.2]" And it is clear that the inhabitants of heaven and earth recognized the descent of the Holy Spirit, especially as He came in the company of the heavenly host. The prophet saw and predicted this in the book of psalms, as in the forty-ninth psalm: "Our God will come clearly, and a fire will go before him, and round him a violent tempest. He will summon the heavens from above and the earth in order to judge his people and gather to himself his saints [Ps. 49.3–5]."

501. And because the Holy Spirit has made previous witness to the house of Israel, and made a covenant of the coming of Christ with heaven and earth, at one time saying: "Pay heed, heavens, and I shall speak, and the earth will hear the words of my mouth [Deut. 32.1]," and at another: "Heaven will hear and the earth give ear, for the Lord has spoken [Is. 1.2],"

502. therefore He will come to judge, to summon heaven and earth, to judge the peoples. Concerning this the Savior of all declared: "He will come and reproach the world for its sins, because they did not believe in me [Jn. 16.8–9]," because the house of Israel was informed of, and familiar with the Spirit through the band of prophets who had arisen and who became famous by their miracles; they also revealed to the heathen races the power of the divine Spirit. And they declared and made known to the kings the saying of Pharoah to Joseph: "We know no one like you who has the Spirit of God [Gen. 41.38]." Likewise Baltasar said to Daniel: "We know that the Holy Spirit of God is in you [Dan. 4.6]."

503. The children of Israel were even more famous as richly endowed with prophets: the great Moses with the seventy-two[1] elders in the desert [Ex. 24.9], and in the promised land all the ranks of prophets who arose in the days of the kings, who are set out in the Books of Kings, who themselves revealed the closeness of the Spirit. Isaiah said: "The Spirit of the Lord is upon me [Is. 61.1]." and Micah: "I shall be filled with the Spirit by the power of the Lord [Micah 3.8]." Ezechiel succinctly revealed the effective power of the Spirit in the story of the vision of the chariots [Ez. 23.24; 26.10]. The same, when he was relating the wonderful vision of resurrection, said: "The hand of the Lord was upon me, and the Holy Spirit with me, and He led me into a valley which was filled with the bones of many hosts; and He

said to me: 'Son of man, will these bones become alive?' And I said: 'Lord, Lord, that you know [Ez. 37.1–3].'"

1. But Ex. 24.9 refers to seventy elders. The number of seventy disciples (§457, cf. Lk. 10.1) is connected by Christian writers with the seventy elders and the seventy tongues divided at Babel; cf. §579, 612. The *Teaching*, however, refers to seventy-two in all of these cases except at §686, following the tradition of seventy-two tongues (cf. Epiphanius, *Adv. omn. Haer.*, II 39.8) rather than the seventy of Clement, Origen, Eusebius. In this connection one may note that the number of seventy scholars who completed the septuagint in seventy days is mentioned by Irenaeus, *Adv. Haer.*, III 21.2, whereas Aristaeus refers to seventy-two, *Letter*, §50, 307. Cf. B. M. Metzger, *Seventy or seventy-two disciples? New Testament Studies*, 5 (1958/9), pp. 299–306.

504. Do you see how the prophet truly indicates and reveals the divine honor of the Holy Spirit? He realized the power of the divinely commanded works over the closely packed old bones, how each one at his breath, being joined and attached and given life, rose up and stood, that not by words and commands alone, but rather by completed deeds you might grasp and understand the profundity of the truth.

505. And then the same mighty and all-powerful Holy Spirit, the searcher of the depths of God [I Cor. 2.10], who by foreshadowing examples announced through the voices of the prophets the life-giving coming of the Son of God, was sent from the divine glory to the gathering of the chosen twelve, "to gather to himself his saints [Ps. 49.5]" and to attest to them truly about the completed deeds which had been done by Christ.

506. "And there appeared to them divided tongues as of fire [Acts 2.3]," that it might visibly glorify the sublimity of the grace. And they were filled with the Holy Spirit and were blamed by their neighbors that "they were drunk [Acts 2.15]." But they were drunk with the cup of prophecy.[1] For they were drunk and rejoiced, and at once they bore the rejoicing of the heights to the whole world. This the prophet relates on their behalf: "I shall be glad and rejoice in you [Ps. 9.3]"; and again: "I shall be drunk at the appearance of the face of your glory [Ps. 16.15]"; and: "Your cup as pure wine has made me drunk [Ps. 22.5]"; and: "Your mercy, Lord, will urge me on [Ps. 22.6]." And clearly the grace of the Holy Spirit has spread out and overrun.

1. Wine is sometimes used metonymously of the Holy Spirit; cf. Lampe, *Lexicon*, s.v. οἶνος.

507. And [the Spirit] was revealed as fire, that the wicked might burn and the elect be filled with the cups of joy of the Spirit, with the gifts of the

inexhaustible treasure which passes not away; and that filled with the un-failing flow of the Spirit, they might at the same time be illuminated by the power of the fiery Spirit. For those who seek blessing they prepared the joy of blessedness; becoming the cupbearers[1] of the whole world they gave drink to the thirsty, but to the disobedient they gave as drink destruction.[2]

> 1. Cupbearers: ꝉꞷɯ.ꞥ.ꞥ.ꞷ/ɭ.ɹ, οἰνοχόοι. In the *Teaching* this is a major theme; see §508 note 1. Cf. also Gregory of Nyssa, *In Cant.*, XIV: (Paul) σκεῦος κατεσκευάσθη πρὸς τὴν οἰνοχοίαν τοῦ λόγου. For this theme in Philo see C. H. Dodd, *The Interpretation of the Fourth Gospel*, pp. 298-299.
>
> 2. The author of the *Teaching* is not here contrasting the divine *sobria ebrietas* with the drunkenness of wine which is ignorance (cf. H. Lewy, *Sobria Ebrietas*, pp. 113, 122) but introducing a major theme: the choice offered by the preaching of the gospel between acceptance and rejection; see below §508-516, 538-542, 544-551.

508. [*The two cups of joy and bitterness: the choice of life and death presented by the Christian gospel*] For the beginning of the wine pouring the mighty prophet, the young Jeremiah, ran and made many tongues drink [Jer. 25. 15] of the cup of the retribution of sins and the bitterness of inescapable death.[1] But these [the Apostles] drank of the fire of the Spirit of joy, and became cupbearers throughout the world. They hastened and served delightful drink in the cups of joyful sweetness to the worthy at the wedding banquet of the kingdom.[2] But for the lazy and negligent, the foolish and imprudent, they mixed and gave as drink the lees of cups of the gall of bitterness [Ps. 74.9; Is. 51.22; Jer. 9.15; 23.15], that as they drank, their lips and their souls might burn.

> 1. The *Teaching* here depends on patristic exegesis of Jer. 25. 15-17; cf. Origen, *In Jer. Hom.*, XII 2, where he contrasts the ποτήριον τῶν χρηστῶν ἔργων with the ποτήριον τῶν ἁμαρτημάτων. But Theodoret, commenting on the same passage, *In Jer.*, XXV: ποτήριον δὲ οἴνου ἀκράτου τὴν δικαίαν τιμωρίαν καλεῖ, idem, *In Ps.*, XI: ποτήριον δὲ ἐνταῦθα τὴν τιμωρίαν ὀνομάζει referring to Ps. 10.6 which is quoted in the *Teaching*, §539; then quoting Ps. 74.9: τοῦτο τὸ ποτήριον ὁ μακάριος Ἰερεμίας τοῖς ἔθνεσι προσενέγκειν ἐκελεύσθη. The *Teaching* has combined Origen's exegesis with the catechetical theme of the choice between the two ways in the *Didache* and Barnabas. Compare the two πίθοι in *Iliad*, 24. 527.
>
> 2. See §510 below.

509. Ananias drank this cup, and his wife Sapphira [Acts 5.1–10], and they were not able to bear the power of the sweet wine. They were thirsty, they drank, they were inebriated and were consumed with thirst from the bile which was hidden in their stomachs. They were dried up by their sins of doubt, and were burnt by the taste of the strength of the fiery cup of wine. A certain woman, Tabitha, also drank this cup [Acts 9.36–41]. A cup of the wine which made her drunk and put her to sleep, again raised her up in the health of righteousness, and raised her up in hope. From the same cup also

drank Cornelius [Acts 10.1–33], who became worthy of the banquet, and gave to many who were with him. The wine pouring of Simon[1] [Acts 8.13] made the beginning of the joys which come from him by the cup which was in his hand.

> 1. Simon the sorcerer?

510. And behold it comes and serves everyone, and has now indeed come even to you.[1] Behold, the chambers of this king are full and the wine pourers ready. The cups are set out to hand, and the banquet is arranged in the palace.[2] He has prepared the sweet and delightful wine of joy as drink for all who wish to drink it in faith. He has prepared also the gall of bitterness of the darkness of evil for the wicked to drink, which burns to destruction.[3]

> 1. See also §541.
>
> 2. The messianic banquet is usually considered to be a future event at which the saved will rejoice, but the *Teaching* here and at §630 uses the theme of the banquet as the occasion on which the choice between salvation and damnation must be made in this world (for there is no repentance after death, §535). The *Teaching* has no interest in making the liturgical parallels explicit.
>
> 3. See also the bitter cup of death in §540, and Ełišē, *History*, p. 188, and the bitter cup of the Jewish pascha in Aphraates, XII 8.

511. So whichever you prefer to drink, the truth is ready to be offered to you by both. Drink wisdom and not foolishness, mercy and not anger, the faith of sweetness and not doubt of unbelief—the burning fire of evil which consumes in Gehenna and in darkness—but the fire of the cups which will illuminate you in your drinking of it, and burn away the rust of the sins of your ignorance, and save your souls through the hope of your faith.

512. The blessed Apostles drank and were given drink and were glad. They gave drink with the two cups to the world, to those who wished to drink what they chose. Behold, the folly of ignorance gave you drink, and the cup of death mixed poison for you. Take, drink in faith the cup of the healing of the life of your souls, that you may live and be saved from the fire which is to come.

513. Behold, the cup of punishment has come to you.[1] Take, drink the cup of peace which is full of profit. Be thirsty for repentance, that there may be added to you the solace of joy. Drink the spirit of adoption and not the spirit of vice, which Saul drank and was exiled. David drank and entered into the joy of his Lord. So also will you, if you only wish. He blesses and makes joyful, He who sent to you these apostles, who came to you for joy bringing two cups, one of threats and the other of delights.

1. I.e., the punishment for martyring Rhipsimē and her companions, as related in the *History*, §211 ff.

514. For He who sent his twelve throughout the whole world as cupbearers, the same also sent these witnesses of his[1] among you. And because you were drunk by the error of your sins, they made you drink the lees of the punishment which has overtaken you. For by their death they became cupbearers to you of the truth of the gospel of God. They preached by their tribulations, and added their blood to the two cups, that they might admonish the folly of the blindness of your hearts, and again prepare these present cups for your joy, that by their death they might make you happy with the cups of life, which they themselves had drunk.

1. I.e., the martyred Rhipsimē and her companions; see also §541 note 1.

515. Because they saw that the Lord and the Creator of the universe had humbled Himself into a cup of humility and degradation of death by his own will, and had drunk endurance of the cup of sufferings freely in humility,[1] therefore all the brave witnesses of the truth and his Divinity gave themselves to tribulation, that by their pains and sufferings which they bore, they might be witnesses of Him who bore them willingly in order to remove our dishonor, and take upon Himself our sufferings, and pay the debt for our death by his own good pleasure. For as He willed, what He willed also occurred; and as He willed, He acted. For He put on our earthly nature[2] and joined[3] it to the unmingled Divinity that He might give us his immortality and impassibility and freedom from suffering. He joined[4] this corruptible flesh to the incorruptible Divinity in order to make our nature incorruptible [I Cor. 15.54].[5]

1. See also §407, 452.
2. Put on our earthly nature: զմեր շողեղէն բնութիւն զգեցաւ. The expression "put on" is frequent in the *Teaching* but usually with reference to flesh; see §377 note 2. This is the only occasion when the *Teaching* uses the word "nature" of Christ's humanity, but see Introduction, pp. 19–20.
3. Joined: խառնեաց, see §369 note 2.
4. See note 3 above.
5. See also §589 ff., Introduction, pp. 17–18, for the major themes in the *Teaching* on the purpose and results of the Incarnation.

516. And these just ones desired to become by their own death witnesses to the Lord's death, who by his own death turned to life the mortality of creation. For death became desirable by the death of our God, who for our sake drank the cup of death and let us drink the cup of immortality. For this death is temporary, that we may be renewed in the glory of the resurrection of immutable and eternal life. As the Lord Himself said in the holy

gospel: "Verily, verily, I say to you, unless the ear of corn fall to the ground and die, the ear remains alone; but in dying it is greatly glorified, and brings forth much fruit [Jn. 12.24]."

517. [*Similes of conversion*] But all lives of earthly beings are similar to the lives of cultivated roots growing in the earth.[1] For the seed is first sown in the womb and then increases and flourishes as a grown man, the image of the Deity. For as we said above, "man was made in the image of God [Gen. 1.26]," in wisdom and rationality, just as we set out for you the lives of those who were examples in the beginning.

1. See also §528–531, 646–650.

518. Then man undertook to cultivate and sow the earth, for the command was laid on him: "What a man will sow, that also will he reap [Gal. 6.7]." And he was endowed with intelligence, for mankind to understand by what had been revealed to sow and reap the hidden invisible things, that they might receive in hope the provisions prepared for them; that whatever a man labored by the divine commands, he might receive the fruit thereof in the next life to come.

519. In the same way as laborers first split the tilled ground and break it up, and plough with furrows the black clodded earth and fertilize it; as they cut with sweating toil the useless sprouting roots and worthless growth of grassy weeds, and then sow the productive seed;

520. so with the preaching of the gospel. Unless one first cuts away the debts of the guilt of one's own wild-growing habits of unworthy and voluntary sins—as now we see with you—unless you extirpate from your minds the wild, harmful and destructive roots of sins, which are rooted in you and have enveloped with their branches your minds, restraining the blossom and preventing the fruit, and altogether drying them up, and throwing you into the doubt of lawlessness or into a dry rocky place, which although one might cultivate, yet it would be barren and fruitless; in the same way, unless you extirpate from yourselves the customs of your upbringing, you cannot receive the seed which will give you profitable fruit.[1]

1. The parallel between preaching and agriculture, based on the gospels and epistles, was a popular one; cf. Clement *Str.*, VII 12: ἐργάζεται τοίνυν ὁ γνωστικὸς ἐν τῷ τοῦ κυρίου ἀμπελῶνι φυτεύων, κλαδεύων, ἀρδεύων, θεῖος ὄντως ὑπάρχων τῶν εἰς πίστιν καταπεφυτευμένων γεωργός . . . αὔξων οὖν τὰ παρ' αὐτῷ κατατιθέμενα σπέρματα καθ' ἣν ἐνετείλατο κύριος γεωργίαν, and Eusebius, *H.e.*, III 37: the μαθηταί of the apostles αὔξοντες εἰς πλέον τὸ κήρυγμα καὶ τὰ σωτήρια σπέρματα τῆς τῶν οὐρανῶν βασιλείας ἀνὰ πᾶσαν εἰς πλάτος ἐπισπείροντες τὴν οἰκουμένην . . . ποιμένας τε καθιστάντες ἑτέρους τούτοις τε ἐγχειρίζοντες τὴν τῶν ἀρτίως εἰσαχθέντων γεωργίαν. On γεωργία, see also §650 note 1.

521.   So, brethren, examine with wise minds your souls and take account of yourselves; consider and see your souls. For God, merciful and compassionate, has visited you and has seen, and did not wish for your destruction, but recently[1] with threats of punishments called you to enter the gate of repentance, that you might live and not die. For the men unworthy of being sought, who spent their lives in their paganism and were not worthy of the finding of their souls, who did not wish to understand their Creator, these the foreknowing wisdom of God abandoned, who would not listen to his commandments; but they were hardened in preparation for the torments in store for them.

1. Recently. Sargisean, *Agatʿangelos*, pp. 388–389, supposes the interval of time implied to be that between Gregory and the composition of the *Teaching*; furthermore, at §572 he sees a reference to the legendary activity in Armenia of Thaddaeus and Bartholomew. But in both cases the *Teaching* refers to the martyrs, Rhipsimē and her companions, as is clear from §514, and notably §541–542.

522.   So you must break up the terrain of your minds, and root out the scandalous sins from your souls, which prevent the growth of righteousness in you, that is these customs of idolatry which have led you astray in the train of your forefathers and have made you err. You are as asleep though awake, mad and stupid; these [gods] who are really nonexistent, of no use or harm, have led you astray in vain, not to profit, but only to vanities, frivolities, superfluous uselessness. They are of no help because they are lifeless, irrational, motionless, and quite unmoving. Some are carved and some hammered, some are of limestone and some cast from metal;[1] they were created by clever minds, fashioned for destruction. Merely in vain do they labor who worship them; they cannot be harmed by them. Not even so much as a bug or a fly, which live uselessly on men, can they chase and expel from the house of their worshippers; not even the spiders, which make their comings and goings over their images and leave their webs around their heads, will they be able to clean from themselves; but covered with dust and eaten by rust they uselessly decay.

1. Cf. Eznik, §299 and Wisdom 13. See also *History*, §73, 234.

523.   The stone images take on the moss of decay, become dirty, green, discolored, and being neglected they become hideous. The wooden images are attacked by worms, and being riddled with holes they disintegrate. The garments thrown around them are eaten by moths and worms, they disintegrate and become rotten and crumble away. For even if foolishness encourages some one to take care of them, to kill his animals in offerings of foul smoke and putrid obscenity, yet the smelly soot and burning smoke accumulate and coagulate around them, blackening them like coal and

changing their color. And the money and labor expended on them become profitless and useless.[1]

1. For this general theme, cf. Clement, *Protrepticus*, §51–52.

524.   And realizing all this, you hasten in error to destroy what is profitable and to prepare for yourselves eternal torments, to come to the inextinguishable fire and undying worm [Mk. 9.44] for nothing. And abandoning your Creator, by your forgetfulness you anger your God. You sowed thorns instead of corn, and thistles instead of rye, and instead of fertile land you have chosen the unfruitful and barren rock.

525.   So then look, stand and face yourselves. Which of you will come forward and reply that any one has heard the voice of your images, or has seen the slightest help come from them, even the least amount in a visible way? But only by dreams and false deceptions and illusions which are of no avail, by these only you have destroyed your souls and cut yourselves off from the Creator.

526.   So the things which are so useless and nothing and of no profit, pluck them out of your souls and cast them away, the arid, dried up things, and take to yourselves what does not maim you but gives health and healing to your souls. Like he who pours off the bile and phlegm[1] of bitterness, and relieving himself of evil humors becomes healthy, so will you, if you abandon the useless, find help for your souls and be saved from the judgment of eternal tortures. For the seed of your idolatry casts [you] into the unquenchable fire of hell, whence there is no possibility of salvation[2]— such fruit does it bear.

1. Cf. the χολή and φλέγμα which cause illness in the body, Plato, *Republic*, 564B, *Timaeus*, 82E.
2. See also §535, John Mandakuni, *Čaṙkʿ*, II, and II Clement, VIII 3: μετὰ γὰρ τὸ ἐξελθεῖν ἡμᾶς ἐκ τοῦ κόσμου οὐκέτι δυνάμεθα ἐκεῖ ἐξομολογήσασθαι ἢ μετανοεῖν ἔτι. Job 7.9 is an important text in this regard.

527.   But the truth of piety which knows God the Creator of all bears the fruit of the joys of the eternal kingdom, and bestows them on those who know the same. The seed of your lawlessness has already been partly revealed to you as the growth of thistles of punishment, that you may learn to cut away its ear, which will soon grow up and reach to you, unless you are first purified to be able to distinguish the thistles from the wheat.

528.   For there comes again another time, sowing and harvest: to sow in the tomb, to harvest again at the resurrection the works of each one's

labors.[1] Be not like the dried up whom the unquenchable fire finds; it will take you as its tinder. But offer to your Lord precious [offerings], the sweetness of your abundant fruit in flowering ripeness. For when He will raise you again from the tomb you will be as wheat, that they may receive you in the granaries of the kingdom in blessing, and that you may bear the fruit given to you, much for one. For as at harvest they pick the thistles from the grain and cast them into the fire, so unexpectedly in the twinkling of an eye, men will rise up from their tombs. They will receive in their souls the Godhead with his commandments, flourishing like ripe and fruitful grain.

1. See also §517–520, 646–650. The parallel between the resurrection of the dead and the cycle of seasons was an important one in the early church; cf. I Clement 24, Cyril Jer., *Cat.*, XVIII 6, Chrysostom, *In Jo. Hom.*, LXVI 3: ποίαν οὖν ἕξουσιν ἀπολογίαν οἱ τῇ ἀναστάσει διαπιστοῦντες, ἐν τοῖς σπέρμασι τοῦ πράγματος καθ᾽ ἑκάστην μελετωμένου τὴν ἡμέραν, καὶ ἐν φυτοῖς, καὶ ἐπὶ τῆς γενέσεως τῆς ἡμετέρας; πρότερον γὰρ δεῖ φθαρῆναι τὸ σπέρμα, καὶ τότε γενέσθαι γένεσιν.

529. And as a simple ear falls upon the earth, grows, takes root, bears a stem, sends out branches, forms knots, increases, becomes full of ears, bearing many from one ear, and prepares them for the use of the sowers; just the same is to be seen here. The souls of the just rise up from the tomb, the same bodies with the same spirit[1] bearing works of the labor of righteousness will rise from the tombs to the kingdom. Each little one, each single soul, will receive and gain countless glorious compensation a myriad and thousand fold. Then, as they rise, they will put on glory,[2] as the grain when it shows maturity in itself is placed and stored in the granaries.

1. On the identity of the body at the resurrection with the mortal body, cf. II Clement 9: ὃν τρόπον γὰρ ἐν τῇ σαρκὶ ἐκλήθητε, καὶ ἐν τῇ σαρκὶ ἐλεύσεσθε ... ἡμεῖς ἐν ταύτῃ τῇ σαρκὶ ἀποληψόμεθα τὸν μισθόν; Aphraates, VIII 3: corpus quod decidit in terram, idem ipsum resurget; Cyril Jer., *Cat.*, XVIII 18: τὸ γὰρ σῶμα τοῦτο ἐγείρεται, οὐ τοιοῦτον μένον ἀσθενές, ἀλλ᾽ αὐτὸ μὲν τοῦτο ἐγείρεται, ἐνδυσάμενον δὲ τὴν ἀφθαρσίαν μεταποιεῖται. On this transformation, cf. Basil, *Hex.*, VIII 8.
2. Cf. Irenaeus, *Fr.*, 7: ἡμεῖς οὖν καὶ σώματα ἀνίστασθαι πεπιστεύκαμεν. εἰ γὰρ καὶ φθείρεται, ἀλλ᾽ οὐκ ἀπόλλυται· τούτων γὰρ τὰ λείψανα γῇ ὑποδεξαμένη τηρεῖ δίκην σπόρου πιαινομένου καὶ τὸ γῆς λιπαρωτέρῳ συμπλεκομένου. αὖθις ὥσπερ κόκκος γυμνὸς σπείρεται, καὶ κελεύσματι τοῦ δημιουργήσαντος Θεοῦ θάλλων, ἠμφιεσμένος καὶ ἔνδοξος ἐγείρεται.

530. In the same way the thorns enveloping the ears[1] of the sinners will grow; then taking form as from a mother, they will bear upwards the fruit of lawless deeds. Just as in the spiritual hymnal [the Psalmist] sings concerning these things: "Fire is fallen, and they did not see the sun; before they have considered their own thorns, like the buckthorn in the anger of the Living one He will burn them up [Ps. 57.10]."

1. Ears: ՀաՍՈ, ears of corn.

531. And what is this saying "before they considered their own thorns"? That is, in carefree insousiance they worked their sins; while they did not know their faults, in advance were prepared their tortures. So also elsewhere [the scripture] says: "Before his day there will come upon him afflictions like water [Job 27.20]." As in the beginning the thorns grew because of the transgression of the sinners, so they envelop the transgressors and grow, and being combustible they will then ignite and burn. But behold, you have been forewarned, that you may be saved from that fearsome fire, that holy seeds may be sown in you and not the thorn which burns.

532. "Sons of men, how long will you be hardhearted? Why do you love vanity and seek falsehood? [Ps. 4.3]" Recognize the wonderful works of God, who was revealed to you that henceforth truth might not abandon all the inhabitants of the earth and that all races of the earth might not be ignorant of Him, but serve Him under one yoke.

533. "Let us break their bonds and cast off from us their yoke [Ps. 2.3]." So break off from your souls the bonds of paganism, and free yourselves from past sins, to rejoice with those who mock at the destruction of the impious. As the book of Wisdom says of those who are to come: "After this I shall mock at their destruction [Wis. 4.18; Prov. 1.26]," and: "He who lives in heaven will mock at them, and the Lord himself will disdain them. Then he will speak with them in his anger, and in his indignation will overthrow them [Ps. 2.4–5]." This is the time of reproach and reprimand, for the Son of God took from the Father his begetter the authority to judge all; He judges those who will not worship the Father, and gives to torments those who will not [worship] the Son or the Spirit.

534. This saying of the Son has given you foreknowledge of the Father: "I was made king by him to tell the commands of the Lord, to shepherd you with a rod of the hardness of iron [Ps. 2.6, 9]," and as a clay vessel to break in pieces those who in disobedience oppose their salvation, for men are clay vessels [Job. 13.12]. Those who are diligent He will fill with rare treasure; but those who are reprobate He will fill with torments and destruction. For the Lord watches from his holy clouds to visit all iniquities of men. "But kings, consider this, be advised all who judge the earth. Serve the Lord with fear, rejoice before Him with trembling. Receive his advice lest the Lord be angry, and you perish from the paths of righteousness. For his anger is kindled over you [Ps. 2.10–12]."

535. You will be blessed if you can supplicate before the Lord and hope in the great mercy of his salvation; He would pardon and forgive your sins.

But if you are obstinate, He will break the teeth in the mouths of the obstinate and impious [Ps. 57.7], and cast you into eternal torments. And the repentance is of no use which comes to mind there [I Jn. 5.16].[1] But see what the prophet cries: "There is no one in hell who confesses to you, and there is no one who in that death remembers you [Ps. 6.6]," because thereafter no one can pass the fixed limit.

1. See §526 note 2.

536.   But this is the time for penitents to find mercy, now, as the prophet says: "God is a just judge, powerful and patient, who does not prolong his anger for ever [Ps. 7.12]." But what does he then go on to say? "If they will not turn back, He has sharpened his sword and drawn his bow, and for them He has prepared the instruments of death, and worked fiery arrows for those who travail lawlessness; and their conception, he says, brings forth sufferings [Ps. 7.13–15]." But to those who hear and believe in his wonders, and return to God the Creator and worship Him, thus he says: "Be encouraged earth, rejoice and be glad, for the Lord has magnified his dealings among you [Joel 2.21]." And the men who do not know their Creator are considered as animals,[1] and so he speaks as if with wild beasts: "Do not fear, wild beast, he says, for pastures have sprung up for you in the plains and rocky places [Joel 2.22]." For the hearts of men were more fruitless than the desert and more dry than the plains.

1. Animals: ԱՆԱՍՈՒՆՍ, ἄλογα.

537.   The vine recalls the tame [beasts] [Joel 2.22],[1] as does the fig tree, fruitful in sweetness according to the divine saying which runs: "Because your words are sweeter in my palate than honey to my mouth [Ps. 118.103]." And again: "You are sweet, Lord, and in your sweetness teach me your righteousness [Ps. 118.68]." And again the prophet calls to the pious and says: "The granaries will be filled with wheat, and the presses will overrun with wine and oil. And I shall compensate for the years in which locusts and grubs and canker-worm and caterpillars ate, my great army which I sent upon you. You will eat and enjoy, and you will bless the Lord your God [Joel 2.24–26]." But to the lawless he says thus: "Set your sickles to work, for the time of harvest has arrived. So in, press the presses, for the presses are full and their vats overflow; for their wickedness has increased. Therefore their voices have cried out in the valley of judgment [Joel 3.13–14]."

1. The *Teaching* contrasts tame beasts (ԾՈՒԱԾԻԱՅՍ) with wild beasts (ԵՐԷՍ ԿԱՅՐԻ, κτήνη τοῦ πεδίου), a contrast not made by Joel but appropriate to this context in order to distinguish those who repent from those who do not.

538.   [*Examples of God's retribution on the unrepentant*] In the times of Abraham, Sodom drank the wine of lawlessness. Then was sought and examined by the Lord from on high, from a hundred[1] to ten [Gen. 18.24–32], and there were not found there ten cups of righteousness. For their grape was a bitter grape, and their cluster the bile of bitterness; the ire of serpents was their wine, the poisoned ire of vipers from which there is no remedy was their cup [Deut. 32.32–33].

1. In Genesis, fifty.

539.   Therefore He made them drink the taste of the fiery cup[1] of wine of their burning, and they burnt by their own cups. Their granaries were full of lawlessness, therefore He pronounced destruction on them [Ez. 28.16]. The tare had come into their fields, therefore his sickle fell to work, and He cut down and burnt them in his fire. As for the net which enveloped them, they were sacrificed to the same net and burnt as incense to the same snare, for they were its catch [Ps. 10.7; Eccles. 9.12; Hab. 1.15–16]. The caterpillar ate them and the grub consumed them, and the locust of their sins fed on them [Joel 1.4]. Therefore suddenly they were dried up. Fire consumed their buildings; fire fell on them and rivers of fire rained on their midst. He raised firewood to fall on them, rivers of fire rose among them and flooded and burnt their land.[2] Their barns were filled with fire, and their presses overflowed with the same. They filled the cups of their sins from the dregs which they drank and were burnt at once. From the cup of Lot, who was among them, they did not drink joy; it became for them a different cup, and it gave them sadness as drink.

1. See §508 note 1; cf. Cyril Jer., *Cat.*, XVII 15, for the purging effects of the fire of the Spirit.
2. The flood of fire; cf. L. Ginzberg, *The Legends of the Jews*, I, p. 153.

540.   The cup of life, from which they did not wish to drink life, gave them as drink the bitterness of death.[1] From the cup of sweetness, which was not sweet on their palate, flowed bitterness; this is the one whose fire did not burn the green grass, but preserved the green and set fire to the dried up and burnt and withered. This cup drank Judas Iscariot and he was consumed, for his tree was arid. The apostles drank this, and blossomed and filled the whole earth with sweet fruit. The odor of their flowers spread throughout the world. Their holiness and their sweet wine give joy to those above and below, angels and men; and the Lord of the temple is glad at them, as at these cups which, behold, have come to give you drink—not the cup of Lot of Abraham's family who was found in Sodom, which gave them no joy and whose like was not found among them.[2]

1. See also §510 note 3.
2. Lot is identified with the fate of Sodom, as in §539, despite the reference in II Peter 2.7 to the "just" Lot.

541. [*The Armenians are exhorted to accept the gospel*] Behold the thirty-seven Christian cups[1] who came to serve you. Its power is fire, its taste sweet; joy is to those who know it, and sadness to those hidden from it. If you drink it worthily, it will burn away your impurity, and your souls will be sanctified. The bodies of the sons of Aaron burned [Lev. 10.2], and the fire did not consume the robes of their priesthood.[2] This cup is accustomed to burn the impure and to preserve the sanctified. So if you desire with love to drink the cup of blessedness, which has sprung forth among you unexpectedly, it will burn away your sins and clean and purify your souls for joy.[3]

1. There is some variation in Agathangelos concerning the number of martyrs including Rhipsimē: thirty-seven out of more than seventy who came from the land of the Romans, §209; Rhipsimē with thirty-three companions, Gaianē with two, §210; but at §737 only thirty-two companions of Rhipsimē are mentioned, the same number as in the Greek version, §83.
2. Cf. *Martyrdom of Matthew*, 23: After Matthew's death ἦν δὲ τὸ σῶμα τοῦ ἀποστόλου ὡς ἐν ὕπνῳ κείμενον καὶ ἡ στολὴ αὐτοῦ καὶ ὁ χίτων αὐτοῦ ἀμίαντα ἀπὸ τοῦ πυρός. The Armenian version, *Ankanon Girk*, III, pp. 437–449, has no reference to this. Cf. also L. Ginzberg, *The Legends of the Jews*, III, p. 23: fire could not injure the garments of the Israelites during their forty years' march.
3. See also §508, 539, 544.

542. But if it should enter your minds that "we have killed the holy martyrs"—just as Paul was unknown to be a vessel of election [Acts 9.15] in the time of his Judaism, who came to the preaching of the Apostles and in persecuting them killed Stephen, who became a witness to the humility [Philipp. 2.7] of the Godhead and also to his majesty—so now do you, who were ignorant, drink this cup which your hands have pressed; for, as they bore witness and died, so they received life for death and came to heavenly fortune.

543. Stephen at the time of his death saw the heavens opened and the Son on the right hand of his Father [Acts 7.55]. And he sought remission for his murderers, and loosed the bonds of their impiety by the intercession of his prayers [Acts 7.60]; he stayed the call for his blood, and made silent the protest of his torment, and begged from the Lord their forgiveness. Therefore Paul bore his cruel yoke,[1] which the ox of the couple carried, and took upon himself his torments and the same cup of his death. He became a witness to his words with him and a companion to his Lord. He saw the same vision [Acts 9.3–6] and heard the same ineffability of words which Stephen had seen and heard.

1. Cf. Eznik, §383, where Paul is called *ծառայակից* (σύζυγος, cf. Philippians 4.3) of the sons of thunder and *քարոզակից* (fellow-preacher) of Barnabas. But in the *Teaching* the yoke refers to martyrdom, not to the tasks common to Paul and the Apostles.

544. You then are the murderers of these victims. Believe their faith and bear their yoke, and throw off from your souls the yoke of sins [Gal. 5.1]; become witnesses of the truth of these preachers. Drink the same cup of spiritual drink and become their companions. Then rivers of benevolent love will descend into the fields of your hearts, to fertilize the soil of your minds with the preaching which will become your own by your powerful faith in it, for you to drink the cup of loving kindness, the purifying fire of election.[1] In the time of the priesthood of Judaism, at the captivity the priests took the living fire of the sacrifices and cast it into the well, and the fire turned into water; and after seventy years, on their return they took the water and cast it round the sacrifices, when the temple was built, and the water returned to the nature of fire [II Macc. 1.19–22]; because according to need it is able to change its form and produce its effects according to the occasion,[2] especially this wonderful fire of the Holy Spirit which appeared in various ways.

1. See also §508, 539, 541.
2. Cf. Cyril Jer., *Cat.*, XVI 12, likening the Spirit to water: ἐπειδὴ ἐξ οὐρανῶν κατέρχεται τὸ τῶν ὄμβρων ὕδωρ, ἐπειδὴ μονοειδὲς μὲν κατέρχεται, πολυειδῶς δὲ ἐνεργεῖ . . . οὐ γὰρ μεταβάλλων ἑαυτὸν ὁ ὑετὸς ἄλλος καὶ ἄλλος κατέρχεται, ἀλλὰ τῇ τῶν ὑποδεχομένων κατασκευῇ συμπεριφερόμενος ἑκάστῳ τὸ πρόσφορον γίνεται· οὕτω καὶ τὸ πνεῦμα τὸ ἅγιον, ἓν ὂν καὶ μονοειδὲς καὶ ἀδιαίρετον, ἑκάστῳ διαιρεῖ τὴν χάριν καθὼς βούλεται.

545. The fire appeared in the midst of the green branches of the briar and kept it unwithered [Ex. 3.2], for the illuminating fire preserved the briar and saved Moses, and he had a cup of joy. Moses drank of it, who had hoped in it. It saved the beasts of Israel and destroyed the possessions of Egypt in the midst of the hail [Ex. 9.25]. And in the midst of the sea He gave Israel to drink of the cup, for they drank the Spirit and sang in the midst of the sea [Ex. 15.1–19], to whom Miriam served wine with the lyre [Ex. 15.20–21], for they passed through the vast sea and gave thanks. The Egyptians also drank of that cup and were given drink from the cup of the column which bound up the wheels of their chariots; its sediment overturned them and struck them to the ground behind it. The people drank the cup of complaint which his anger had mixed; He gave them a cup of scrutiny to drink, where they were condemned.

546. [*Examples of God's providence*] The holy column, which with clouds of air sheltered them in the heat of the desert during the day and gave them light and warmth in the cold of the frosts of the first watch [Ex. 13.21–22],

the same pillar changing with the times, prepared what was necessary according to their needs.[1] On one occasion He caused the rock to pour forth in abundance for the thirsty rivers of sweet water [Ex. 17.1–7]—for Christ Himself was this,[2] who in every way has all fulness—and filled them and was kind to them, once in the sweetness of bread, another time with the birds [Ex. 16.13–15]; another time He poured forth for them the sweetness of fountains [Ex. 15.27], and the cup of the Holy Spirit made them glad.

1. The *Teaching* interprets the column as the Holy Spirit, in accordance with an old tradition; cf. Daniélou, *Bible*, pp. 92–93. The column was also interpreted as a figure of Christ Himself; cf. Clement, *Str.*, I 24.

2. Cf. Origen, *Selecta in Ex.*, commenting on Ex. 17.6: πέτρα παρεικάζεται ὁ Χριστὸς διὰ τὸ ἄγειστον καὶ ἀκλόνητον, quoted almost verbatim by Cyril Alex., *Glaphyra in Ex.*, 3: πέτρα παρεικάζεται διὰ τὸ ἄθραυστον καὶ ἀκλόνητον. Cf. also I Cor. 10.4: ἡ πέτρα δὲ ἦν ὁ Χριστός. Somewhat differently Aphraates, XII 8, on Ex. 17.6: Illis eduxit (viz. Moses) aquam de petra; nobis aquas vivas Salvator de ventre suo fluere fecit (Jn. 7.38).

547. But in accordance with their hardheadedness and obstinate conduct, He mixed and gave them the cup of anger. For this cup, be it fire or water, is able to change its power into whatever it wills. Now it becomes snow, and now ice, now rain; now it turns to fire, and now to lightning, or dew which nourishes plants to give food to the wild beasts and birds, game and animals, and to prepare the food of men and the needs of creatures. The same is able spiritually to bedew and nurture the seed which is pleasing to the will of the All-highest, to prepare the food of incorruption for the rational flock.

548. Sometimes as sweet and useful rain, which makes the earth rich and productive, casting heat with a burning flash of lightning to water the plants, it gives the branches and blossoms moisture with dew for joy. It demands double satisfaction for the gifts of the bestower, when for increase of help He gives this cup as drink. For even the clouds as servants of his commands pour forth. For although they fill the face of heaven with rain, yet at their coming and raining, in giving and pouring on the earth, when He wishes He brings near the useful [clouds], but when He does not, [He brings] cruel frost and snow and deleterious ice; with burning rays He consumes, and with blight prepares destruction; with the blowing of venomous winds of inflexible bitterness, with burning wind He dries up the leafy, verdant plants, burning right down to the stubble.

549. [*God's appearances to men*] With the clouds He fulfills his commands, for it is something natural [for Him] to appear with clouds from the beginning like a giver of commands and server of wine to men, now in anger, now in mercy. For when God wished to appear to men, restraining his strength in Himself He hid Himself, and kept Himself veiled in the cloud, for men were

quite unable to endure the vision of the Godhead. But He closed the heavens as with a curtain, veiling Himself, lest the creatures being unable to bear Him should burn up.[1]

1. Curtain: ᵫᵖᵚᴢᵚᴴᵢ. That man cannot grasp God is a common theme in the *Teaching*; cf. Chrysostom, commenting on the veil of Heb. 6.19, *Hom.* 13 in II *Cor.* 4. 13: καταπέτασμα γὰρ ἐνταῦθα τὸν οὐρανὸν ἐκάλεσε . . . ὅτι καθάπερ τὸ καταπέτασμα ἀπὸ τῆς ἔξω σκηνῆς διεῖργε τὰ ἅγια τῶν ἁγίων, οὕτω δὴ καὶ ὁ οὐρανὸς οὗτος, ὥσπερ καταπέτασμα, μέσος τῆς κτίσεως παρεμβεβλημένος ἀπὸ τῆς ἔξω σκηνῆς, τοῦτ' ἐστι, τοῦ κόσμου τούτου τοῦ βλεπομένου, διεῖργε τὰ ἅγια τῶν ἁγίων, τὰ ἄνω λέγων καὶ τὰ ὑπὲρ αὐτῶν.

550. Although He appeared then at various times to various of the worthy, He appeared according to the capability of those seeing Him to see, that they might be able to understand; as to Moses or all the people on the mountain of Sinai He came down and appeared enveloped with the cloud,[1] and there spoke with them [Ex. 19.9]. He in all ages appears similarly with a cloud. He appeared to the holy prophet Ezechiel, who was full of the Spirit, in a famous vision; but without a cloud no human person ever saw Him. As the inspired prophet in his vision narrates and says: "I saw that a spirit rose and came from the northern regions, and a great cloud in it and strong light around it; and fire and thunder came from it, and in the midst of it a vision of the sun and rays of fire [Ez. 1.4]."

1. The cloud was often associated with the Holy Spirit (e.g., by Gregory of Nyssa, *De Vita Moysis*: ὁ ὁδηγὸς ἡ νεφέλη, τοῦτο γὰρ ὄνομα τῷ ὁδηγοῦντι, ὅπερ καλῶς τοῖς πρὸ ἡμῶν εἰς τὴν τοῦ ἁγίου πνεύματος μετελήφθη χάριν), but the *Teaching* associates it with the inability of men to perceive God; cf. Gregory Nazianzenus' interpretation of the cloud in Ex. 14.20 as the limitation set on human knowledge by the bodily senses, *Or.*, XXVIII 12: διὰ τοῦτο μέσος ἡμῶν τε καὶ Θεοῦ ὁ σωματικὸς οὗτος ἵσταται γνόφος, ὥσπερ ἡ νεφέλη τὸ πάλαι τῶν Αἰγυπτίων καὶ τῶν Ἑβραίων. But in the next paragraph of the *Teaching* the role of the clouds as ministering to God's commands is stressed; cf. Is. 5.6: ταῖς νεφέλαις ἐντελοῦμαι, and its interpretation as angels or the prophets.

551. [God appeared as] light and fire, and not without a cloud. For the light is to illuminate the good, and the fire to burn up the wicked with wrath. But the cloud is for both, to serve drink to both. For the fire burns up the sinners; and the light serves the Spirit of the grace of adoption to the good, but to the evil serves sparks and flame and smoke of suffocating affliction and torments. Similarly the clouds are the servants of his majesty, as the seer narrates: "The clouds are the dust of his feet [Nahum 1.3]."[1]

1. See also §550 note 1 and Cyril Jer., *Cat.*, IX 9.

552. [*Predictions of God's retribution on the wicked*] And because of the abundant increase in impiety, he said: "He reproves the sea and dries it up, and destroys all the rivers [Nahum 1.4]," that He might dry up the sea of

sins and restrain the rivers of lawlessness, and purify the infectious and the unwholesome and the muddy and the complacent; and that the salvation of those who took refuge and hoped in Him might increase and spread, and the river without sins flow more strongly. Therefore the other prophet says in the same dance of his song: "You will scatter the rivers and make the earth tremble by the force of your rain, who pass through it [Ps. 73.15; 106.33]." For He will pour the waters of violence from above over the waters, that He may expel and reject the bitter waters. For He who is pure and clean has entered it to cast out the impure and execrable.[1]

1. The reference is to baptism: the destructive waters are those of the flood, or the Red Sea, and Christ has sanctified the water of baptism by his own baptism; see §413 note 2, 415 note 3. Cf. Cyril Jer., *Cat.*, III 5: ἐλευθερία τῷ Ἰσραὴλ ἀπὸ τοῦ Φαραὼ διὰ τῆς θαλάσσης· καὶ ἐλευθερία ἁμαρτιῶν τῷ κοσμῷ διὰ τοῦ λουτροῦ τοῦ ὕδατος ἐν ῥήματι Θεοῦ; and also XIX 3: μετάβηθί μοι λοιπὸν ἀπὸ τῶν παλαιῶν ἐπὶ τὰ νέα, ἀπὸ τοῦ τύπου ἐπὶ τὴν ἀλήθειαν ... ἐκεῖνος ὑποβρύχιος γέγονεν ἐν θαλάσσῃ καὶ οὗτος (Satan) ἐν τῷ σωτηρίῳ ὕδατι ἀφανίζεται.

553. As the other seer sang to the same effect, and explained the same in brief: "You prepared willing rain, O God, for your inheritance; for although it was ill, yet you confirmed it [Ps. 67.10]." For they were caught in a sea of sins, and were ill with the same malady, and tied in bonds of impiety. Therefore emptying the bottomless sea of unwholesomeness, and drying up the source of their spring, He will send rain of reprimand on men. Just as looking to this the prophet sang: "The depths called to you from the deep at the voice of your waterfalls [Ps. 41.8]." For like spiritual waterfalls the heavenly words come from above over the precipice and will destroy thoroughly the unwholesome and diseased.

554. And the healing dew became health-giving according to the saying: "The dew which falls from you is their healing [Is. 26.19]."[1] that they might return to Him in fear. For those who in love did not return to Him, with fear of menaces He made his inheritance, like you. For He will cast out the flood of sins from you and then will give you the abundance of his grace.

1. See §486 note 2.

555. For from you will spring "and flow righteousness as rivers, and justice as the waters of floods will be increased [Amos 5.24]." And He will rain his knowledge of your life on you from the clouds of mercy, according to the saying: "You prepared willing rain, O God, for your inheritance; for although it was ill, yet you confirmed it [Ps. 67.10]"; and: "Torrents of delight you will give the worthy to drink [Ps. 35.9]," according to the spiritual word of the singer who says: "From you, Lord, is the source of life, and by your light we see the light [Ps. 35.10]"; and: "Make your mercy shine on

those who know you [Ps. 35.11]." Then He shines on those who know Him, and springs of wisdom from the same source of light pour out on them, but on the unwise, burning, flooding, fiery, and flaming rivers.

556. And because like fire sins were burning on earth, in order to give light, that they might be exposed by the vengeance which was to come upon them, the foreknowing prophecy anticipated the confirmation of the events of its own sayings, as it says: "I saw in man the sins like a sea, increased, pouring out [Gen. 6.5, 11]." Just as the parable once was explained in the days of the epoch of Noah, in the sins covering the earth like the sea, in the same way the waters swamped the earth and increased for the destruction of mankind.

557. But the holy prophets produced many parables[1] of the things to be, inducing fear by the events that they might perchance be able to save them from their various impieties. Therefore frequently they gave examples: now the burning of Sodom, now the drowning of mankind at the time of the flood, now the plagues of Egypt and those of many others; and the lawlessness He calls extensive as the sea, and promises to make it disappear from the earth, and again promises to set righteousness on the earth, and to increase it more than the flood, and to make justice to flourish.

1. Parables: ᴡᴘᴡᴘᴡ; see Introduction, p. 16.

558. Therefore at the passing of mankind through the passage of the sea, the prophet cries out and says: "They shall pass through the strait sea, and will smite the waves of the sea"—that is the impieties—and "the gulfs of the rivers will dry up [Zech. 10.11]"—that is the abundant flow of sins. Concerning this the other prophet says: "Over the rivers will you be angry, Lord, and will your wrath be over the seas and your anger over the rivers [Hab. 3.8]?"

559. For He will bring the rain of abundance; and the holy waters, the currents of life, will reject the waters of impiety and will cover on earth the bitterness of the evil of ignorance and impiety of men.[1] As the prophet says: "The earth will be filled with the knowledge of the Lord as the many waters cover the seas [Is. 11.9; Hab. 2.14]." This he says concerning the waters which are destructive, the waters that destroy and drown, that He covers these waters which gave[2] the earth muddy deceit to drink, which more and more on account of the deceit abounded in idolatries and raged in the world. For He will raise up the spiritual cloud which appeared to the prophet

Ezechiel [Ez. 1.4], for the same cloud will pour upon men the grace of knowledge, and the same will turn the dryness to fertility and plants.

1. See also §552 and note 1.
2. The verb is singular, probably reflecting a Greek source *τὰ ὕδατα ἐπότισε.

560. But around the dessicated who do not wish to come into obedience He will spread the fiery rain of lightning to burn them up, to consume and destroy them; He will offer them the cup of bitterness to drink. As in the tenth psalm the seer sings: "He will rain upon the sinners traps, fire and sulphur; this tempest is the share of their cup [Ps. 10.7]."

561. "For the Lord is just and loves righteousness [Ps. 10.8]," and in righteousness He wishes to call you to Himself for adoption. For the spiritual cloud of divine truth[1] is accustomed to rain into the souls of men the teaching of knowledge, and plant in the hearts of men the fear of the worship of God, and to pour out the love of Christ the Creator on his creatures, and by the will of the same to raise them to the height of his Divinity, which[2] you must accept.

1. See also §550 note 1.
2. I.e., the knowledge from the spiritual cloud of divine truth.

562. [*The martyred Rhipsimē and her companions will intercede for the Armenians*] For if the clouds, which are servants, receive the command from the Lord and come down from the heights to the deep abyss of the seas and near the *ether* fill out and swell up, circumscribing the multitude of the waters, rising up, spreading out, hiding the face of heaven full of thunder and with dewy liberality fulfill the commands of the Creator in pouring out [rain] upon those below; how much more did these martyrs, who have been elevated to the love of the Deity, to whom God inclined, receive even more the grace of the Spirit and were even more filled with his gifts? They gave their bodies as treasure for the Lord[1] that they might receive them again and renew the outworn.[2] And filled with the divine words they labored, and with great travail preached and rained on you the rain of heavenly profits, and thundered on you light and fire together, and more than the divine cloud poured assistance on you. Instead of the frightening rain and thunder with clouds, God thundered on you even more frightening things and willed your life and salvation.

1. So Origen, *In Num. Hom.*, XI 2: (in the martyrs) Dominus . . . habet thesauros suos.
2. See also §602. But the martyrs do not wait for the general resurrection; see §563 note 1 below.

563. They, who hated this world and all that is on earth, and loved heaven and the commandments of the king the Creator, wait on Him who received them and their souls in the upper realms of light; they have been taken up into the heavenly city and have become sharers in the joy of those in heaven. They are alive[1] and have been changed from corruptibility to incorruptibility, from death to immortality. For they overcame the desires of the flesh and have shared in the divine glory and have been renewed into ineffable glory and saved from destruction. Their bones have become temples[2] of the Spirit of the Godhead because they are living with their God, and their holy souls have been cared for and preserved alive.

1. See also §572, 731, and the *Martyrdom of Polycarp*, 14.2: εὐλογῶ σε, ὅτι ἠξίωσάς με τῆς ἡμέρας καὶ ὥρας ταύτης, τοῦ λαβεῖν με μέρος ἐν ἀριθμῷ τῶν μαρτύρων ἐν τῷ ποτηρίῳ τοῦ Χριστοῦ σου εἰς ἀνάστασιν ζωῆς αἰωνίου ψυχῆς τε καὶ σώματος ἐν ἀφθαρσίᾳ πνεύματος ἁγίου· ἐν οἷς προσδεχθείην ἐνώπιόν σου σήμερον ἐν θυσίᾳ πίονι καὶ προσδεκτῇ. See also §586 note 1.
2. See §564 note 1 below.

564. Their bodies and their bones are temples of God in your midst,[1] for in no other way can you reconcile God with yourselves and approach God, except by the intercession of their prayers,[2] and unless you accept this faith by which they lived and became worthy to ascend to the living sea, from there to pour on you rivers of preaching of the divine words and to serve you the cup of creative love, if you can accept it. For He will abandon no one to go according to the desires of their souls; but whether you wish or not, nevertheless what God wills, that you must perform.[3]

1. See also §583, 597. The bodies of all living Christians should be temples of the Godhead, but the dead bodies of the martyrs are so-called because of the efficacy of prayer made over them; cf. the second canon attributed to Abraham, bishop of the Mamikoneans, *Kanonagirkᶜ*, I, pp. 502–504.
2. See also §572, 586, 597, 718. Cf. also the letter about martyrs sent from Lyons and Vienne to the churches in Asia and Phrygia, Eusebius, *H.e.*, V 1.45: διὰ γὰρ τῶν ζώντων ἐζωοποιοῦντο τὰ νεκρά, καὶ μάρτυρες τοῖς μὴ μάρτυσιν ἐχαρίζοντο. More explicitly the evidence from the catacombs at Rome indicates the early belief in the martyrs' intercession; cf. H. Delehaye, *Les Origines du culte des martyrs*, Bruxelles 1912.
3. A statement strangely at variance with the general tenor of the *Teaching*.

565. [*The saving mercy of Christ*] For when God saw that the race of men had become weak and was perishing by its sins of infirmity, He came as a doctor[1] to heal them, lest they die of the infirmity of their sins. To this the prophet bears witness and says: "Although it was ill, yet you confirmed it [Ps. 67.10]." But the same compassionate and merciful one, who from the beginning was eternal, the establisher and Creator of all, the same Himself is the doctor of his creatures. He made his light shine on those who fear Him,

as the prophecy says: "On you who fear my name the sun of righteousness will arise, and healing is in his wings [Mal. 4.2]."

1. See also §452, but here "doctor" has a less literally physical application; cf. Cyril Jer., *Cat.*, X 13: Ἰησοῦς τοίνυν ἐστὶ κατὰ μὲν Ἑβραίους σωτήρ, κατὰ δὲ τὴν Ἑλλάδα γλῶσσαν, ὁ ἰώμενος, ἐπειδὴ ἰατρός ἐστι ⟨ψυχῶν⟩ καὶ σωμάτων καὶ θεραπευτὴν πνευμάτων· τυφλῶν μὲν αἰσθητῶν θεραπευτής, φωταγωγῶν δὲ τὰς διανοίας· χωλῶν φαινομένων ἰατρός, καὶ ποδηγῶν τοὺς ἁμαρτωλοὺς εἰς μετάνοιαν.

566. Who is the sun of righteousness[1] if not He who humbled Himself and cast his rays on all the infirm and those who had fallen by sin into woe? He is the same who proceeded from the Father.[2] For it is only He who can illuminate the darkened spirits of men and bring joy to the souls fallen into the shade.[3] He Himself it is who visited our destruction, by whose rays all creatures live who by Him came into being. Similarly the ornament of heaven, that is the luminaries, make their light to shine by looking at his rays in the midst of creation, to give light to the earth;[4] and the heavens and the world are full of his light. His spirit is the radiance of the splendor of his own being.[5] He humbled Himself by the will of his compassion and came to illuminate the creatures. For they were in darkness, and He came to give and cast his light [Is. 49.9; Jn. 12.46].

1. Cf. the long list of epithets, including this one, applied to Christ in Eusebius, *De eccl. Theologia*, I 20.
2. See §362 note 1. But the term "proceeded," ᴅᴡᴦʙᴀᴦ, is here reminiscent of Heb. 7.14, ἀνατέταλκεν; cf. Is. 11.1.
3. Cf. Clement, *Protrep.*, XI 114, quoting Mal. 4.2: καταψεκάζει τὴν δρόσον τῆς ἀληθείας, and ibid., 113: ὁ Λόγος ὁ φωτίσας ἡμᾶς . . . ὁ τὸν ἐν σκότει κατορωρυγμένον νοῦν ἐναργῆ ποιησάμενος, καὶ τὰ φωσφόρα τῆς ψυχῆς ἀποξύνας ὄμματα. There are overtones here, and perhaps in the *Teaching*, of the Platonic myth of the cave, but biblical inspiration is more likely in the *Teaching*, as in the last sentence of this paragraph.
4. See also §365 and note 1.
5. ᴌᴏᴦᴘ ᴌᴘᴡ ᴌᴚᴎᴊᴘ ᴅᴡᴘᴡᴘᴡᴊᴩᴦ ᴌᴘᴩᴌ ᴌᴘᴩᴌᴡᴌᴌ. Radiance: ᴌᴚᴎᴊᴘ, which in the singular renders ἀπαύγασμα in Wisdom 7.26 (but in Heb. 1.3 ἀπαύγασμα is rendered by "light" in the Armenian version). The *Teaching* does not refer to Christ's relationship to the Father or Spirit; the spirit here means Christ's divinity (see §567); cf. Athanasius, *Ad Serapionem*, IV 19: περὶ ἑαυτοῦ εἰρηκέναι τὸ πνεῦμα (i.e., Mt. 12.31) . . . ἵν᾽ ἐκ δὲ τοῦ πνεύματος τὴν πνευματικὴν ἑαυτοῦ καὶ νοητὴν καὶ ἀληθεστάτην θεότητα δηλώσῃ.

567. But if they will not wish to open their hearts to the rays of his Godhead, He will utterly burn them up, according to the saying: "Fire was kindled from my anger; it will burn and go down to the bottommost hell, it will consume the earth and all plants of their earth; they will be burned with fire, the foundations of their hills will be burned up [Deut. 32.22]." Why, or wherefore, or how will it approach and burn up the foundations? Because their sins were founded and strengthened on earth, therefore with foundations

and roots He will burn up the evil, and utterly root out error from the earth, and efface the folly of idolatry and cast it out, as in the beginning of your torments it was shown to you.[1]

1. The torments are those inflicted on Trdat and those who put the martyrs to death. The reference is to Gregory's preliminary remarks before the long catechism, *History*, §226–242.

568. For when He speaks of the simile of the sea and of the filtering and purification of sins, He drowns there the cruel according to the likeness of their disobedient, hardhearted, and recalcitrant mode of life, destroying in the waters the unbridled and insolent host of Pharoah with its various companies and many chariots and lances of armed cavalry and innumerable excited horses. For in a moderate amount irrigation is most necessary for all sown plants; but when it is excessive and immoderate, it devastates, ruins, and destroys, and when it is multiplied greatly, it floods and effaces without memorial. In the same way the light is desirable to our eyes, but when it becomes excessively hot it destroys them, like the army of the Egyptians who opposed Moses and were burned up by the anger of God.

569. But this dry earth is our habitation, and all assistance and nourishment for our lives [comes] from it and [grows] on it, and the food for our growth, like milk from a mother, comes to us from it. Therefore this earth, our protector, has split and been cleft, it has opened its depths; it has hidden, submerged, and quite swallowed up and escorted alive to hell the Levites, those who dared to mock and despise Moses [Num. 16.32; 26.10; Deut. 11.6], the chosen and loved of God [Deut. 33.1].

570. At that time this occurred, but now God has sent his Son to mankind, who came and walked on earth and sent his disciples throughout the whole world. These blessed ones,[1] who have come as far as you, have shown you not only mere words, but also signs of their miracles through your punishments.

1. I.e., Rhipsimē and her companions, classed with the apostles as in §572 and 541. Other early martyrs were sometimes called apostles; cf. the variants to the title of the Πράξεις Παύλου καὶ Θέκλης which include: μαρτύριον τῆς ἁγίας καὶ ἰσαποστόλου (and also ἀποστόλου) Θέκλης, L.B.I. p. 235.

571. Those who reproached the servant of God, Moses, became worthy of such punishment.[1] But those who dared to oppose the Son of God, of what punishment and vengeance will they be worthy? For they who renounced an earthly lawgiver became liable to so much anger; but those who renounced a heavenly, how much more will they meet with torments? For the Lord,

the Son of God, who was sent by the Father, when He sent his own beloved apostles through all the earth thus pronounced judgment and decreed, saying: "Who receives you receives me, and who receives me receives my Father [Mt. 10.40; Jn. 13.20]."

1. The Levites, see §569.

572. Although yesterday you killed them, yet they are God's and now are living and will live for ever. By their intercession you will be reconciled with God according to the instruction of the companion apostle to these apostles of yours,[1] the great Paul, who said: "Through us be reconciled with God by the death of his Son [II Cor. 5.18]." For the Son of God died and lived, and likewise his beloved martyrs are alive and intercede for you.[2]

1. See §570 note 1, 521 note 1.
2. See also §564 note 2.

573. [*Christ's call to the eternal kingdom*] For the Son of God Himself preached to you, and He Himself is the server of joyful words. He invites you to the kingdom; He is the minister of his blessings; He raises his arms, and passing to the center of the earth [I Pet. 3.19] becomes the bestower of gifts to his worthy ones.[1] He casts fear on, and brings retribution to, those who do not know Him. He is the finder of those who have lost his mercy. He is the guide of those who have gone astray, who have erred from his ways. He is the haven for those whom the waves of the impiety of sin have enveloped —like you. He is the liberator from slavery of those who were held captive in their sins—like you. He is the healer of the wounded, who were hurt by impiety—like you. He is the helper of those who are deprived of help in knowing Him. He is the hope of those who hope in Him [and] in the everlasting, eternal, perpetual, ineffable, unending kingdom. He cares for his creatures with gentleness, and in his pity gives nourishment to the evil and the good, but also warns all men in order to make them worthy to approach the adoption of the call of the Godhead.

1. Cf. S. Der Nersessian, *An Armenian Version of the Homilies on the Harrowing of Hell, Dumbarton Oaks Papers*, 8 (1954), pp. 203–224, and idem, *A Homily on the Raising of Lazarus and the Harrowing of Hell*, in *Biblical and Patristic Studies in Memory of R. P. Casey*, ed. J. N. Birdsall and R. W. Thomson, Freiburg, 1963, pp. 219–234.

574. But let it be clear to you that this is so, that God the benevolent wishes to make you his own heirs. Up to now you did not know God, you were slaves to those who were not real[1] gods. But now become aware of God, especially that God knows that you had gone astray to feeble creatures and vain worship and were subject to the yoke of the slavery of sin. But now

you have been freed from that useless yoke of slavery to desire, from serfdom [Rom. 6.17], into Christ Jesus our Lord, the Son of God.

1. Real: ի իսկ; cf. Eznik, §392.

575. Take care lest you abandon what has been promised, for if those were not able to be saved who dared to abandon the earthly giver of commandments, how much more will we [not be saved] if we turn our backs on the heavenly lawgiver? He whose voice at that time moved the earth again also now promises and says: "Again another time I shall move not only the earth, but also the heavens [Haggai 2.6]." "But the saying 'again another time' indicates the moving of the things which are shaken, as of things which are made, that that which is immovable may remain firm [Heb. 12.26–7]."

576. Therefore be subject in your hearts to the immovable kingdom and you will receive grace, whereby you will serve God with eagerness. For God is a burning fire who will burn up your sins and hallow your souls as in the founts of essai of the skillful smiths, of the silversmiths, to separate the rust from the pure [Mal. 3.2–3]. What is chosen is purified and becomes precious, but what is not is burned up and consumed; just as the prophet says: "The light of Israel will become fire, and he will hallow it in a burning flame [Is. 10.17]." And it will make the lawlessness like grass, as he says: "It will kindle around him and devour him like grass. In that day all the mountains will be destroyed and hills and forests, and it will consume from the breath to the body, and who lives will be as one saved from flaming fire, and who remains among them, he says, will be numbered [Is. 10.16–19]."

577. [*The tower of Babel contrasted with the cross of Christ*] But in those former times after the flood, when mankind multiplied on the face of the earth, they enjoyed the liberality of the attentions of God, And becoming puffed up, they plotted disturbance and, losing control of themselves, went mad. They came to a certain place and decided on a vain plan, to build for the worship of [pagan] temples an impossibly high tower, which they set up in the plain of Senear in the land of the Assyrians [Gen. 11.1–9].[1] They built for the worship of demons, attaching to themselves the name of "temple builder," to bequeath it to their sons. And boasting in their vain glory, they set to work and labored at their work in clay of lawlessness, as the foolish first race sought to leave provision of iniquity for the descendants of the races which would come after them.

1. See also §297.

578. The Lord God, looking down on their lack of intelligence, mixed and gave them confusion of many tongues to drink. There He confused them one with another, whence the same place inherited the name Babel of confusion [Gen. 11.9]. They were scattered and separated from each other, and as a consequence no man understood the language of his neighbor. And being thus disunited from each other, they were separated, and their work was abandoned, and what they had formerly put up, they themselves destroyed. Having drunk, they spoke in each one's tongue, learning it from the Creator and Founder of all things. They were confused and scattered and separated from each other.

579. And a terrible fire mixed with wind and vapor of the Spirit of God, who is accustomed to confirm mankind on the right road and to keep them from the useless paths, to guide into righteousness and to confirm all men—this fire fell down from above and cut down the tower and made it crumble and collapse, knocking it down to the plain and scattering it. When this sudden obstacle to their impieties occurred, they were scattered according to the will of God over the earth following the lot of each one. Seventy-two patriarchs were set over the [various] tongues, and were divided and established each one in his own borders.[1]

   1. See also §503 note 1.

580. But a certain person who was of the first Hebrew race did not enter the plan to build what quickly crumbles and did not join what is soon destroyed—for such was the plan. Therefore he preserved his own tongue.[1] He first knew the Creator with his offspring, as we have narrated in the beginning,[2] undertaking the service of God; and they were called God's own people.[3] From him [are descended] the inspired prophets; "whence also Christ according to the flesh, who is above all, God blessed for ever [Rom. 9.5]"; whence also the disciples,[4] the evangelists with the new and gracious gift of the testaments, who are also his witnesses to the power of the deeds, signs, and miracles which were performed at his coming. They administered his grace, they received in their mouths the fire of the life of the Spirit, and with the fire purified the salt of the world [Mt. 5.13; Mk. 9.50]. They raised from their downfall the fallen of all the world. They destroyed and burned and consumed the lawlessness of the world, according to the likeness of the high tower about which we have spoken.

   1. I.e., Abraham and Hebrew.
   2. §298 ff.
   3. God's own people: *Joղովուրդ ձեռնական Աստուծոյ. Ձեռնական,* not found in the Armenian bible, means "own," "particular," and also "client," "protegé."
   4. See also §433.

581. In place of the lofty and quickly ruined tower, the cross of truth has been set up,[1] whose power is eternal and its glory God. As the prophet says: "To you the Lord will be revealed, and his glory will hide you. Kings will come to your light, and gentiles to the rising of your light [Is. 60.2–4]."

   1. See also §585 note 1.

582. Behold those reigning, who boasted in the crucified Savior and who are witnesses to his Divinity: "Who died with Christ, with Him also reign [II Tim. 2.12]." For they were offered to death for the name of God [II Cor.4.11], and behold the life of Jesus is revealed in the mortal bodies of those who love Christ.[1] They are apparently dead but hiddenly are alive; they preached openly their own life and gave life as drink to you who are dead in your sins.

   1. See also §564.

583. For God was revealed to you in their bones, since they took into themselves the light of the passion of the cross, and by the same sufferings of Christ they patterned[1] the patience of the Savior in themselves, to illuminate the darkness which was attached to your souls. As the prophet says: "Darkness hid the earth, and fog enveloped the gentiles [Is. 60.2]." In truth darkness and fog envelop the paganism of your souls with these ignorant customs, like the tower of error where the races of mankind conceived the worship of lawlessness, offering worship to lifeless and living creatures instead of to the Creator.

   1. Patterned: *աւրինակեալ;* see also §407 note 1. For the patience of Christ, see also §452 and note 2.

584. For although in their counsels was conceived lawlessness in the corrupting worship of the tower, for which reason they were scattered over the earth and confused in tongues, nevertheless they did not abandon the same, as the prophet says in the same psalter:[1] "Behold they have travailed with lawlessness, they have conceived evil and given birth to lawlessness [Ps. 7.15]." For after the collapse of the tower and the abandoning of each one's deeds of lawlessness, they fashioned handmade [images] which they adored. Just as the other prophet says: "They said to the wood: 'you are my father'; and they said to the stone: 'you gave birth to us'; and they turned their backs to me and not their faces [Jer. 2.27]."

   1. But the previous quotation is from Isaiah. Cf. the mistake in §398.

585. Therefore instead of the wood which they worshipped, He set up his cross that He might send out the light of its rays to all creatures who were

sitting in darkness and in the shadow of death [Ps. 106.10; Lk. 1.79]. He will burn the useless according to the prophet's saying: "The light of Israel will become fire, and He will hallow it in a fiery flame [Is. 10.17]." The tower stirred the wrath of the anger of the Creator to scatter them and confuse their tongues. But from the cross[1] mercy was elicited to gather together the scattered of the races of the sons of Adam. And instead of the old and futile stone worship, He made the faith of their martyrs firm as a rock that they might be immovable and firm [I Cor. 15.58].

1. The opposition of the tower and the cross is a key feature of the *Teaching*; cf. §628–629, 631. The tower stands for scattering (as Gen. 11.8), the cross for gathering (as Jn. 12.32). The arms of the cross gather Jews and Gentiles; see §489 and note 1.

586. And let us build with you on the foundation of the faith of the apostles and prophets. Let us receive the fire of the grace of the Spirit. He who burned and demolished the tower of error, the same will build us up on the firmness of the faith and will lead us into unity by his foundations of the firmness of the faith, by which sins will be burned away, and righteousness will be revealed through the cross, on which the Lord was made manifest, on which the Lord hung, whence his glory arose and filled the earth, and to which [testified] the martyrs, kings and reigning with Christ,[1] by whom you are reconciled with God through the death of his Son.[2]

1. Cf. Dionysius of Alexandria's account of martyrs in Alexandria under Decius, Eusebius, *H.e.*, VI 42.5: οἱ θεῖοι μάρτυρες παρ' ἡμῖν, οἱ νῦν τοῦ Χριστοῦ πάρεδροι καὶ τῆς βασιλείας αὐτοῦ κοινωνοί. See also §563 note 1.
2. See also §564 note 2.

587. [*The benefits for men of Christ's incarnation*] For this reason the Son of God humbled Himself to take the flesh of mankind and be humbled to the indignity of death, even to burial, that He might render those made worthy similar to the image of the Divinity by his love for men,[1] those who had been called brothers on account of the infinite love with which He loved mankind, that He Himself might be the firstborn among many brothers [Rom. 8.29]. On account of his love for men He thus pronounced, the Son of God Himself said: "They are my sisters and brothers who do the will of my Father who is in heaven [Mt. 12.50; Mk. 3.35; Lk. 8.21]." For the Son came and fulfilled the will of the Father.

1. See §369 note 2, 385 note 1, 589 note 1.

588. And what is the will of the Father except to receive again into the kingdom the sons of men who had rejected it, and to raise up into life those who had fallen down into death, and to make the servants of the Father,

whose[1] only begotten Son He is by nature, sons by grace. And therefore the Lord of hosts Himself[2] came down to the weakness of the state of men, that by that same weakness He might seize those who had become weak into the power of the glory of the rank of the Godhead and render them worthy of the adoption of grace.

1. Whose: որ ... որդի է միածին, a Syriacism; see §269 note 1.
2. See §363 note 2.

589. He Himself came down willingly to join[1] his loved ones to the Godhead. Those who in worthy love are modeled[2] on the divine love He named his brothers, and taught them the natural love of his Father's wisdom, and nourished, exhorted, and warmed them in the compassion of the Father's care, and gave the saints the power to become sons of God, those who believed in his name [Jn. 1.12]. He showed them the Father of grace, his begettor, and taught them to call Him their own Father [Mt. 6.9; Lk. 11.2] and showed them the benevolence of his Father that they might become worthy through their benevolence like the Father's to be called brothers of the true Son. The Son took them up and brought them near to the Father: "Behold me and my children whom the Father gave me [Is. 8.18]." And again He speaks to the Father and says: "I shall tell your name to my brothers, and in the midst of the congregations I shall bless you [Ps. 21.23]," just as He said to the disciples: "Everything that the Father has said to me I showed you, for I know you are friends of mine [Jn. 15.15]."

1. See §369 note 2, 385 note 1.
2. See also §407 note 1.

590. The true Son of God made those obedient to his Divinity his true witnesses and confidants, those who were steeped in his love and kept his commandments. He so raised and elevated them to his Divinity that He called to the Father: "Therefore they are not of the world, as I also am not of the world [Jn. 17.16]." "And I shall beg the Father that he send the Holy Spirit the Comforter to you, the first fruits,[1] who will join you to the Godhead,[2] who will dwell in you for ever, whom this world does not see, speak of, or know [Jn. 14.16–17]." He made them the first temple of the Godhead on earth and the house of the lodging of the Holy Spirit. "I and my Father, He says, will come and make our dwelling with you [Jn. 14.23]." And the treasure of the love, power, majesty, and mystery of the Father prepared them and was known to them before the world.

1. Added to the quotation from John by assimilation with II Cor. 1.22, 5.5, Eph. 1.14.
2. A further addition, but without scriptural authority, based on an idea important to the *Teaching*; cf. §589 and 369 note 2.

591. And because mankind could not bear the yoke of the commands of righteousness, therefore they fell under the necessity of death from sins. And as no man was able to bridge the breach [Eph. 2.14][1]—by enslaved races this could not be done, over whom through Adam's transgression death had gained power and had swallowed them up, as it is said: "By Adam we all died [I Cor. 15.22]"—then the Son of God took the form of Adam in the likeness of a servant [Philipp. 2.7], and became Himself like one of mankind, and came to bridge the separated, to build up what was destroyed. As the prophet says: "The ruins will be built up for ever [Is. 58.12; Ez. 36.33]." [He came] to take the body of the form of his just ones and through the same body to complete all righteousness. As He said to John: "Now it is thus fitting, that we should fulfill all righteousness [Mt. 3.15]."

> 1. Bridge the gap : ‍ցանկել զկրռամանունւթիւն; cf. Ps. 143.14 κατάπτωμα φραγμοῦ, or Judges 21.15 διακοπή. (This latter term is used by Gregory of Nyssa, *Or. cat.*, 35, to refer to the break with sin effected at baptism.) The *Teaching* is following the usual patristic exegesis of Eph. 2.14.

592. For the Lord Himself in a servant's body fulfilled all righteousness, in order to give the victory to the same body which He had joined and united to the Godhead,[1] that as they were in debt through the one body of Adam, so through the one body of the Lord they might be freed from slavery to sin [I Cor. 15.22], by that liberty which is above all liberties [Rom. 8.21].

> 1. See §369 note 2, and Introduction, pp. 18–19.

593. For the sake of their liberation He descended to slavery, that through his own body He might fulfill and complete all measures of the orders of the works of righteousness, that He might at once remove the needs of the weakness of the body of sin and once offer[1] Himself to his Father, and once in Himself make a satisfying offering of Himself [Heb. 9.25] as a sacrifice of reconciliation to his Father, and by the same sacrifice offer with it the faith of our confession. For He it was who conquered and fulfilled and broke and abolished the sentence of death that the gospel of life might become assured and true and infallible. For we shall all be made alive in Christ Jesus [I Cor. 15.22].

> 1. Offer: քահանայագէ, ἱερατεύειν.

594. And what is the saying: "He fulfilled the will of his Father [Jn. 4.34]," except that by his own body He will exalt the name of victory of the fulfillment of righteousness? He attained the goal of victory for all bodily creatures, to take away the dishonor from the sons of Adam, and to pour away

the poison of death and efface the sting of hell, that we may be bold in saying: "Where is your victory, death, or where are your stings, hell? [I Cor. 15.55]," to wipe away for ever all tears from all faces [Is. 25.8], to remove mourning and sadness and give serenity and joy.

595. And as He Himself was humbled from the heights, even so He raised to his Divinity those He knew to be worthy.[1] And He made them treasure-houses of the love of his will, and a temple of the dwelling of the Holy Spirit [I Cor. 6.19], that they might be submerged[2] in the Godhead. For by his own body, which was like theirs,[3] He drew them first to Himself and by them will draw all men to their joy. Just as the foretelling wise prophet in wonder at this said: "We shall be glad at the joy of your race, and we shall give praise with your inheritance [Ps. 105.5]." For the inheritance of the Father is the only-begotten Son, and the races who rejoice are the just fellow members[4] of the Lord's body. For He Himself exalted the praise of righteousness with all bodies of men, who was the heir of the Father and the inheritor of all creatures [Heb. 1.2]. Those who bore witness to Him He made sharers of his joy, for they were related[5] to his body, and all related[6] men will share in the joy of the martyrs who are their relatives.

> 1. See also §587, 589 and note 1.
> 2. Submerged: ընդզմեալ; see §378 note 3.
> 3. Like theirs: ազգակից, of the same race.
> 4. Fellow members: մարմնակից.բ, σύσσωμοι as Eph. 3.6.
> 5. Related: տոհմակից, of the same family.
> 6. See note 5 above.

596. [*The martyrs live and intercede for men*] The Lord first freed them from this earthly order and raised them from this earth as ranks of angels and divine beings,[1] that they themselves, being raised to the Godhead, might elevate all those related to them to the same love of the Godhead to which they themselves had attained. For they first were made worthy to know the mysteries of the Godhead, and through them all creatures have known "what the world does not see and does not know [Jn. 14.17]." For they first were separated and cut off from this world and then attained by the love of their Lord to the power of his Spirit. "Know, He says, that He will dwell in you for ever [Jn. 14.16]."

> 1. See also §586 note 2: θεῖοι μάρτυρες.

597. Do you see the declaration, for He said: "For ever He will dwell in you"? For as in their life, so now and for ever the interceding Spirit dwells in the bones of these [martyrs][1] who have been made worthy of adoption, by whom you will be reconciled with God through the death of his Son.[2]

For these holy martyrs by the same Spirit of which they were made worthy by the same will be intercessors for you, that there may be absolution for you also, ignorant and transgressors.[3] For the Son of God, who in Himself showed the example of life to his own beloved martyrs, said to them: "I am alive and you will live in me. For I am with the Father, and you are with me and I with you. For who receives my commandments and keeps them, he it is who loves me, and he will be loved by my Father, and I shall love him and shall reveal myself to him [Jn. 14.19–21]."

1. See also §563, 564 and note 1.
2. See also §564 and note 2.
3. See also §574, 630.

598. So they loved the Lord more than their own [natural] ability. For they saw that the Lord and Creator gave Himself for them, and they gave themselves to death in return for his death. And they were joined to the love of his Divinity and became dwelling places of his majesty. They saw that the Lord offered Himself as a sacrifice to the Father, therefore they themselves like lambs offered themselves to death that they might become a sacrifice to the Son of God.[1] For the Son of God fulfilled the will of his Father, whereas they fulfilled the will of the Son of God. The Son of God drew them to Himself and through them the whole world.

1. Cf. Ignatius, *Romans*, IV: λιτανεύσατε τὸν Χριστὸν ὑπὲρ ἐμοῦ, ἵνα διὰ τῶν ὀργάνων τούτων (i.e., the wild beasts) θυσία εὑρεθῶ; ibid., VI: ἐπιτρέψατέ μοι μιμητὴν εἶναι τοῦ πάθους τοῦ Θεοῦ μου; and Polycarp, *Ep.*, VIII: μιμηταὶ οὖν γενώμεθα τῆς ὑπομονῆς αὐτοῦ, καὶ ἐὰν πάσχωμεν διὰ τὸ ὄνομα αὐτοῦ, δοξάζωμεν αὐτόν. τοῦτον γὰρ ἡμῖν τὸν ὑπογραμμὸν ἔθηκε δι' ἑαυτοῦ, καὶ ἡμεῖς τοῦτο ἐπιστεύσαμεν.

599. They received a command from the Lord to despise this world and all that is in the world [Mt. 6.24 ff; Lk. 16.13], that they might despise this fleeting life in the world, that they might despise also the tribulations in it on account of the righteousness which will come, for they are the blessings and the seeds of the eternal kingdom, that they might despise and reject, cast aside and abandon their own works of vanity, that they might be saved from eternal torments.

600. He said: "Do not fear those who kill the body and cannot kill the spirit, but fear him who will cast the spirit and the body into the hell of fire [Mt. 10.28; Lk. 12.4–5]," that they might abandon the evil and choose the good, that they might desire and hasten to holiness, and inherit the heavenly light and eternal glory, and become heirs to the immortality of the divine eternal glory.

601. The Son of God said: "Enter through the narrow gate; for narrow is the gate which leads to the good and strait the road which leads to eternal life [Mt. 7.13–14]." For by tribulation and pain they will come to the unfading kingdom which is in store for them, when Christ will be revealed again with the eternal gifts at the resurrection, bringing immortality and retribution according to their deeds [Rom. 2.6], as we shall tell you in its own place.[1]

1. See §376 note 2.

602. [*The similes of the serpent and dove*] "And become, He says, wise as serpents [Mt. 10.16]." What is the wisdom of the serpent except that as he grows old and sees his body decaying, he brings out the secrets of his wisdom? For he goes to a place where the cavity is narrow, and it is his practice to slough off the skin of his aged body; he strips it away and returns again to childhood, and being renewed, he enlivens his old age. Even so the just strip off from their souls the ephemeral impurities of the body that they may enter the narrow gate and obtain the immortal kingdom.[1] For those who have loved the Lord are alive for ever, because He spoke thus: "Who believes in me, even though he die, is alive [Jn. 11.25]." For "I am resurrection and life" said the Son of God, who by the will of the Father, as we said above, tasted death for our sake [Heb. 2.9] that He might save all nations from corruption. But now that He sits on the right hand of the Father, He prepares everything and bestows it on those who have hoped in Him.

1. Cyril Jer., *Cat.*, III 7, develops this theme of the snake sloughing off its skin à propos of baptism: πᾶς γὰρ ὄφις εἰς στένον ἐνδύνας ἀποτίθεται τὸ γῆρας, καὶ τὴν παλαιότητα διὰ τῆς ἀποθλίψεως ἐκδυσάμενος, νεάζει λοιπὸν τῷ σώματι· οὕτως εἴσελθε καὶ σὺ διὰ τῆς στενῆς καὶ τεθλιμμένης θύρας· ἀπόθλιψον σεαυτὸν διὰ τῆς νηστείας, ἐκβίασαί σου τὴν ἀπώλειαν· ἀπόδυσαι τὸν παλαιὸν ἄνθρωπον σὺν ταῖς πράξεσιν αὐτοῦ, καὶ εἰπὲ τὸ ἐν ᾄσμασιν ἐκεῖνο· ἐξεδυσάμην τὸν χιτῶνά μου, πῶς ἐνδύσομαι αὐτόν;

603. "Be simple, He says, like doves [Mt. 10.16]." Firstly, because the dove is benevolent and gentle and only wishes to live close to men, for God also is benevolent and wishes always to dwell in the midst of his saints. And secondly, if any dove raises many times its eggs or young, it never in doubt abandons the place of its nest. In the same way, although the insults of men are frequent and untiring against the Creator[1] from whom the wants of their nourishment are provided, and they do not recognize Him, yet He did not abandon and withdraw from his creatures but continually visits them and seeks to find those who have been destroyed, saying: "Today you will hear my voice [Ps. 94.8; Jn. 10.16; Heb. 3.15]." And He wills, for the reason that

He sent his Son, that He may make all men his heirs by grace; that they may learn the wisdom of the serpent, to strip off from their souls the old man of ignorance and impiety, and receive the harmless and pure simplicity of the dove,[2] which bears in itself the blessings of the Godhead. For the Holy Spirit when He was revealed to the world, as we narrated above,[3] appeared in the bodily form of a dove in order to show the abundance of benevolent and loyal love.

1. Creator: աշաբղաւ[ծ]աււ, abstract noun for substantive, as §607 note 2, 640 note 3, 666 note 1, *History*, §718 etc.

2. Cf. Origen, *In Luc. Hom.*, XVII: Descendit enim spiritus sanctus super Salvatorem in specie columbae, avis mansuetae, innocentis et simplicis. Unde et nobis praecipitur, ut imitemur innocentium columborum. See also §418 note 1. For the combination of wisdom and simplicity, cf. Clement, *Str.*, VII 13: γνωστικὸς ... μίξας οὖν τῇ περιστερᾷ τὸν ὄφιν τελείως ἅμα καὶ εὐσυνειδήτως βιοῖ, πίστιν ἐλπίδι κεράσας πρὸς τὴν τοῦ μέλλοντος ἀπεκδοχήν.

3. See §418 ff.

604. For those who wish to offer hospitality to the Spirit of the Godhead will take from the vision the blessings of the harmless and pure dove. As the Lord said to the disciples: "Be kind to the wicked and your enemies, even though you are persecuted by all for the sake of righteousness, because your Father is kind. He makes his sun to shine on the good and on the evil, and brings rain on the just and on the sinners, that you may become kind sons of your kind Father [Mt. 5.44–45]."

605. But those who stand in this loyalty to the command of righteousness will take the form of a dove with rapid wings and will fly on the wings of the Holy Spirit to attain the kingdom of heaven, for which the saints remained yearning on earth. To this the prophet aspired and awaited with desire, saying: "Would that someone would give me wings as of a dove that I might fly up [Ps. 54.7]." This the blessed Paul, the fellow apostle of your apostles, explained in the letter of consolation by which he comforted the Thessalonians: "We who are alive and who remain are caught up with the dead in the clouds to meet the Lord in the air, and so we shall be forever with the Lord [I Thess. 4.17]." They will be joined to the band of Christ, flying the swift flight of shining-feathered white doves, who have taken and represented in themselves the form of the Son of God who appeared to them. And the same [form] He ordered them to show in themselves that He might make spiritual wings to grow on them so that they could join the divine band.[1]

1. The *Teaching* does not interpret Ps. 54.7 mystically, as was usual (cf. Lampe, *Lexicon*, s.v. περιστερά), but literally of the second coming, as at §659. See also §606 note 1.

606. But in wonder the heavenly hosts of light will ask when they see the lower bands of human saints coming up from below towards the Lord: "Who are these flying like clouds, and like doves with their young, in flocks coming to me? [Is. 60.8]"[1] Then they will hear the reply from the Lord Himself: "These have hoped in me. I shall lead them to the hill of my holiness and shall make them rejoice in my temple [Is. 56.7]." And all who see them will know that "they are the seed blessed from God [Is. 65.23]," and with joy will rejoice in the Lord. Then the Lord will say: "Be my sons and daughters [II Cor. 6.18]." Then will be aroused the compassion of the Creator's love, according to the word of the prophet: "As a father has compassion on his sons, the Lord will have compassion on those who fear him [Ps. 102.13]."

1. Cf. Cyril Jer., *Cat.*, XVIII 34, speaking of the last things: ἤγγικε γὰρ ἡ ἀπολύτρωσις ὑμῶν καὶ τὴν ὑμετέραν ἐκδέχεται σωτηρίαν ὁ τῶν ἀγγέλων ἐπουράνιος στρατός ... then he quotes Is. 60.8, adding: νεφέλαι γὰρ διὰ τὸ πνευμάτικον, καὶ περιστεραὶ διὰ τὸ ἀκέραιον.

607. For "now, looking with hope, we see all this as if looking through a mirror, but then face to face [I Cor. 13.12]." And we are renewed into the same renewal, to glory from glory [II Cor. 3.18], as the Lord's Spirit who tries and chooses all and renews whom He finds worthy. In the furnaces of testing[1] of the smelting house of election He places the tongues of the apostles that by them He may make election of all the world. For both the temple of the Godhead and the furnaces of the earth have become dwelling places of the Creator.[2]

1. See also §632.

2. Creator: աշաբղաւ[ծ]ււււ, abstract for substantive; see also §603 note 1.

608. Of this the first laborers, the prophets, handing down to all nations these things to come, first informed their own Jewish race and then warned all nations of the world: "The congregations to gather together, and kings to serve the Lord [Ps. 101.23]."

609. And again, referring to themselves, they indicated the apostles as their future sons and called to the Lord, as if speaking of themselves and their sons who would be scattered over the earth:[1] "Instead of your fathers they will be your sons, and you will set them up as princes in all the land [Ps. 44.17]." They are established and rule the earth[2] to bring all men back to one authority under obedience, to the service of freedom by their own will, that all may become heirs of the kingdom by goodness of their own doing, with their princes.

1. See also §697 note 2. The apostles were considered to be heirs to the prophets; cf. Irenaeus, *Adv. Haer.*, IV 36.5: Qui igitur nos per Apostolos undique vocavit Deus, hic per prophetas vocabat eos qui olim fuerunt. Somewhat differently, Chrysostom, *In Jo. Hom.*, XXXIV 2: οἱ προφῆταί εἰσιν οἱ σπείραντες· ἀλλ' οὐκ αὐτοὶ ἐθέρισαν, ἀλλ' οἱ ἀπόστολοι.

2. The apostles' task extended to the whole world, as opposed to the prophets' limited sphere; cf. Chrysostom, *In Mat. Hom.*, XV 6, quoting Mt. 5.13: ὁρᾷ πῶς κατὰ μικρὸν δείκνυσι καὶ τῶν προφήτων εἶναι βελτίους (i.e. the apostles), οὐ γὰρ τῆς Παλαιστίνης διδασκάλους εἶναί φησι, ἀλλὰ τῆς γῆς ἁπάσης.

610. Just as the Lord Himself speaks of the future through the prophets: "I shall make your princes peace, and your exactors righteousness [Is. 60.17]." Whereby the apostles drank the cup of visitation and will give the world the cup of peace to drink. Therefore the prophets anticipated the future by their foreseeing: "Thus says the Lord to me: 'Cast your silver into the furnace and test if it be pure, as I was tested for them.' And I took the thirty pieces of silver and cast them into the Lord's house into the furnace [Zech. 11.13]."

611. [*The testing of the Apostles*] But because the Son of God was to come and descend and raise all nations to the Godhead, therefore a scrutiny was made of all men in the form of the law of their not tasting of the fruit of the tree [Gen. 2.17], that they might become worthy to receive the gracious gift of immortality.[1] So also the Lord through the humility of his body and abject appearance will test and examine the strong in faith who in his humble form saw and heard that He was God—how and why they will believe in the elevation of his nature. Concerning this He quoted and said: "As I also was tested for them [Zech. 11.13]." But He made them united, revealing them as one house united in thought and faith through the truth, preaching the same message, with articulated members, one temple of the Godhead,[2] by which He will examine the whole world concerning their faith in his coming.

1. Cf. Athanasius, *De Incarnatione*, 3.
2. See also §613.

612. But because the fire of sin had consumed and completely destroyed the nature of mankind, for sins were aflame in the likeness of fire, the anger of God's exasperation was awakened to seek vengeance. Truly few remained according to the saying: "And those who remain will be numbered [Is. 10.19]." But first He numbered and revealed the established twelve, set as laborers according to the tribes of the race of Israel.[1] He also according to the former tongues of all divided nations revealed the seventy-two, as we said above,[2] that by them He might gather into unity the former schism of the nations and tongues.[3]

1. Cf. Mt. 19.28; Lk. 22.30; Irenaeus, *Adv. Haer.*, IV 21.3: Peregre nascebatur duodecim-tribus genus Israel, quoniam et Christus peregre incipiebat duodecastylum firmamentum Ecclesiae generare.
2. See §503 note 1.
3. It is the apostles and their successors who carry out the gathering of the scattered, of which the cross is the symbol; see §585 note 1.

613. But they at first were few in number. Therefore the Son of God Himself came to teach them with united faith to choose the one and the same gathering. Therefore He came and said: "The harvest is great and the laborers few. Pray therefore the Lord of the harvest that he may send laborers to the work of his harvest [Mt. 9.37–38; Lk. 10.2]." And by this He Himself requested from them love for each other, and He united them and established them as his temple on earth,[1] and through them tested the whole universe.

1. The church and Christians are frequently described metonymously as the temple of God; see also §564 note 1. As applied to the apostles only, this depends on Jn. 20.22.

614. And this is the fire of the Spirit which was revealed in the days of Pentecost, who came and rested on the tongues of the Apostles, who came and gathered the scattered ones, and they began to speak tongues [Acts 2.4–11] to the former scattered tongues. Because the seed of lawlessness had fallen into the womb of the mind of the first witless men, therefore they received the embryo of impiety and, putting their hands around their sides, they conceived the birth of idolatry and brought it forth [James 1.15]. But the fruit of this was the diverse and dissident separation, one from another going astray; and separated each from his brother, they were scattered.

615. But the former sought from each other the united, harmonious gathering. Therefore He commanded that they themselves first gather together by their own wits that they might learn to bring into unity the peoples of all nations; that He might first make them prepared dwelling places, and then send to them the Spirit of his Godhead.[1] The Spirit, taking the love of the Father of the Son, hastened and came to them to dwell first in them and through them in all creatures. "I and my Father, He says, will come and make our dwelling with him [Jn. 14.23]." And by the love for each other which He taught them, He says: "Pray the lord of the harvest that he may send workers to the task of his harvest [Mt. 9.38; Lk. 10.2]."

1. The apostles were the first Christians; cf. the use of ἀπαρχή in Cyril Alex., *Glaph. in Gen.*, 4: τῶν ἁγίων ἀποστόλων ὁ χορὸς ὡς ἀπαρχὴ γεγονὼς τῶν ἡγιασμένων ἐν πνεύματι. The unity of the apostles is frequently stressed in the *Teaching*; cf. §661.

616. Is He Himself not able without their prayers to do this, who merely by a sign[1] created all creatures? But because charity is completely honorable to the Godhead, as the Godhead is loving, so He wills that by loving each other they may become worthy of the Godhead through inoffensiveness to each other.

1. Merely by a sign: ա-նշ-ա-ր-կ-ե-լ-ո-յ-ն, τῷ νεύειν, e.g., Jn. 13.24, Acts 24.10. Cf. Athanasius, *C. Gentes*, 44: ὁ τοῦ Θεοῦ Λόγος ἑνὶ καὶ ἁπλῷ νεύματι, τῇ ἑαυτοῦ δυνάμει τόν τε ὁρατὸν κόσμον καὶ τοὺς ἀοράτους δυνάμεις κινεῖ καὶ συνέχει, or Eusebius, *H.e.*, I 2.5: τὸν μὲν πατέρα καὶ ποιητήν . . . ὡς ἂν πανηγεμόνα βασιλικῷ νεύματι προστάττοντα, Who is contrasted with the Logos, τὸν δὲ τούτῳ δευτερεύοντα θεῖον λόγον . . . ταῖς πατρικαῖς ἐπιτάξεσιν ὑπουργοῦντα.

617. As soil and winds and plants from one earth have origins separate from each other, yet are creatures of one Creator, so they will love first the Creator[1] and will be loved by Him. And living pleasingly to Him, they will be able to obtain the kingdom of heaven. For in self-love there is no charity but selfishness which is not pleasing to the will of the Creator; for which reason sin from the beginning entered the world.[2] But because the Godhead is loving, therefore He made them his companions that they might love each other and come as messengers[3] to the world and pray and send workers to the tasks of their Lord's crops.

1. Creator: ա-ր-ա-ր-չ-ո-ւ-թ-ի-ւ-ն, as §603 note 1.
2. See also §262 and note 4.
3. Messengers: հ-ր-ա-ւ-ի-ր-ա-կ; see §484 and note 1, 573, 630, 672 note 2, and the մ-շ-ա-կ-ո-ւ-ա-կ-ք of §507 and note 1. հ-ր-ա-ւ-ի-ր-ա-կ occurs once in the Armenian bible, at Jer. 31.6; the Syriac reads nāṭorā᾽ (watchman), the LXX has a widely variant text.

618. [*Return to the tower of Babel as a type of the cross of Christ*] For the first conception of self-willed mankind brought forth the schism of confusion of tongues. The same is also seen with respect to the Jewish people from the narrative of the prophets which says: "Well, ask and see, has it ever been heard that men have conceived and given birth, putting their hands on their loins and seeking remedy? For behold I see every man and his hand on his side; I look at man, and all faces have turned into the color of paleness [Jer. 30.6]."

619. Indeed they conceived in the impieties of the idolatry of their pagan customs, and placing their hands on their sides, they had regard to gaining profit for themselves from their vain works. Whence they found woe, the color of pain of childbirth from the recompence of their reproach, giving birth to captivity. And they brought forth from the womb the dissolution of destruction and scattering as their progeny instead of the fruit of the

womb. And migrating among foreign nations in place of the love of the marriage chambers they wandered. In return for their state of revolt they received destruction from their Creator, from the nearby Lord.

620. In the same way the first nations, in return for daring to turn their backs away from their Lord who had made them from nothing, and for taking refuge in a tower built of bricks and mortar and tar, conceived with the same pain through their lawless worship and were scattered, torn apart, separated, divided from each other; and they gave birth over the face of the earth, each one privately by himself, to isolation of evil life in themselves as fruit of the womb in the matrix; and in the likeness of mothers they received, conceived, and bore.

621. And bearing in mind the punishment of the earlier flood they began to build the tower, as if they expected to be saved by this same building when it should come. And they did not attend to the Creator to cease from their lawlessness and to be saved by deeds pleasing to Him. And of his will and creation, either before or after, or of Him who was the Creator from the beginning, they took no thought. And all coming together, they were no longer aware of each other's conception by which they were weighed down.

622. Therefore the All-seeing, when He saw what was displeasing to his will among them and their ignorance and lack of understanding, the Godhead decided to bring forth their conception. And God said: "Let us go down and descend and confound their tongues [Gen. 11.7]." He did not say: "Go, descend and confound their tongues," as the kind of command which was suitable for the Godhead, but: "Let us go, He said, let us descend and confound." By saying "let us confound" He revealed the unanimity of the deed, and truly He set this pattern both in creating man and in dividing the tongues.[1]

1. See also §275 and note 1.

623. Because the Godhead was to take upon Himself humanity for our salvation, He taught the number of the Persons of the Trinity to the Apostles so that according to this example they might teach all men who would be in the whole world [Mt. 28.19] that knees might bend in humility before the revealed hypostasis of the three consubstantial Persons,[1] at the sole worshipped Lord. But the conception of these others had brought forth confusion of voices unintelligible to each other.

1. On these technical terms see Introduction, p. 13.

624. So what did these first nations say at the building of the tower? "Come, let us build a tower, that its summit may reach the heavens [Gen.11.4]." They were unable to reach the height which their pride had promised, of which they had boasted, but they destroyed, brought down, and broke the building of their unity of mind and language. They did not bring up the tower to the heavens as they said, for it was on earth and there the building remained; but thence they descended to destruction and division and scattering. They conceived lawlessness, they gave birth to the division of many tongues, so that a man could not understand his fellow's language; and separated from each other, they were scattered.

625. But the Godhead appeared at that time in a mystery[1] and was revealed in these times clearly [Col. 1.26]. He was truly disclosed that all might know, see, and believe. He sowed in the souls of the prophets the grace of foreknowledge of the Holy Spirit that they might conceive the gospel of truth of the coming of the Godhead to all creatures;[2] and that these others might sow over all the world,[3] and conceive the mystery of the expectation of life, to bear the birth of immortality; that they might conceive hope and love, first for the Godhead of creation, and then the love of charity, to keep accord with each other by sincere and undeceitful love.

> 1. Mystery: *խորհուրդ*; see also §374 note 2, and §332, 393, 407 note 1.
> 2. See also §318 ff.
> 3. I.e., the apostles, contrasted with the prophets; see §609 note 2.

626. This He Himself explained when He came: "On these two commandments hang all the law and the prophets [Mt. 22.40]." First to love the Godhead with all one's heart and soul and with all one's power—which is the first. And the second is to love one's neighbor as oneself. But the third is to hear the word of the gospel of the Godhead without doubting and to believe it.[1] By this they conceived rapidity of hastening, whereby they were borne on the flight and wings of the Holy Spirit to join the band of Christ, to conceive the hope of faith and bring those once captured to birth in the kingdom. Just as the prophet cries for all creatures to the Father, as on behalf of all, as for all seeing the adoption of grace which is prepared for us, saying: "Like the pains of childbirth when she has reached the time of delivery and cries out in her pangs [Is. 26.17]."

> 1. The three commandments derive from the three imperatives in the passage parallel to the quotation from Matthew, Mk. 12.29–31.

627. But what are the pains which have arrived, which will force the pangs of crying out, except repentance and confession conceived by contrition,[1]

according to the saying: "So we have been to your beloved [Is. 26.17]"? Of what beloved then does the prophet speak unless he speaks about his Son who was to come, in whom was the expectation of all creatures [Rom. 8.19]? Who came and fulfilled in Himself everything, just as they said to Him, crying out: "Lord, we have conceived in awe and fear; we have been in pain and brought forth the spirit of your salvation [Is. 26.18]."

> 1. On the importance of contrition and tears with confession as a part of repentance, cf. John Mandakuni, *Čařkᶜ*, II, and *Yačaxapatum*, XIX. See also §535–536.

628. Instead of the tower the Lord set up the wood of the cross, according to the prophecy which says: "Behold I set up a sign above the Gentiles [Is. 11.12]"—that is the saving cross on which the Lord Himself [hung] and from which He effects life for the world.[1]

> 1. See also §488–489, 585 note 1.

629. But "Come, they said, let us build a tower so that its top reaches heaven [Gen. 11.4]." And the one occurred according to this same plan of theirs; but the other was not so. Now the tower is the cross on which hung the Son of God. The cross is on the earth and the body on it. But the Godhead who reaches above the heavens, beyond the infinite, limitless nature of material creatures, was contained and nailed to the wood of the cross, filling and extended in both the material and immaterial spheres;[1] such was also He who dwelt in the hearts of the Apostles and of all the saints with the Father and his Holy Spirit, who inspired tongues in place of the confused tongues. For from the first tower was scattering, but from the cross, gathering; from the one expulsion to torments, and from the other, approach to the kingdom.

> 1. God on the cross links this world with eternity; see §489 note 1, and the *Acts of Andrew*, James, *Apocryphal N.T.*, pp. 359–360: O cross, planted upon the earth and having thy fruit in the heavens.

630. The Apostles conceived love for their fellowmen and brought forth all creatures and joined them to the Godhead. They handed themselves over at the accusation of their fellows because they had spoken God. Therefore like enemies they were condemned to death for their benefits; the messengers[1] received evil for good, who came to call everyone to the marriage[2] of the love of the Godhead. They received death with torments instead of finding praises and honor from them, as you have done to yours. For you acted in ignorance, since you had not attained truly to goodness.

> 1. Messengers: *հրաւիրակք*; see §617 note 3.
> 2. See also §508, 510 note 2.

631. From the first tower came scattering of tongues; and now the Lord Himself has gathered the scattered of the races and attached them to his body,[1] which He took from us and in which He hung on the wood, to join them into one faith of united worship. They received a command to love the Lord and to do his will that they might save from eternal death the souls of their relations[2]—that is all men. For the Lord Himself came and died for all that He might raise all to immortality. But these were sent as preachers of his will, to make all aware of the salvation and benefits of the Godhead who had been among them.

    1. See §369 note 2, and Introduction, pp. 18–19.
    2. Relations: *ırnçfıuflyp*; see §595 note 5.

632. [*Return to the testing of the Apostles*] Therefore the Apostles conceived by the Holy Spirit and brought forth tongues speaking of immortality to all. For the Spirit of the Godhead came Himself to try and examine all, like silver in a furnace, by the tongues of the Apostles. Like his saying for all, as for the world, speaking like a trumpet by his power, the prophet cries: "Try us, God, and examine us, even as silver is tried [Ps. 65.10]."

633. Truly the just were tested as in a furnace through the Holy Spirit for He first tested them in breathing the power of the Spirit. "He breathed on them and said: 'receive the holy Spirit' [Jn. 20.22]," that He might choose them first like silver, that the impurity might be burned up. For the house of the Lord was his own divine body.[1] They were also the furnace of purification for the world. The valiant Apostles were cast into the furnace, at first twelve in number. One of them was burnt, dissolved, and destroyed, Judas the son of destruction; like copper he was consumed and destroyed in the fire.

    1. Cf. Proverbs 9.1 and the interpretation of Gregory of Nyssa, *C. Eun.*, III: τὴν τῆς σαρκὸς τοῦ κυρίου κατασκευὴν διὰ τοῦ λόγου αἰνίσσεται. οὐ γὰρ ἐν ἀλλοτρίῳ οἰκοδομήματι ἡ ἀληθινὴ σοφία κατῴκησεν, ἀλλ' ἑαυτῇ τὸ οἰκητήριον ἐκ τοῦ παρθενικοῦ σώματος ᾠκοδομήσατο; or Chrysostom, *Frag. in Prov.*, IX: αὐτὸ ἑαυτῷ κατεσκεύασεν οἶκον τὴν ἐκ Παρθένου σάρκα. Cf. also the title to Ps. 29.1, and Basil, *In Ps. Hom.*, XXIX 1: κατὰ δὲ τὸ νοητόν, τὴν ἐνσωμάτωσιν τοῦ Θεοῦ Λόγου σημαίνειν.

634. The eleven were hallowed and chosen like silver in a furnace, and they became chosen vessels of ability for the needs of the Creator. They were tested in various ways by tribulations and torments which they endured from men, from those to whom they spoke profit. Firm in love they gave witness to their fellowmen from whom they received torments that they might ful-fill the commands of the Lord who had sent them. They brought the love of

profit to their companions by suffering tribulations that they might despise transitory things. For when the Creator of the world will be revealed again, they will reign with Him in an eternal kingdom, as truly says the prophecy of the same Psalmist concerning them: "You have proved us, O God, and tried us as silver is tried. You have brought us down into the trap, and placed afflictions on our backs, and have made men to pass over our heads [Ps. 65.10–12]."

635. For He tested them by the fire of the Spirit and at the hands of men, that in the process of testing their fortitude might be revealed through their tribulations for the sake of righteousness, just as you know testing from those who in your country in front of you were proved martyrs to the Godhead. For they loved the hope of the promised coming again of the Son of God. They took the fire of the living Spirit into themselves, and they became worthy to receive the flowing fountains of immortality. Therefore they were able to face, pass by, and despise the torments by fire and the sins frozen by ice.[1] Truly they despised sin and with it the tribulations to come, and they thanked the Giver of grace: "We have passed through fire and water, and you have brought us to rest [Ps. 65.12]."

    1. The ice seems to be suggested by the water of the following quotation. At §511 the *Teaching* speaks of the rust of sins.

636. For first they passed through fire and water and the sword of sin and despised the fire of sin and the water of lawlessness and the sword of trial and torments, and they received the illuminating fire of life and the water of renewal and the sword, that is, "the Word of God which is sharper than all double-edged and steel swords and is able to strike, cut, and penetrate to the separation of soul, body, and breath [Heb. 4.12]."

637. Therefore the prophet earlier exposed this: "Two-edged swords are in their hands [Ps. 149.6]," by which they will cut and strike once for all the lawlessness of the impieties and extirpate them from the earth. And what will they do to the harvested and the cut? He says: "The winds will take them, and the clouds will scatter them, and the whirlwind will pile them up like bushes [Is. 41.16; 40.24]." Those piled up will be cast into the inextinguishable fire. For this is indeed the task of the true laborers—to gather into barns the useful and profitable harvest, and to feed the thorn and buckthorn to the fire.

638. [*The Apostles bring the gospel to the world*] They first tried themselves and then became the furnace of the world. They received the fire of life.

Again they entered the furnace like silver, were smelted, purified, and forged in the love of the Creator; they were taken from the furnace of the foundry and hammered into trumpets[1] for the service of the Lord's commands; they called out and filled the world. Trumpets called to trumpets, and companion said to companion: "Preach day by day his salvation. Relate to the gentiles his glory, and to all the congregations his wonders. For great is the Lord and greatly blessed, terrible is he above all idols [Ps. 95.2–4]." And: "All the idols of the heathen are nothing, but the Lord made the heavens [Ps. 95.5]." Instead of the sculptured images, the Apostles were called hammered trumpets that they might completely fill all the world, according to the saying: "Throughout all the earth went their speech, and their words to the ends of the world [Ps. 18.5; Rom. 10.18]."

1. Cf. Ps. 46.6, and Chrysostom's comment, *Expositio in Ps.*, XLVI 5: οὐκ ἂν δέ τις ἁμάρτοι σάλπιγγας τὰ στόματα τῶν ἀποστόλων εἰπών; cf. also John Awjnec̣i, *Opera*, VII 20, pp. 236–238. Aphraates likens Christian preachers (kāroze᾽ d᾽idtā᾽) to trumpets, and Ephrem compares the two testaments of the church to trumpets, *De Fide*, 21. Cf. the μεγάλη σάλπιγξ of the Spirit, Theodoret, *Eranistes*, III. See also §658–659 below.

639. They are furnaces of the world, and the fire of the life of the Spirit is on their tongues that they may test all the world and that they may call out again on behalf of the Lord the revelation of the true nature of the Godhead: "See, see that I am, and there is no other God save me;" and: "I put to death and I bring to life. I strike and I heal, and there is no one who will take you from my hands;" and: "I shall sharpen like lightning my sword, and cast my right hand in search of vengeance. I shall exact retribution of my enemies [Deut. 32.39–41]."

640. The tongues of the Apostles conceived the immensity of their faith and brought forth tongues which they did not know. They called out as trumpets the absolute authority of lordship and brought the numberless multitude of mankind to the ranks of the angels and the service of the Son of God, that instead of the fallen angels who had been cast down from the divine service of light the sons of men might become angels,[1] that they might be raised up and take their place, that the same set number[2] of glorious ones[3] might remain complete and unabated, so that from the equivalent numbers of glorious ones praise might be increased and magnified, whence by comparison: "Glory in the highest to God and on earth peace, goodwill to men [Lk. 2.14]."

1. See also §414.
2. See §297 note 1, 321.
3. Glorious ones: խառատորութեանն, abstract noun for substantive; see §603 note 1.

641. [*Trees and plants in spring as examples of the resurrection*] The Apostles became trumpets which sound the time for the world, that they might place in the hearts of all the world the expectation of the appointed time, to serve the trumpet [which announces] the coming of the Lord. For with the same voices they will come, and at that time make known the same sound of the trumpet; raised from the sleep of death to the spring,[1] they will show the blossom of each one's plant. When they later come to this spring, they will bear the appropriate form from the root of each one's seeds,

1. See also §528 and note 1.

642. one like a sweet-tasting and beautiful palm tree, as says the predicting prophecy: "The righteous like palm trees will blossom and like the cedars of Lebanon become many. They will be planted in the house of the Lord, and in the courts of our God they will flower [Ps. 91.13–14]." And again our Lord Jesus Christ Himself, in his gospel which brings good news and life, clearly gives knowledge to all: "From a fig tree learn the parable, for when the branches are tender and bear leaves, you will know that the spring is near [Mt. 24.32]."

643. For all groups of trees are good similes and examples, bearing the appearance of each one's form; and never do they change the varieties of their flowers, tastes, smell, or leaves. For the palm tree will bear its own form and color and taste and product and what is natural to its root and the growth of its plant. Likewise the fig tree also has the form of its own leaves and structure of bark and distinct kind of fruit, and the others are separate from it. For the red apple has its own form, and the red pear its own, and the red peach its own. And they are from the same nature, yet various; for each one of them will give off its own individual smell.[1]

1. Cf. Ephrem, *De Fide*, §36, 76.

644. Likewise the lemon and balsamon, and laurel and beautiful olive tree, and quince and myrtle, and nut and almond, and jujube and holly, and mulberry and grenadine and cornel tree. And all trees, fruit-bearing and flowering, leaf-bearing and tuft-bearing, lofty and great, like the cedar and cypress, and pine and oak, and laurel and plantain, and poplar and buck thorn, and vine and poplar, and willow and box tree.

645. Likewise the various kinds and colors of flowers, like the mandrake and rose, and lily and soldanel, and jasmin and lotus, and sumach and narcissus, and arum and lungwort, and hyacinth and poppy and violet. And of

all the other fragrant flowers and trees, the budding shoots will appear in spring after the winter.

646.   Similar is also the resurrection of the dead. For after the world was created, no one of them in autumn or spring replaced its companion or gave its own form to a plant of similar origin. But from the beginning of their creation, from the time of creation to the time of passing away, although in autumn the growing plants are continually stunted, they dry up and lose their leaves, those that were flourishing take on winter's garb, are covered with ice, snow, and frost, and buffeted by the fierceness [of winter] the roots of the flowers decay, with the numerous trees in the various parks and the forests of high cedars and growing pines with many buds; yet coming to the time of spring, receiving light from the clouds, shaken by thunder, beaten by the rain, touched by dew, increasing and growing in the summer, they bear each one its own kind of flower. According to each one's nature its appearance remains in its own form and does not change from itself to another, or from its companion to its own likeness, but according to the establishment of the Orderer it remains thus in its own nature;[1] firmly and unalterably disposed according to the Creator's command, they grow and blossom.

1. On all this paragraph cf. Cyril Jer., *Cat.*, IX 10.

647.   The small green herbs are different and separate in form from each other, like the alga and oat and rush, and whatever is similar to them; and likewise seeds of use to men, like corn and rye, and barley and millet, and yellow millet and lentil, and pea and rice, and bean and chick-pea, and many other seeds which no one can number. Each in its own time in spring shows its resurrection by shoots and taste and smell, by buds, flowers, and fruit. And the flowering plants cover their nakedness according to each one's fashion.

648.   Just so the minds and bodies of men at the great Spring will be nourished by the divine dew and spring up from their tombs. For at once around the dry bones will be arranged in order flesh and nerves, and cartileges and fibres, clothed with skin and adorned with hair.[1] And each one's spirit will return to him and each one's likeness to himself. For they will carry the appearance of each one's works on their heads, like fruits of sweetness and crops of delightfulness, with spices and oil and flowers and odors, with the splendor of abundant branches and leaves nurtured on water. This the Psalmist in prophecy sang: "He will become as a tree planted in water courses, which will give its fruit in its time, and its leaves will not fall;

and everything he does will go well for him [Ps. 1.3]." And again: "They will flower in the city of the Lord like the grass of the earth [Ps. 71.16]." And: "They will be blessed for ever [Ps. 36.26]."[2]

1. This follows the *Apocalypse of Peter*, James, *Apocryphal N.T.*, p. 512, rather than Ezekiel 37.
2. Cf. *Ad Diognetum*, XII: εἴσεσθε ὅσα παρέχει ὁ Θεὸς τοῖς ἀγαπῶσιν ὀρθῶς, οἱ γενόμενοι παράδεισος τρυφῆς, πάγκαρπον ξύλον εὐθαλοῦν ἀνατείλαντες ἐν ἑαυτοῖς, ποικίλοις καρποῖς κεκοσμημένοι.

649.   And indeed the spring that brings growth teaches men an example of the resurrection of the dead, because flowers and trees are adorned, and thorns too spring up—like buckthorn and thistle, nettle and plantago, butcher's broom and poisonous thorn, hawthorn and prickly thorn, darnel and cardoon and harmful dodder, and whatever is similar to these—they all grow each one in the likeness of its nature. And the useful flowers and buds of trees in the woods attain in spring to their own nature.

650.   The minds of men, which are plants of the garden and flowers of the beds of the Godhead, are able to bear in themselves of their own will the likenesses and examples of the leaves and flowers and odors and fruits.[1] For some produce bitter fruit, and some sweet; some produce fruit, and some thorns; some bring forth righteousness, and some sin; some become flowers in order to come to the honorable table of the king and be prepared as decorous crowns for the joy of the worthy, according to the prognostic saying of the Holy Spirit through the mouth of the prophet Isaiah: "Then will you become a garland of delight in the hand of the Lord and a crown of the kingdom in the hand of God. And they will call you 'my will' and your land 'the building of habitation.' [Is. 62.3–4]"

1. Cf. Cyril Jer., *Procat.*, 1: ἤδη τὰ νοητὰ ἄνθη συλλέγετε πρὸς πλοκὴν ἐπουρανίων στεφάνων and XIV 10, commenting on Song 2.11, on which see also Gregory of Nyssa, *In Cant*, V: ἄνθη δὲ τῆς ζωῆς ἡμῶν αἱ ἀρεταί. Cf. also Eusebius, *De Solemn. Pasch*: χωραὶ δὲ πᾶσαι, πρὸς τοῦ γεωργοῦ Λόγου τῆς κατὰ ψυχὴν γεωργίας (on γεωργία, cf. §520 note 1) τυχοῦσαι, τὰ ὡραῖα τῆς ἀρέτης ἄνθη βεβλαστήκασιν, and Cyril Alex., *Hom. Pasc.*, II 3: ἔδει καὶ τὴν ἀνθρώπου φύσιν χλοηροφορούσαις ταῖς ἀρούραις φιλονεικεῖν. καὶ τοῖς τῆς εὐσεβείας, ἵν᾽ οὕτως εἴπω, βλαστήμασι περιανθιζομένην ὁρᾶσθαι.

651.   The building is to be in the divine, brilliant, shining, perfect, and immutable city. For now all plants stand bound in their own nature; but only the plants which are men are able to change each one's disposition of nature into various forms. Now, just as they wish, they bury this plant in their souls and with the same are buried in tombs, that is death, the autumn not of grass but of men, which gathers them into barns. But the spring, not of grass or

trees but of men, produces these forms which you buried with you in the tomb. For if like a flower, or odiferous and sweet in righteousness, you sleep in the tomb, with you righteousness soon grows at your resurrection. But if you are buried with sins in the tomb of your name,[1] with you grow for your spring thorns at your resurrection, and they will grow up around you.

    1. In the tomb of your name: ի քո անուն (nom.) զերեզմանի (loc.); see also §706: they were so named by the Father who sent them, անուանեցան յառաքիչէ (nom.) ի Հաւրէ (abl.).

652.   Well then, hear the great John, how he preaches to the Jewish race of Abraham: "Make therefore for yourselves fruit worthy of repentance, and do not strike yourselves and say 'we have Abraham for father.' I say to you that God can raise up from these stones sons for Abraham [Mt. 3.8–9; Lk. 3.8]." Not that He deprived Abraham in any way of the patriarchate, but that they might be worthy sons of his and not unworthy. He cares for the useful, but for the useless grass and thorns what will He wish to do? He first dries up and parches that in which He finds no fruit.

653.   So consider the parable of the fig tree and see: the Lord came to the fig tree to find fruit on it and found none, for it was not yet the time for bearing fruit. And He cursed it: "From henceforth may no one eat fruit from you [Mk. 11.14]." Because all leaf-bearing and flower-bearing plants in [their own] time bear fruit, why then did He curse it because it was not the time of its fruit? Truly if there were any need, was He not able—who by his word alone commanded the world to bring forth the trees and make appear above the earth the multitude of cedars with each one's fruit, and all plants with each one's seed according to its kind—also to prepare for the needy the fruit of the tree at that time?

654.   But not unjustly did He bring this withering on the tree, as He was quick to say: "From the fig tree learn the parable [Mt. 24.32; Mk. 13.28]." The fig tree supports the example of fruitless men, for He will dry up the thorns of fruitless righteousness. Hear the great prophet, the forerunner John the Baptist: "So the axe is set to the root of the tree; every tree which will not produce good fruit, they will chop down and prepare as fuel for fire [Mt. 3.10]." And the prophet Isaiah: "Sinners will be like thorns, burned and rejected [Is. 33.12]." But tending for the grass with the living water in the kingdom, in that spring He will renew and nurture it; they will give fruit, one a hundredfold, and one two-hundredfold, and one three-hundredfold, that is, according to their labors the rewarding gifts of each one's illuminating faith.

655.   [*Birds in spring as examples of the resurrection*] Now in the spring which brings vegetation and flowers, which brings the renewal of the beauty of spring after the oldness of winter, the flying birds also know the time of each one's coming, just as in this regard the prophet Jeremiah spoke, adducing the circumstances of his own time for a likeness of the types of reproach, and indicated the future by saying: "Truly the swallow and turtledove and crane, birds of the field, know the time of each one's coming [Jer. 8.7]." For by the time of the spring and by each one's coming they show the time of the life of joy for men, in raising their voices, in singing, chirping, and in the building of their nests.

656.   The swallow loves man; when men see it, they know by it the green ears of corn of the growth of spring. The turtledove appears as loving its consort, it fills listening men with soft and sweet voice; constructing a nest of soft and gentle brush, it prepares a refuge for the eggs of its two-winged offspring.

657.   Similarly groups of cranes come in the spring time, they gather together and settle. They go flying high; with their airy wings and claws they tread their unsupported journey and fix their path. Becoming trumpets, raising a screeching cry, they arouse from sleep the works of laborers to the awakening of tasks profitable for men and hasten on the early [risers] to the oxen.

658.   The birds are nature's trumpets for the exhortation of virtue.[1] As the bee and ant [Prov. 6.6, 8] become teachers or reprovers for the wicked,[2] in the same way the birds are like a loud sounding trumpet to give warning to all of the Lord's coming in the resurrection of the dead. As in the hymns of inspired wisdom of the Song of Solomon he says: "The prisoners will awake at the voice of the bird [Eccl. 12.3–4]." And who are the prisoners, if not the gathered spirits [I Pet. 3.19], kept under the commandment, who are each to put on his own body, and according to their works to receive each his own dispensation, the fruit of each one's sown labor, just as we narrated above and shall further relate to you?[3]

    1. Cf. Origen, *Sel. in Jer.*, commenting on Jer. 8.7: τρυγὼν καὶ χελιδὼν ἀγροῦ στρουθία· οἱ συνετοὶ ἀκροαταὶ καὶ οἱ εἰς τὸ λέγειν κρείττονα ἱκανοὶ ἐφύλαξαν ἐν καιρῷ ποιεῖσθαι τὰς ἰδίας εἰσόδους, ὥστε τὸ λεγόμενον καθικνεῖσθαι τῶν ἀκουόντων, συντρεχούσης τῆς εἰσόδου τῆς χελιδόνος τῇ εἰσόδῳ τῆς τρυγόνος.
    2. Cf. Cyril Jer., *Cat.*, IX 13: ὅταν γάρ τις ἀργὴν ἔχῃ τὴν νεότητα, τότε ὑπὸ τῶν ἀλόγων ζώων διδάσκεται, διελεγχόμενος ὑπὸ τῆς θείας γραφῆς λεγούσης, he then quotes Prov. 6.6, 8.
    3. See also §650, 376 note 2.

659.   The blessed Apostles became heralding trumpets[1] to prepare all hearers to be ready to wait on the divine trumpet of the coming, that all might be

freely joined to that troop of birds,[2] whence the sound of the warning trumpet of the resurrection will blow, that they too may be worthy to acquire their wings and rise to the heights and see the Lord of heights without shame, that Lord who knows from afar, and who saves those who walk in tribulation, those who for righteousness' sake imposed trials of endurance on themselves for the love of God.

1. See §638 note 1.
2. See also §605–606.

660.   They have fulfilled the will of their Lord for they loved each other; for He so loved them that He gave Himself for his friends [Jn. 3.16; 15.13–14]. They received the command to love each other that thereby they might receive in themselves the promised grace.

661.   [*The Spirit gives the Apostles knowledge of the Trinity and understanding of the Old Testament prophecies*] Therefore they showed the love of hidden hearts openly by gathering with one accord in the upper room [Acts 2.1], where the Holy Spirit came and found them and made his dwelling in them that He might fill their desire which they had for the Lord and completely fulfill his promises. For He had said: "I go and I send the Comforter to you, who will come and have compassion on your hearts. For he glorifies me, for he receives from me and will tell you [Jn. 16.7, 14]." He will fulfill the love of the Trinity for unity in the unity[1] of those who have received from the Lord the commandment: "Go throughout the whole world and make disciples of all tongues and baptize them in the name of the Father, Son, and Holy Spirit. And teach them all to keep what I have spoken with you. And I am with you all the days of your lives until the end of the world [Mt. 28.19–20]."

1. See also §615.

662.   He gave them knowledge of the truth of the Trinity, the consubstantial lordship, the hypostasis of three Persons, that according to this pattern[1] they might make disciples of all men, and baptize them in the name of the Father, Son, and Holy Spirit.

1. Pattern: *աւրինակ*; cf. Introduction, p. 16.

663.   But because they received the power of the Holy Spirit, they also received the knowledge of all races and divided tongues that they might be able to teach the commands of the Godhead to men of all lands throughout

the universe, and the love of the Creator towards his creatures, and his humbling for our elevation, and the hope of immortality after the resurrection of the dead; and that this very immortality Himself, the power and Godhead of the Son [Rom. 1.20],[1] for our salvation came and put on humanity, especially for the renewal of all his creatures [II Cor. 5.17], that He might give this knowledge to all those on whom[2] these great blessings had been bestowed.[3]

1. The immortality, power, and Godhead: these three nouns in the Armenian version render the ἥ τε ἀίδιος αὐτοῦ δύναμις καὶ θειότης of Rom. 1.20.
2. On whom: *որ նոքա*, a Syriacism; see §269 note 1.
3. For the main themes of the redemption, here summarized, see Introduction, pp. 17–18.

664.   Then were fulfilled the predicted gifts of the prophecies through them: "In that day the captains of Juda will say in their hearts, 'let us go and find the inhabitants of Jerusalem in the Lord Omnipotent, their God' [Zech. 12.5]." For first from there they gave knowledge to their own race, and from Jerusalem they spread the worship of God throughout the whole universe.

665.   And because the Lord sprang from the whole race of Juda, therefore they were called captains of the house of Juda. This the Apostle Paul explained and elucidated, saying: "We are the captains of the mysteries of God [I Cor. 4.1]." The same Spirit truly says somewhere through the mouth of the prophet: "In that day, says the Lord, I shall place the captains of the house of Juda as torches burning in the midst of woods, and as lamps of fire in a sheaf, and they will consume all the peoples round about on your right and on your left [Zech. 12.6]." And further on he continues: "I shall pour on the house of David and on Jerusalem the spirit of grace and mercy, and they will return to me [Zech. 12.10]." The Holy Spirit Himself came and fulfilled this, who was sent by the Father and the Son. For as the Son was sent and came through the Father and the Spirit, so the Spirit was sent through the Father and the Son,[1] that the united and consubstantial hypostasis might be revealed.

1. On the procession of the Son and Spirit see Introduction, p.13.

666.   He came to the city of Jerusalem and found them together, and filled their hearts with a single power, that the sayings of the same Spirit's predictions through the mouth of the prophet[1] Joel might be fulfilled: "And it will come to pass after these latter days, says God, I shall pour of my Spirit on all flesh; and your sons and your daughters will prophesy, and your young men will see visions, and dreams will be revealed to your old

men, and on my servants and my handmaids I shall pour of my spirit, and they will prophesy. I shall give signs in heaven above and on earth below, blood and fire and tempest of smoke; the sun will turn to darkness and the moon to blood before the great and glorious day of the Lord will come. And it will come to pass that all who call on the name of the Lord will live [Joel 2.28–31; Acts 2.17–21]."

1. Prophet: ⟨Armenian⟩, abstract for substantive; see also §603 note 1.

667. [*The six days of creation and the six ages of the world*] And what is the saying "in the latter days"? Because when God made the creatures, He began on the first day and on the sixth completed everything through his omnipotent, effortless, tireless, and unslackening power; and He rested from all his works, and the seventh day He called rest [Gen. 2.2–3].

668. But when the Godhead saw that man had slipped, fallen, and lapsed from keeping the commandments—since he had not remained in virtue as He wished, but had fallen under punishment and correction in the judgment of righteousness, he had been seized by death from outside, he had been wounded and hurt, and had been submerged in cares, agitation, trouble, sweat of evils, restless trembling agitation—He did not go back on the word He had spoken, that is, the death which He had imposed.[1] But [according to] the time of creation which He had accomplished on the sixth day by reckoning, in the same fashion, in order that his greatness might be manifest, He measured six thousand years of time for the evils and sweat of toils and travail of the world. He measured a thousand years for each day according to the six first days, in which might take place the births and sowings of many, and the growth of creation.[2]

1. See also §283.
2. See also §366. This typology of the week has its origins in Judaism, where the seventh day represents the world to come. On the other hand, some early Christian writers saw the seven ages as representing the time of this world and the eighth day as the eternal rest, e.g., Barnabas, XV. But the tradition established by Irenaeus is followed here: the end of the temporal world will occur at the end of six thousand years, the seventh age is the age of rest, as §670 below; cf. Irenaeus, *Adv. Haer.*, V 28.3; Daniélou, *Theology*, pp. 396–404; and A. Luneau, *L'Histoire du salut, la doctrine des âges du monde*, Paris, 1964. For Armenian parallels, cf. Ps-Ełišē, *Matenagrutʿiwnkʿ*, pp. 254, 323–324, John Awjnecʿi, *De Officiis Ecclesiae, Opera*, p. 216.

669. In which also [might occur] the trials of the proving of the good, that He might effect the election to their recompense, the expectation of the liberal promises for the patience of the just in their tribulations, which are furnaces in a sabbath of years of toil; as the prophet cried to all, warned and said:

"A thousand years in the eyes of the Lord are as the passing of a single day [Ps. 89.4]."

670. For in the first [age] was the beginning, and in the sixth was the renewal which He effected by his own coming, and [when] He granted the descent of the Spirit. And in the same thousand will be the end, wherefore it is called the last, in which He is to come again, bringing with Him the mystery of the time of the seventh day, the rest and gifts without number and without measure. But because He Himself calls the seventh day of his own creation rest, therefore He commands the seventh day to be kept holy and delightful that all may know the day of delight by the resting of the Creator and observe it. For likewise in the seventh age He will give rest to the weary who have worked in the six ages of their time. Just as with Him they worked in their time, so also with Him they will rest in that long year without limit, and with Him will rejoice.

671. The Spirit of God in this sixth [age] appeared to fulfill his predicted promises, the sayings through the mouths of the prophets. The grace of the Holy Spirit was poured out in the last times and was spread over the great variety of peoples; it flowed with the great force of a multitude of waters.

672. They prophesied the hidden mysteries, they suddenly spoke all tongues, they enabled all races to rise together to the kingdom. They received the revelations of visions, they related to all the dispensation of the ineffable Word, they revealed the mystery of the eternal marriage of the Son of God,[1] that is the rising to adoption, and the rejoicing with the Father through the same Son and Spirit. They became *samandra*[2] to call every one to the pool of baptism, to wash off the filth of the satanic smoke, to put on robes of light[3] and enter the rejoicing of the marriage feast, where Christ the groom will rejoice with the bride, that is, with the just among men;[4] those who have suffered with Christ will also reign with Him [II Tim. 2.12].

1. See §441 note 1, and §672 note 4 below.
2. Samandra: ⟨Armenian⟩; cf. Pʿawstos, III 14: "those worthy and ready for his resurrection He chose, instructed, and sent as ⟨Armenian⟩ to invite us to the light of salvation," and John Awjnecʿi, *Opera*, p. 236.
3. See also §412 note 3.
4. The just as the bride of Christ: the church or the soul are the usual interpretations of the "bride"; cf. Lampe, *Lexicon*, s.v. νύμφη. Theodoret, *In Cant. Proem.*, speaks of the just souls: τὴν μὲν νύμφην ἐκ πολλῶν λέγει συγκεκροτημένην· ἡρμοσάμην γάρ, λέγει, ὑμᾶς, οὐ σέ, ὡς εἶναι δηλονότι τὰς εὐσεβεῖς καὶ τελείας ἐν ἀρετῇ ψυχάς. The *Teaching* here as elsewhere is free of parallels involving the mystical ascent of the soul to God; see §441 note 2.

673. The grace of the Spirit was revealed and poured out on all men, to make all worthy of the newly-bestowed, newly-given grace of the Godhead. On sons and daughters, old men and youths, servants and handmaids [Joel 2.28–29; Acts 2.17–18], He bestowed in common the grace of the Holy Spirit to remove the distinction so that "there be no distinction, neither of Jew nor Gentile, servant nor master, man nor woman, that all together may be worthy of Christ [Gal. 3.27]." And not just this, but He also opened the door of forgiveness to evil-workers, that even taxcollectors and harlots and murderous brigands, and indeed even his own crucifiers, might be evangelists of his working of salvation, of his bringing of forgiveness, and of his bestowing of the kingdom on all.

674. All were filled with the surge of the power of the Holy Spirit. They went throughout the world to give knowledge of the wonders of the Godhead to the tongues of many races, to teach the signs which He gave in heaven above and on earth below, according to the promise: "I shall give signs in heaven above and on earth below [Joel 2.30; Acts 2.19]." The sign to the heavenly beings [is that] they saw the Son of God incarnate above in heaven, and with Him the obedient fellowmen reigning with Him and joined and united to the ranks of the angels.[1]

   1. See also §414 and note 1.

675. But on earth below this is the sign, that men saw on earth the same unique Son of God, humbled and incarnate and on the cross, shedding his own blood, whence[1] the fire should be lit for the Apostles, and lamps should come into their tongues, to consume, burn up, and cast out the sins of all men.[2] For the Son of God Himself became a lamb [Jn. 1.29, 36], and was offered to his Father as a sacrifice of reconciliation on the cross [II Cor. 5.18], and He took away altogether the sins of the world.

   1. The fire of the Spirit from the cross is also mentioned in §585–586.
   2. Cf. Cyril Jer., *Cat.*, XVII 15, after quoting Acts 2.3–4: πυρὸς μετέλαβον, οὐ καταφλεκτικοῦ, ἀλλὰ σωτηριώδους πυρός, ἀφανίζοντος μὲν ἀκάνθας ἁμαρτίων, λαμπρύνοντος δὲ τὴν ψυχήν.

676. "Fire, he says, and blood and whirlwind of smoke [Joel 2.30]." Fire is the sanctifier, the Holy Spirit which has sanctified and sanctifies all, and they are sanctified by the blood of Christ. But those who will not wish to be sanctified, but cause the smoke to rise, have as the example of the revelation the nakedness of the conflagration. And his blood which He made their salvation, the same blood He will cause to be their destruction, which is the kingdom for the worthy. The sun turned to darkness[1] and the moon to blood [Joel 2.31; Acts 2.20] when they saw the Lord suffering on the cross.

For that was not the fearful day when He is to come, the day of judging and justifying all by judgment, but the day of salvation which justifies all by grace [Rom. 3.26].

   1. Joel 2.31 is referred to here, but cf. Amos 8.9, Zech. 14.6–7, Mt. 27.45, Mk. 15.33, Lk. 23.44–45.

677. For the sun and moon became heralds at that time. For the sun protested by darkening its light, by revealing to all the Lord on the cross; and being unable to bear that vision, it became dark, for it could not endure to see the indignities of the Lord.[1] The moon also showed marvels, for in a likeness, as in a mirror, it showed to all creatures the blood in itself, above in the heights—the salvation of all lands which will receive with their minds this blood as their kingdom.[2] But from those who despise it and will not come to such a giving of presents the moon will show the blood ever flowing from their bodies, which will produce the undying worms of continuous torments of destruction in hell.

   1. Cf. Cyril Jer., *Cat.*, IV 10: (Christ) ἐγνωρίσθη δὲ ὑπὸ τῆς κτίσεως ὅτι Θεὸς ἦν. ὁ γὰρ ἥλιος δεσπότην ἀτιμαζόμενον ἰδών, ἐξελίμπανεν τρέμων, οὐ φέρων τὴν θέαν.
   2. Cf. I Clement, XII 7: διὰ τοῦ αἵματος τοῦ κυρίου λύτρωσις ἔσται πᾶσιν τοῖς πιστεύουσιν καὶ ἐλπίζουσιν ἐπὶ τὸν Θεόν.

678. Therefore [the prophet] says: "I shall give signs in heaven above and on earth below [Joel 2.30; Acts 2.19]." The Lord below on earth on the cross, the luminaries in the heights as heralds to bring warning throughout the world: "Blood and fire and whirlwind of smoke [Joel 2.30]." Two things were intended: one, the gospel of life; the other, the terror of the threatened punishments. "The sun will turn to darkness and the moon to blood, before the great and glorious day of the Lord comes [Joel 2.31]." That is, he indicates the day of the coming of retribution, for that indeed is the great and glorious day.

679. Until that [day] comes whoever will invoke the name of the Lord will live by his grace [Acts 2.21; Rom. 10.13]. For God descended to earth and raised mankind to heaven[1] and joined these earthly creatures to the spiritual ones.[2] He renewed and rejuvenated creation once and for all. He opened the womb of baptism that they might be renewed and born again as children of the kingdom by baptism.[3] For the Apostles acted as the womb of baptism, they gave birth to all the world again and brought them to the innocence of children's unadulterated milk, to make them all sons of God and heirs of the salvation of Christ. As the blessed Paul said: "My children, of whom I travail in birth again until Christ be figured in you [Gal. 4.19]."

1. See also §381, and Athanasius, *De Incarnatione*, 54: αὐτὸς γὰρ ἐνηνθρώπησεν ἵνα ἡμεῖς θεοποιηθῶμεν. See also J. Gross, *La Divinisation du chrétien d'après les Pères grecs*, Paris 1938.
2. See also §414 note 1.
3. See also §412 and note 1.

680. [*The regeneration of the world by baptism*] They regenerated all the world for his sake, since they had received the power of Him, the Ancient of Days, who became a child.[1] As the divine wisdom sang previously: "The king will return to childhood [Ps. 102.5]." For the world returned to childhood since they saw the Lord made a child.

1. ֍ֆատուրքն մանկացաւ; see §363 note 2.

681. The Apostles brought forth the whole world afresh by water and the Spirit. They seasoned everyone by fire,[1] for they received the command: "Every one will be seasoned by fire [Mk. 9.49]." They were joined indissolubly to the Godhead and illumined. They made the world rejoice and showered [all] with gifts. For who have been once baptized into Christ have put on Christ and his Spirit [Gal 3.27]." From the spring of light they drank grace, and by its fearful signs, by its fiery power, they were seasoned and confirmed from the corruption of their impure sins of paganism into health of healing.

1. See also §639.

682. With dewy abundance and spiritual rain they fattened the abandoned fleshly lands of men's hearts. And they brought as a vast sea, peace, and as an abundant river, salvation, and as perpetually flowing fountains, greeting and faith, like cups of joy the love of the Godhead, like fire to plant awe and fear in the hearts of men. For in the same way as the smith takes iron and forges it, throwing it into the furnace of fire and making it glow at red heat, just so the just have been plunged into the furnace of righteousness and dyed in the hues and colors of the Holy Spirit.[1] They have put on Christ Himself in person and like a light have kindled the love of the Godhead in themselves. They have received power from on high, like strong workers they have hastened to fill all tongues with the seed of the service of God.

1. Cf. Chrysostom, *In Ep. I ad Cor. Hom.*, XL 2, though he has specifically baptism in mind: καὶ ὥσπερ σίδηρον ἢ χρυσὸν ἀναχωνεύων, καθαρὸν καὶ καινὸν ἄνωθεν ποιεῖς· οὕτω δὴ καὶ τὸ πνεῦμα τὸ ἅγιον ὥσπερ ἐν χωνευτηρίῳ τῷ βαπτίσματι ἀναχωνεῦον αὐτὴν (i.e., the soul) καὶ δαπανῶν τὰ ἁμαρτήματα, χρυσίου παντὸς καθαροῦ καθαρώτερον ἀποστίλβειν παρασκευάζει.

683. They became lighted torches[1] as on a candlestick,[2] that is, on the cross. And by the power of the same they shone and illumined the world; they expelled the obscurity of darkness from all men, to make them receptive to

the divine love. They spread through the world to become heralds of the truth. "For there is no opposition or difference, neither of Jew nor Gentile, neither of slave nor lord, neither of man nor woman; for all will be one in Christ [Gal. 3.27]."

1. Torches: ջրաջունլք, λύχνοι as Lk. 12.35.
2. Candlestick: աշտանակ, λυχνία as Lk. 8.16; cf. §581.

684. And many from the Jewish race, themselves also Apostles, true firm pillars,[1] and many of the Gentiles, took the example of these same upon themselves and bore it, many free and many slaves. The free ran from freedom to the kingdom through Him who as king was humbled [Philipp. 2.8] for their sake from his eminence; the slaves from slavery to freedom through Him who took the form of a servant [Philipp. 2.7] and freed all from servitude to darkness. Now the Jews, the fathers and prophets, handed down to their nation the earlier mystery. But when the promise of the gospel arrived [Acts 13.32], then the sun of righteousness [Mal. 4.2] arose clearly in their midst, who is Christ Himself.[2] And of those for whom eternal life is prepared, who believed in Him, some became preachers and apostles to the world, the first martyrs.[3] And there arose some also from the Gentiles; they swelled the ranks of believers and rows of martyrs, and filled the whole earth. For not only by men, but also by holy women the gospel of life was preached throughout the whole world.[4] For women also were blessed on account of the virgin birth which was of woman.[5]

1. True firm pillars: բուն սիւնք հաստատունք; cf. Irenaeus, *Adv. Haer.*, IV 21.3: duodecastylum firmamentum ecclesiae, and ps-Chrysostom, *In duodecim Apostolos Sermo*: τῆς ὀρθοδοξίας ἀμετάθετοι στῦλοι. The metaphor is very common.
2. See also §566 note 1.
3. Martyrs: վկայք, which has the same ambiguity as μάρτυς, witness or martyr.
4. Cf. Athanasius, *De Incarnatione*, 27: καὶ μελετῶσι κατ' αὐτοῦ (i.e., a martyr's death) ταῖς ἀσκήσεσιν, οἱ μόνον ἄνδρες, ἀλλὰ καὶ γυναῖκες· οὕτως ἀσθενὴς γέγονεν (i.e., death), ὡς καὶ γυναῖκας τὰς ἀπατηθείσας τὸ πρὶν παρ' αὐτοῦ νῦν παίζειν αὐτὸν ὡς νεκρὸν καὶ παρειμένον.
5. Cf. Origen, *In Luc. Hom.*, VIII: ὥσπερ ἤρξατο ἡ ἁμαρτιά ἀπὸ τῆς γυναικος . . . οὕτω καὶ τὰ ἀγαθὰ ἀπὸ τῶν γυναικῶν ἤρξατο (but Origen is referring only to Elisabeth and Mary as mothers of John and Jesus).

685. [*The Apostles divide the various nations between them*] The real pillars,[1] the Apostles, the companions,[2] who spoke all tongues, went throughout the world; they took lots[3] and divided up all races. He sent them and gave them power to work signs and miracles, to raise the dead, heal the sick, restore the infirm to health, make the lame to walk, open the eyes of the blind, restore hearing to the deaf and let the dumb speak, purify lepers and cast out all pains and torments, put to flight the demons, the enemies of

mankind, and trample under foot Satan, the guardian of the sins of the error of mankind; to inform everyone of the worship of God and remove errors, to confirm all races in believing the commands of the Creator.

   1. Real pillars: ﬓﬔﬖ ﬗ﬘﬙﬚﬛, as P̔awstos, IV 4. See also §684 note 1.

   2. Companions: ﬓﬔﬗ﬘﬙﬚﬛, which has primarily the connotation or a couple or pair; the apostles are enumerated in pairs in §686.

   3. They took lots: ﬓﬔﬗ﬘﬙﬚﬛. The dividing of the various countries among the apostles is an important feature of the apocryphal Acts; cf. Acts of Thomas 1, Acts of Andrew, and Matthias 1. See also Eusebius, *H.e.*, III 1.1: τῶν δὲ ἱερῶν τοῦ σωτῆρος ἡμῶν ἀποστόλων τε καὶ μαθητῶν ἐφ᾽ ἅπασαν κατασπαρέντων τὴν οἰκουμένην, Θωμᾶς μέν, ὡς ἡ παράδοσις περιέχει, τὴν Παρθίαν εἴληχεν.

686. The heads of the Christian band of crusading[1] Apostles were Peter and Andrew, James and John, Philip and Bartholomew, Thomas and Matthew, James and Simon, Thaddaeus and Barsabbas, Matathias and James, Mark and Luke, Paul and Barnabas;[2] and still others who were like these, who were seventy more,[3] who received power from the Lord to walk on the viper and asp and to trample the power of the enemy [Ps. 90.13; Mk. 16.17–18; Lk. 10.19], to become the light of the world [Mt. 5.14], and season and salt [Mt. 5.13; Mk. 9.50] the disorder of the evil of men's ignorance with the salt of the Holy Spirit of the Godhead. Like brave champions, like valiant battle-loving soldiers,[4] they threw themselves into the struggle of virtue. They bore afflictions of tortures, that through their labors and efforts, by the strength of their patience, not as a gift but for their [just] reward, they might gain for themselves the kingdom of God through the struggles of their combats. When the brave soldiers[4] clothed themselves with faith and love [I Thess. 5.8], like breastplates of armour against which the arrows of deceit of the enemy's intrigue can work nothing, they put on the hope of salvation as an inviolable headpiece, and hastening throughout the world they despoiled all nations. They received also the examples of patience already given and passed them on to others by letter.[5] The lives of their predecessors they held as examples: "Take as an example, brethren, the long suffering of the prophets who spoke in the name of the Lord [James 5.10]," and: "You have heard the patience of Job and seen the end of the Lord [James 5.11]."

   1. Crusading: ﬓﬔﬖﬗ, σταυροφόρος,; cf. the group of Maštoc̔'s disciples described by Koriun, III 1, as the ﬓﬔﬖﬗ ﬘﬙﬚﬛. Cf. Eusebius, *Vita Const.*, II, title to ch. 9.

   2. The apostles are mentioned in pairs, as Mk. 6.7 and Lk. 10.1; cf. Chrysostom, *In Mat. Hom.*, XXXII 2, where he discusses the pairing (συζυγία) of the apostles. The list in the *Teaching* does not follow exactly any of those in the N.T. but is closest to Mt. 10.2–4 The title "apostle" is never explicitly applied to the seventy in the gospels but was reserved for the twelve; this exclusive usage was soon dropped.

   3. See §503 note 1.

   4. Soldiers: ﬓﬔﬖﬗ﬘, the word means a "brave soldier" and is also used of martyrs.

   5. See also §699 note 4.

687. For the Lord taught them the same patience: "Blessed will you be when they will insult and persecute and put you to death for my sake. Rejoice and be glad, for your reward is great in heaven [Mt. 5.11–14]." And He gave an example: "Likewise they persecuted the prophets who were before you," and: "You are the salt of the earth and the light of the world." And He gave them Himself as an example, who in Himself had fulfilled everything, just as they showed others: "We have also seen the Lord Himself in person [Acts 9.27; I Jn. 1.2]."

688. They spread throughout all nations to give knowledge of the Godhead, to inform all of the Godhead, as the prophet previously sang, as if by foreknowledge from them,[1] by the prediction of the Holy Spirit: "Hear this, all nations, and pay heed, all you who dwell in the world; the births of the earth and the sons of men at once great and poor [Ps. 48.2–3]." And thus they were spread through the world and divided into all tongues, to which bore witness the visiting Jews from all parts: "We hear in our own language [Acts 2.8]," who had gathered and saw the Apostles in one place before their scattering over all the world.

   1. See also §609 and note 1.

689. Some took their own Jewish region and taught while others spread over all the world. Some to the Medes, some to the Parthians, some to Chuzastan, and some to Mesopotamia; one to the region of the Gamri, one to Pontus, one to Asia, one to Phrygia, one to Pamphylia, one to Egypt, one to the land of the Indians, one to the region of the Libyans, one to the region of the Cyrenians, one to the regions of the Dalmatians, one to the region of the Spaniards, one to the region of Azot, one to the region of Thrace, one to Laconia, one to Cappadocia, one to Bithynia.[1] No one is able to count or reckon, but "their word went throughout the whole earth and their speech as far as the ends of the world [Ps. 18.5; Rom. 10.18]."

   1. This list is a composite of Acts 2.9–11, I Peter 1.1, and other references in the Acts and apocryphal Acts, but with curious omissions, as Crete and Gaul. On the various lands visited by the apostles, cf. Eusebius, *H.e.*, III 1, or Gregory Naz., *Or.*, XXXIII 11.

690. Thus they preached throughout the world "to illumine all men who were to come into the world [Jn. 1.9]," to give repentance of salvation to all, to wash all men and deliver them from the bonds of darkness by baptism, to stamp all nations as the band of Christ, to make the Spirit of God dwell

in men's hearts, to unite and join them to the love of the Son of God, that the heart of all might cry as one, and to unite all the world in saying: "Abba, Father [Rom. 8.15; Gal. 4.6]"; that the name of bondage might be taken away, and the name of adoption be placed on them by the grace of Christ; to enable them to eat the flesh of the Son of God and drink the life-giving blood,[1] that thereby they might bring all the world into the inheritance of Christ, to become heirs of God and fellow heirs of Christ.

1. See also §432 and note 3, and in the *History*, §81, 84, 834.

691. So they strengthened them in the intentions of their will by their hope in Christ. Hear them and believe in the truth of the gospel of your salvation; believe in them and be baptized into the Spirit of the gospel of holiness, who is the guarantee of our inheritance to salvation and admission to the praise of his glory [Eph. 1.14].

692. They ran throughout the whole world, to the ends of the earth, in order to complete the preaching of the word of life. Hosts of angels, spiritual and fiery,[1] gathered for the comforting of the Apostles, for they were their companions in both their journeys [Acts 27.23][2] and bonds of imprisonment [Acts 5.19; 12.7; 16.26], whence by the grace of God they delivered the Apostles. They were guided by the commanding Holy Spirit to every city and country to make the faith of Christ universally known; and we also, though lesser, will carry the truth of the more excellent through the guidance of the commanding Holy Spirit.

1. See also §262 note 2.
2. Cf. Origen, *In Num. Hom.*, XI 4: ipsi apostoli angelis utantur adiutoribus ad explendum praedicationis suae munus et opus evangelii consummandum.

693. For so He commanded—to teach all nations [Mt. 28.19]. He sent them through the world, inviting all the Gentiles to obedience to the faith, to preach the gospel without fear by the guidance of the Holy Spirit. They freely preached the kingdom of God and taught about the Lord Jesus Christ with all unrestrained and unimpeded frankness [Acts 4.31].

694. [*The preaching of the Apostles*] After this the Christian band of the Apostles, who by the grace of the Holy Spirit had advanced through all regions under heaven, with all signs and miracles and power of grace, made warning to each part, and announced the word of life, and encouraged the Christians with the hope of the resurrection. For by their graceful words and deeds each decision fixed by the command of the Holy Spirit was revealed. This Paul indicated: "From Jerusalem to Illyricum it has fallen to

me to fulfill the gospel of Christ [Rom. 15.19]." And again: "Who wrought Peter for circumcision has strengthened me for the Gentiles [Gal. 2.8]."

695. So the divinely appointed time stands at hand for every one to attain the Christ-given salvation.[1] Just as Paul replied to the Athenians: "God winked at the times of ignorance but now commands all men to repent [Acts 17.30]," similarly Peter also in his Catholic epistle indicates: "The time past was sufficient for the will of the Gentiles to be done, but from now they will live according to the will of God [I Pet. 4.2–3]."

1. See also §535–536.

696. But not at once and suddenly according to the power of the Holy Spirit did they extend the newly-bestowed, unaccustomed wonders, but at first very gently, according to the condition of the world,[1] they spoke in parables and with skill.[2] Therefore Paul revealed: "I have fed you with milk in Christ and not solid food, for you were not able to bear it [I Cor. 3.2]," just as was previously ordained by the Mosaic laws of the all-wise God, first by sacrifices and sabbaths and establishing of festivals; later He separated them from these and showed them better things by the prophets who arose, by whom He said: "I am sated with your sacrifices [Is. 1.11]." And: "Not on account of your offerings do I reprimand you [Ps. 49.8]." But: "Offer to God a sacrifice of blessing [Ps. 49.14]." And: "What does the Lord seek from you, O man, except to do righteousness and justice, and to be prepared to follow the Lord? [Micah 6.8]"

1. See also §309 note 1, 698–699.
2. They spoke in parables and with skill: *առակարանութեամբ* (cf. §407) *եւ արուեստաբանութեամբ*; cf. Koriun, I 2. On the influence of Koriun on Agathangelos see Introduction, pp. 36–37.

697. The same canon was observed by the Apostles. For the law and interpreters of the law[1] of the one God were known as the first and the second.[2] This the Lord revealed, saying: "Now the word is true, that it is one who sows and another who reaps. I have sent you to reap what you have not worked. Others have labored and you have entered into their labors. For he who sows and he who reaps will rejoice together [Jn. 4.37–38]."

1. Interpreters of the law: *օրինադպաnու* ; cf. Eusebius, *Vita Const.*, 17, where he calls the apostles νομοθέτας καὶ νομοδιδασκάλους.
2. The phrase refers to the prophets and the apostles who were their heirs, with perhaps overtones of the distinction between the law of the letter and of the spirit; cf. Origen, *In Gen. Hom.*, IX 1: Primas tabulas legis in littera confregit Moyses et abiecit; secundam legem in spiritu suscepit, et sunt firmiora secunda quam prima. But here the *Teaching* is following Chrysostom, *In Jo. Hom.*, XXXIV 2: οἱ προφῆταί εἰσιν οἱ σπείραντες· ἀλλ' οὐκ αὐτοὶ ἐθέρισαν, ἀλλ' οἱ ἀπόστολοι, as proved by the following quotation. See also §609 note 1.

698. They were instructed in the art of preaching by the Savior of all, Christ, who "began to do and to teach [Acts 1.1]." For Christ Himself did not then in the beginning speak the highest and most incomprehensible things, but first with humble and symbolic[1] words and healing of pains informed and instructed them. To them He said: "If I have spoken earthly things to you and you have not believed, how will you believe if I speak heavenly things? [Jn. 3.12]" But after that, as to perfected people, He taught the truth very frankly and sublimely. In the same way the Apostles also worked in barbarian regions.

1. Symbolic: ꭓꭔꮃꮮꮃꮯꮃꮲ; see Introduction, p. 16.

699. Therefore by synodal command [Acts 15.6 ff][1] the Apostles handed down[2] to the neophyte Gentiles the easiest things and at first kept them away from food of idols and fornication and corpses and blood [Acts 15. 20]. But when they had expounded to every one and borne witness by the Holy Spirit to the Jews and Gentiles about the hopeful faith in the Lord Jesus Christ—as Peter earlier said to the Jews: "We are his witnesses, and the Holy Spirit whom God gave to those who obey him [Acts 5.32]"; but Paul with fearful care at Miletus before the unanimous gathering recalled the commands of tradition[3] and vowed: "I was not afraid of profitable things in public and at home to give witness to Jews and Gentiles of repentance to God and of faith in our Lord Jesus Christ [Acts 20.20]"; which he affirmed, saying: "I give witness to you on this day, that I am pure from the blood of all. For I have not shunned from declaring to you the entire will of God [Acts 20.26]"—then they came to blessedness and attained the mind of the Holy Spirit, to recall the divinely spoken and divinely given teaching of the Only-begotten of God, that they might set it in writing[4] and establish it for all nations and times to come under the heavens, "to illuminate all men who were to come into the world [Jn. 1.9]." Especially moved by the influence of the Spirit, they succeeded in this undertaking. It was this that the Savior of all indicated in his teaching to the holy disciples, when saying: "I have still much to tell you, but you are unable to bear it now. When the Spirit of truth comes, he will lead you with all truth [Jn. 16.12]."

1. Synodal command: the council at Jerusalem (Acts 15) is specifically referred to here, but cf. the title of the *Constitutiones Apostolorum*: διαταγαὶ τῶν ἁγίων ἀποστόλων (or διατάξεις) and ibid., VIII 4: ἅμα τοίνυν ὑπάρχοντες ἡμεῖς οἱ δεκαδύο τοῦ κυρίου ἀπόστολοι τάσδε τὰς θείας ὑμῖν ἐντελλόμεθα διατάξεις περὶ παντὸς ἐκκλησιαστικοῦ τύπου.
2. Handed down: ꮃꮮꮃꮲꮮꮣ; cf. the title ἀποστολικὴ παράδοσις.
3. See also note 2 above.
4. The gospels are intended here, in §700 the epistles; cf. Justin, *I Apologia*, LXVI 3: οἱ μὲν γὰρ ἀπόστολοι ἐν τοῖς γενομένοις ὑπ' αὐτῶν ἀπομνημονεύμασιν, ἃ καλεῖται εὐαγγέλια, οὕτως παρέδωκαν.

700. [*The writing of the gospels and epistles*] He made allusion to his life-giving gospel: "This gospel of the kingdom will be preached throughout the whole world for a witness to all Gentiles, and then the end will come [Mt. 24.14]." The Apostles, the witnesses of the same truth, taking from the holy gospel and prophetic writings, composed inspired and apostolic letters, that they might be kept as everlasting canons for those under instruction, and having especial regard to the perfection of the churches they added to them afterwards by speaking more things orally.[1] As Paul made clear, saying: "We speak wisdom with the perfected, the wisdom not of this world and not of the princes of this world who come to nought, but we speak the wisdom of God in a hidden mystery, which before the ages God ordained for our glory, which none of the princes of this world knew. For if they had known, they would not have crucified the Lord of glory [I Cor. 2.6–8]." They were illumined and adorned with wisdom, saying: "We have not received the spirit of this world, but the Spirit which is from God, that by it we may know what has been granted us by God [I Cor. 2.13]."

1. Cf. Chrysostom, *In Ep. II ad Thess. Hom.*, IV 2, after quoting II Thess. 2.15: ἐντεῦθεν δῆλον ὅτι οὐ πάντα δι' ἐπιστολῆς παρεδίδοσαν, ἀλλὰ πολλὰ καὶ ἀγράφως· ὁμοίως δὲ κἀκεῖνα καὶ ταῦτά ἐστιν ἀξιόπιστα.

701. Then those who had seen God and were filled and imbued with the Spirit took the divine gospel and established it in writing[1] and defined the one tradition as four gospels;[2] not elaborating it with incompatible material, but by the all-knowing Spirit of God relating the single truth of the commands of Christ, which one can see foreordained in the prophets. For what the great Moses by the grace of the Spirit previously spoke in parables as due to occur, the same was repeated with inspired words by the prophets who came later, by whom was revealed the power of the bountiful Spirit.

1. Cf. Irenaeus, *Adv. Haer.*, III 5.1: Traditione igitur quae est ab apostolis sic se habente in ecclesia et permanente apud nos, revertamur ad eam quae est ex scripturis ostensionem eorum qui evangelium conscripserunt apostolorum.
2. Cf. Irenaeus, *Adv. Haer.*, III 11.8: ὁ Λόγος . . . ἔδωκεν ἡμῖν τετράμορφον τὸ εὐαγγέλιον, ἑνὶ δὲ πνεύματι συνεχόμενον, and Clement Alex., *Str.*, VII 17: μία γὰρ ἡ πάντων γέγονε τῶν ἀποστόλων ὥσπερ διδασκαλία, οὕτως δὲ καὶ ἡ παράδοσις.

702. [*The Trinity, the keystone of Christian truth*] Rising then on the wings of the Spirit, the evangelists of Christ passed through the heavens and were raised over the altars of heaven. There above, at the divine throne, they were informed by the Holy Spirit of the profundities of God [I Cor. 2.10], and they learned of the only-begotten Son in the bosom of his Father [Jn. 1.18].[1] And He established them in such exactness of truth with knowledge of Himself, as also the Father knows his Only-begotten. By Him they

were illumined and received the ineffable to declare: "From the beginning was the Word, and the Word was with God and the Word was God. He was from the beginning with God. Everything was made through Him, and without Him nothing was made [Jn. 1.1–3]." Do you see how he omitted no details of the wisdom of the knowledge of God, but at once brings the totality by saying: "He was from the beginning, and He was with God and He was God, and everything was made through Him?" And now the essential personality of the Son has been made known, and his consubstantial and divine honor and his omnipotent power.

1. Cf. Chrysostom, *In Jo. Hom.*, II 4, commenting on John 1.1: ὅρα γοῦν εὐθὺς ἐκ προοιμίων ποῦ τὴν ψυχὴν πτερώσας καὶ τὴν διανοίαν ἀνήγαγε τῶν ἀκουόντων . . . ὑπὲρ τοὺς ἀγγέλους χειραγωγεῖ καὶ ὑπεράνω τῶν Χερουβὶμ καὶ τῶν Σεραφίμ, καὶ ὑπὲρ τοὺς θρόνους, καὶ ὑπὲρ τὰς ἀρχάς, καὶ ὑπὲρ τὰς ἐξουσίας, καὶ πάσης ἁπλῶς ἐπεκείνα κτίσεως ὁδοιπορεῖν ἀναπείθει.

703. At first the all-loving Christ made his beloved disciples aware of God by innumerable wonders, that they might be instructed and informed of the beauty and form and consubstantial nature of the three perfect Persons, for not by the wisdom of their own weak intelligence would they have attained the inscrutable knowledge of God.[1] But God Himself in his benevolence revealed from heaven: "This is my beloved Son, hear Him [Mt. 17.5; Mk. 9.7; Lk. 9.35]." To Him Peter bore witness in his Catholic epistle: "We did not follow elaborated fables when we showed you the power and coming of our Lord Jesus Christ, but we ourselves were eyewitnesses of his greatness. For He received from God and from the Father glory and honor, when there came a voice from the majesty of glory: 'this is my beloved Son with whom I am pleased.' This voice we heard coming from heaven, we who were with Him on the holy mountain [II Pet. 1.16–18]."

1. See also §309 note 1, 356 note 2.

704. In the same way the Son also came and revealed the greatness of the Father: "I came not to fulfill my own will but the will of Him who sent me [Jn. 6.38]." With abundant indications in his teaching, He extolled the glory of the Father and revealed his consubstantial will: "The words which I speak with you I do not speak by myself, but the Father who dwells in me, He works these deeds [Jn. 14.10]." In the same way He spoke concerning the Holy Spirit: "The Spirit of truth will lead you with all truth. For He will not speak anything by Himself, but what He hears He will speak, and He will show you what is to come. He will glorify me, for He will receive from mine and tell you. Everything that the Father has is mine. Therefore I said that He will take from mine and tell it you [Jn. 16.13–15]."

705. See the unity and identity of will and truth. See how He clearly showed and revealed the essence of the three Persons, saying: "Not of Himself will the Holy Spirit speak, because He will take of mine and tell you. For everything that the Father has is mine." See the Father, perfect; the Son, true; and the Spirit, certain. He indicated the indivisible[1] and consubstantial nature[2] of the divine hypostasis, saying: "I came from the Father and entered into the world [Jn. 16.28]." Similarly also about the true Spirit: "The Spirit of truth who comes from the Father [Jn. 15.26]."

1. Indivisible: անբռշական, ἀμερής.
2. Nature: պայման, lit. condition.

706. He decrees concerning the unity of the consubstantial Trinity, saying: "God is a Spirit [Jn. 4.24]." He shows concerning Himself and the true Spirit their inseparability[1] from the Father. For although the Apostles were so named by the Father who sent them,[2] yet united with Him and without separation they fulfilled their consubstantial[3] task, saying: "No one has ascended to heaven except He who descended from heaven—the Son of man who is in heaven [Jn. 3.13]." Do you see that He descended to earth and is in heaven? To Him the evangelist John bore witness: "No one has ever seen God; but the only-begotten Son who is in the bosom of the Father, He has told of Him [Jn. 1.18]." Consider what he says: "Who is in the bosom of the Father, He has told of Him." For Him whom they saw beside themselves, the same they knew to be in the bosom of the Father. O wonderfully gifted ones, who have acquired the knowledge of God[4]—what majesty have they now attained!

1. Inseparability: անբաժանութիւն; cf. §385 note 1.
2. See §651 note 1.
3. Consubstantial: միասնական, a frequent term; cf. Introduction, p. 13, but elsewhere used of the relation between the three Persons of the Trinity.
4. Ո զարմանալի պարգեւելոցն եւ աստուածացելոց միխակելոցն, a genitive of exclamation, a Greek not an Armenian construction; cf. Jensen, *Altarmenische Grammatik*, p. 190.

707. Similarly also it is of the true Spirit that one must understand the saying: "The Spirit of truth who comes from the Father [Jn. 15.26]." He comes from, yet is not separated, He flows forth and is not consumed.[1] And once and for all He speaks of the really true, united equality:[2] "I am in the Father and the Father in me. And who has seen me has seen my Father [Jn. 10.38; 14.9–11]," not because any boundaries enclose the Divinity, or that the Father is in heaven and the only-begotten Son and the true Spirit on earth, by whom everything is filled, and He is in all and over all.

1. On the procession of the Holy Spirit see Introduction, p. 13.
2. Equality: մասշբան, equilibrium, ἰσορροπία.

708. Concerning all this He preached and taught his disciples and invited them to the guidance of the Holy Spirit. To them He also said: "I have many more things to tell you, but you are not able to bear them now. But when the Spirit of truth comes, He will inform you and lead you with all truth [Jn. 16.12–13]." Concerning this Peter also indicated, receiving the Holy Spirit: "I remember the word of the Lord which He said: 'John baptized in water, but you will be baptized by the Holy Spirit.' [Acts 11.16]" And [he said this] not only to them but also to those who would come to God through them.

709. Just so the blessed Luke at the beginning of his gospel declared: "Many have intended to set forth in order the story concerning the things which have been established among us, as they who were from the beginning eyewitnesses and servants of the Word have handed down to us [Lk. 1.1–2]." From them also he set down the gospel of the Lord. He also appeared to Paul in a most wonderful and awesome inspiration, concerning which he himself in wonder narrates: "Whether with the body or without the body I know not. But I know he was elevated to the third part[1] of heaven and to paradise and heard ineffable words [II Cor. 12.3–4]." Concerning which he also says: "I have not received from a man or heard of any one but from the revelation of Jesus Christ [Gal. 1.12]." He also boasts of being an eyewitness: "I saw the Lord Jesus Christ with my own eyes [I Cor. 9.1]."

1. The third part of heaven: this is not the text of Paul, but the interpretation followed by Eznik in his refutation of Marcion, *De Deo*, §380.

710. But although he was sent by Christ with such high honor and glorious signs, yet he rendered obedience to the twelve, writing to the Corinthians: "For I formerly handed this down to you, which I myself had received [I Cor. 15.3]." Similarly also to the Hebrews: "How shall we be saved if we neglect such salvation, which took its beginning at being spoken by the Lord, and was confirmed for us by those who heard? [Heb. 2.3]" By which it is clear that the grace of the one power illuminated all, and they were inspired for a witness to the single truth. For Paul says: "We have all drunk the one Spirit [I Cor. 12.13]." Whereby they began to noise abroad with a voice that reached to heaven the honor of the consubstantial glory of the Only-begotten, with the prophetic words which the theologian[1] had spoken previously: "In the beginning was the Word, and He was with God and He was God, and everything was made through Him [Jn. 1.1–3]." Luke also speaks concerning the Apostles: "In the beginning we were eyewitnesses and servants of the Word [Lk. 1.2]." The same again John also says in his Catholic epistle: "Who was from the beginning, of Him we heard, on Him we looked, and our hands touched the Word of life [I Jn. 1.1]."

1. The theologian: աստուածաբանութե; cf. Origen, *Fr. in Jo.*, 1: ὁ θεολόγος γράφει, then he quotes Jn. 1.1: or Athanasius, *C. Gentes*, 42: ὁ θεολόγος ἀνήρ.

711. "And the Word was with God [Jn. 1.1]." Saying this he bore witness to the saying of the Lord: "Father, give me the glory which I had with you before the creation of the world [Jn. 17.5, 24]." Paul also refers to this: "He considered it no usurpation to be equal with God [Philipp. 2.6]." Similarly John also in his Apostolic letter: "Who was with the Father and appeared to us [I Jn. 1.2]." "And the Word was God [Jn. 1.1]." As Christ also said: "What the Father has, I also have [Jn. 16.15]." Again John in his letter says: "He is the true God [I Jn. 5.20]." Likewise Paul: "In the appearance of the glory of the great God and our Savior Jesus Christ, who gave Himself for us [Tit. 2.13–14]."

712. So in unity and spontaneously by our own will "let us come to the faith and knowledge of the Son of God, to a perfect man and the measure of the stature of the fullness of Christ [Eph. 4.13]," because Christ gave his teaching intending it for the audience of many, by which command He invited all nations of the earth, through the forthright teaching: "Go to all the Gentiles, teach and baptize them in the name of the Father and the Son and the Holy Spirit [Mt. 28.19]."

713. It was with particular solicitude for the many[1] that He wished to reveal his glorious coming, how He will come to be revealed to the patient for their long-suffering and to his hopeful servants. So must one understand the first coming of Christ and the descent of the divine Spirit on the tenth day at the feast of Pentecost [Acts 2.1]. No dwelling was necessary for the stay of the only-begotten Son of God in his ascension to the height of heaven, or for the Holy Spirit descending on the company of the Apostles, by whom heaven and earth are filled. But thus God in his benevolence wished, that after a wait of ten days for the Apostles, He might call to the upper room the gift-bearing Spirit, the Comforter of all. And everywhere He provides opportunities to men for [working] his own benevolence, that through these small opportunities offered from above He may become a ready dispenser of infinite rewards.[2] And what truly more measureless and immeasurable than this will there be, when rising from heaven in the glory of the Father, He will come, and before all the host of his angels take by hand each of his beloved and bring them to Himself, and give them the enjoyment of eternal life in his divine dwelling?[3]

1. The many, as in §712, means the Gentiles.
2. See also §270 and note 1.
3. See also §605.

714. Because God, who lacks nothing, arranges his kingdom for his beloved as regions of paradise, a wonderful dwelling near to God, there to settle and install near Himself for their delight all worthy rational creatures, spiritual and bodily, therefore the Savior of all gave the gospel to his disciples and encouraged them: "Where I am there will you be also, and at all times you will see my glory [Jn. 17.24]." And the other more sublime [saying]: "In that day you will know that I am in the Father, and you in me and I in you [Jn. 14.20]." In this same respect it is most profitable to mention the saying: "What eye has not seen, nor ear heard, and has not fallen into the heart of man, God has prepared for those who love Him [I Cor. 2.9]," and the saying of the blessed Paul: "Thanks be to Christ for his ineffable gifts [II Cor. 9.15]."

715. The end of the teaching of Saint Gregory which was granted him by God, to illuminate through faith and baptism the hearts which were in darkness of this land Armenia. And he made them all firm believers in Christ, that they might praise the holy names of the Father, Son, and Holy Spirit.

Abbreviations

A.F. I and II	*The Apostolic Fathers*, ed. K. Lake, Loeb Classical Library, 24, 25, Cambridge, Mass. 1912, 1913	G.C.S.	*Die Griechischen Christlichen Schriftsteller der ersten drei Jahrhunderte*, Leipzig
Bihlmeyer-Schneemelcher	*Die Apostolischen Väter*, Neuarbeitung der Funkschen Ausgabe von K. Bihlmeyer, 2te auflage von W. Schneemelcher, Erster Teil, Tübingen 1956	Jaeger	W. Jaeger, *Gregorii Nysseni Opera*, Leiden
		J.T.S.	*Journal of Theological Studies*, Oxford
		L.B.	R. A. Lipsius and M. Bonnet, *Acta Apostolorum Apocrypha*, 2 vols, Leipzig 1891–1903
C.S.C.O.	*Corpus Scriptorum Christianorum Orientalium*, Louvain	P.G.	*Patrologiae Cursus completus, Series graeca*, ed. J.-P. Migne, Paris
		S.C.	*Sources chrétiennes*, Paris
		S.D.	*Studies and Documents*, London and Philadelphia
		T.S.	*Texts and Studies*, Cambridge

Sources

Armenian Sources

Agatʿangełos, *History = Patmutʿiwn Hayocʿ*, ed. K. Tēr Mkrtčʿean and St. Kanayeancʿ, Tiflis 1909, text reprinted without apparatus in *Łukasean Matenadaran*, 15, Tiflis 1914.

———— *Teaching = History* §259–715.

Ankanon Girkʿ, 3 vols., Venice 1896, 1898, 1904.

Casey, *Armenian Version* = R. P. Casey, *The Armenian Version of the Pseudo-Athanasian Letter to the Antiochenes and of the Expositio Fidei*, S.D. 15, London 1947.

Ełišē, *History = Vasn Vardanacʿ ew Hayocʿ Paterazmi*, ed. E. Tēr Minasean, Erevan 1957.

———— *On the Passion = I čʿarčʿarans Teaṙn*, in *Matenagrutʿiwnkʿ*, Venice 1859.

———— Elisée Vardapet, *Questions et réponses sur la Genèse*, publié par N. Akinian, traduit par S. Kogian, Vienna 1928.

Ephrem, *Commentaire de l'Evangile concordant; version arménienne*, ed. L. Leloir, *CSCO*, 137, 145, Louvain 1953, 1954.

———— *Commentary on Genesis*, in *Matenagrutʿiwnkʿ*, I, Venice 1836.

Eznik, *De Deo*, ed. L. Mariès and Ch. Mercier, *Patrologia Orientalis*, XXVIII 3, 4, Paris 1959.

Girkʿ Tʿłtʿocʿ, ed. Y. Izmireancʿ, Tiflis 1901.

Irenaeus, *Dem.* = *Des heiligen Irenäus Schrift zum Erweise der apostolischen Verkündigung*, ed. K. Ter-Mekerttschian and E. Ter Minassiantz, *Texte und Untersuchungen*, Band 31, Heft 1, Leipzig 1907.

John Awjnecʿi, *Opera*, Venice 1834.

John Mandakuni, *Čaṙkʿ*, Venice 1860.

Kanonagirkʿ = Kanonagirkʿ Hayocʿ, I, ed. V. Hakobyan, Erevan 1964.

Koriun, *Koriwn, Varkʿ S. Maštocʿi*, ed. N. Akinian, *Texte und Untersuchungen der altarmenischen Literatur*, Band 1, Heft 1, Vienna 1952.

Knikʿ Hawatoy, ed. K. Tēr Mkrtčʿean, Ējmiacin 1914.

Łazar, *History = Patmutʿiwn Hayocʿ*, ed. G. Tēr Mkrtčʿean and St. Malxasean, Tiflis 1904.

———— *Letter*, printed in the above edition, pp. 185–204.

Moses Dasxurancʿi = Moses Kałankatuacʿi, *Patmutʿiwn Ałuanicʿ Ašxarhi*, *Łukasean Matenadaran*, 8, Tiflis 1912. English translation by C. J. F. Dowsett, *The History of the Caucasian Albanians by Movsēs Dasxurancʿi*, London Oriental Series, 8, Oxford 1961.

Moses Xorenacʿi, *Patmutʿiwn Hayocʿ*, *Łukasean Matenadaran*, 10, Tiflis 1913.

Pʿawstos Buzandacʿi, *Patmutʿiwn Hayocʿ*, Venice 1933.

Timotheus Älurus' *Widerlegung*, ed. K. Ter Mekerttschian and E. Ter Minassiantz, Leipzig 1908.

Yač. = Grigori Lusaworčʿi *Yačaxapatum Čaṙkʿ*, Venice 1954.

GREEK SOURCES

Acts of Andrew, L.B. II.

Acts of Andrew and Matthias, L.B. II.

Acts of Thomas, L.B. II.

Apoc. Bar. = *Apocalypse of Baruch*, ed. M. R. James, *Apocrypha Anecdota*, T.S. 5, Cambridge 1897.

Apostolic Constitutions, ed. F. X. Funk, Paderborn 1905.

Aristaeus, *Letter* = *La Lettre d'Aristée à Philocrate*, ed. A. Pelletier, Paris 1962.

Ascension of Isaiah, ed. R. H. Charles, London 1900.

Athanasius, *Ad Adelphium*, P.G. 26.

——— *Ad Serapionem*, P.G. 26, trad. J. Lebon, S.C. 15, Paris 1947.

——— *Contra Gentes*, P.G. 25, trad. P. Th. Camelot, S.C. 18, Paris 1947.

——— *De Incarnatione*, P.G. 25, *The De Incarnatione of Athanasius*, S.D. 14; Part I, *The Long Recension Manuscripts*, by G. J. Ryan, 1945; Part II, *The Short Recension*, by R. P. Casey, 1946.

——— (ps.) *The Dialogues of Athanasius and Zacchaeus and of Timothy and Aquila*, ed. F. C. Conybeare, *Anecdota Oxoniensia*, I 8, Oxford 1899.

——— (ps.) *Expositio Fidei*, P.G. 25. See also Casey, *Armenian Version*.

——— (ps.) *Quaestiones ad Antiochum*, P.G. 28.

Barnabas, A.F. I, Bihlmeyer-Schneemelcher.

Basil (of Caesarea) *Hex.* = *Hexaemeron*, P.G. 29, *L'Hexaéméron de saint Basile*, ed. S. Giet, Paris 1950.

——— *In Ps. Hom.* = *Homiliae in Psalmos*, P.G. 29.

——— (ps.) *Historia mystagogica*, ed. F. E. Brightman, J.T.S. 9 (1908).

Chrysostom, *In Gen. Hom.* = *Homiliae in Genesin*, P.G. 53, 54.

——— *In Gen. Sermones*, P.G. 54.

——— *Expositio in Ps.*, P.G. 55.

——— *Frag. in Prov.*, P.G. 64.

——— *In Mat. Hom.*, P.G. 57.

——— *In Jo. Hom.*, P.G. 59.

——— *In Ep. I ad Cor. Hom.*, P.G. 61.

——— *In Ep. II ad Thess. Hom.*, P.G. 62.

——— *In Heb. Hom.*, P.G. 63.

——— *De Incomprehensibili Dei natura*, P.G. 48, trad. R. Flacelière, S.C. 28, Paris 1951.

——— *Huit Catéchèses baptismales inédites*, ed. A. Wenger, S.C. 50, Paris 1957.

——— (ps.) *In duodecim Apostolos Sermo*, P.G. 59.

I and II Clement, A.F. I, Bihlmeyer-Schneemelcher.

Clementine Recognitions, P.G. 1.

Clement (of Alexandria), *Eclogae*, P.G. 9, ed. O. Stählin, G.C.S. 17, Leipzig 1909.

——— *Protrepticus*, P.G. 8, ed. O. Stählin, G.C.S. 12, Leipzig 1905, and ed. C. Mondésert S.C. 2, Paris 1949.

——— *Quis dives salvetur*, P.G. 8, ed. O. Stählin, G.C.S. 17, Leipzig 1909.

——— *Str.* = *Stromateis*, P.G. 9, ed. O. Stählin, G.C.S. 15, 17, Leipzig, 1906, 1909.

Cyril Alex. (= of Alexandria), *Glaph Gen.* = *Glaphyra in Genesin*, P.G. 69.

——— *Glaph. in Ex.*, P.G. 69.

——— *Comm. in Is.*, P.G. 70.

——— *In Jo.*, P. E. Pusey, *Cyrilli in Joannis Evangelium*, 3 vols., Oxford 1872.

——— *Hom. Pasc.* = *Homiliae Pascales*, P.G. 77.

Cyril Jer. (= of Jerusalem), *Procat.*, *Cat.* = *Procatechesis* and *Catecheses*, P.G. 33, vol. I ed. G. C. Reischl, Munich 1848; vol. II ed. J. Rupp, Munich 1860.

Didache, A.F. I, Bihlmeyer-Schneemelcher, J.-P. Audet, *La Didachè*, Paris 1956.

Ad Diognetum, P.G. 2, A.F. II, Bihlmeyer-Schneemelcher.

Epiphanius, *Adv. Haer.* = *Panarion*, P.G. 41, 42, ed. K. Holl, G.C.S. 25, 31, 37, Leipzig 1915, 1922, 1933.

Eusebius, *De eccl. theologia*, P.G. 24, ed. E. Klostermann, G.C.S. 14, Leipzig 1906.

——— *Dem. ev.* = *Demonstratio evangelica*, P.G. 22, ed. I. A. Heikel, G.C.S. 23, Leipzig 1913.

——— *De Solemn. Pasch.*, P.G. 24.

——— *H.e.* = *Historia ecclesiastica*, P.G. 20, ed. E. Schwartz, G.C.S. 9, Leipzig 1903.

——— *Vita Const.*, P.G. 20, ed. I. A. Heikel, G.C.S. 7, Leipzig 1902.

Gregory Nazianzenus, *Or.* = *Orationes*, P.G. 35, 36.

Gregory of Nyssa, *C. Eun.* = *Contra Eunomium*, P.G. 45, Jaeger I, II, Leiden 1960.

——— *De Hominis Opificio*, P.G. 44, *La Création de l'homme*, trad. J. Laplace, S.C. 6, Paris 1944.

——— *De Vita Moysis*, P.G. 44, Jaeger VII, Leiden, 1964, *Vie de Moise*, trad. J. Daniélou, S.C. 1, Paris 1942.

——— *In Cant. Hom.*, P.G. 44, Jaeger VI, Leiden 1960.

——— *In Christi Res. Hom.*, P.G. 46, Jaeger IX, Leiden 1967.

——— *Or. cat.* = *Oratio catechetica*, P.G. 45, *The Catechetical Oration of Gregory of Nyssa*, ed. J. H. Srawley, Cambridge 1903.

Hippolytus, *Antichr.* = *Demonstratio de Christo et Antichristo*, P.G. 10, ed. G. N. Bonwetsch and H. Achelis, G.C.S. 1, Leipzig 1897.

——— *Fr. in Psalmos*, P.G. 10, G.C.S. 1.

——— *Ref. omn. Haer.*, ed. P. Wendland, G.C.S. 26, Leipzig 1916.

Ignatius, *Eph.* = *Epistula ad Ephesios*, P.G. 5, A.F. I, Bihlmeyer-Schneemelcher.

——— *Romans*, P.G. 5, A.F. I, Bihlmeyer-Schneemelcher.

Irenaeus, *Adv. Haer.*, P.G. 7, ed. W. W. Harvey, 2 vols., Cambridge 1857, *Contre les Hérésies*, IV, ed. A. Rousseau et al., S.C. 100, Paris 1965.

——— *Dem.* = *Démonstration de la Prédication apostolique*, trad. L. M. Froidevaux, S.C. 62, Paris 1959. For Armenian text see under Armenian Sources.

——— *Fr.* = *Fragmenta*, P.G. 7, Harvey, vol. II.

Justin, *I Apol.*, P.G. 6, ed. E. J. Goodspeed, *Die Älteste Apologeten*, Göttingen 1915.

——— *Dial.*, P.G. 6, ed. E. J. Goodspeed.

Martyrdom of Matthew, see Acts of Andrew and Matthias.

Martyrdom of Polycarp, A.F. II, Bihlmeyer-Schneemelcher.

Melito, *Pascal Homily*, ed. C. Bonner, S.D. 12, London 1940, ed. M. Testuz, *Papyrus Bodmer*, 1960.

Methodius, *Res.* = *De Resurrectione Mortuorum*, P.G. 18, ed. G. N. Bonwetsch, G.C.S. 27, Leipzig 1917.

Oracula Sibyllina, ed. J. Geffcken, G.C.S. 8, Leipzig 1902.

Origen, *In Gen. Hom.*, P.G. 12, ed. W. A. Baehrens, G.C.S. 29, Leipzig 1920.

——— *In Ex. Hom.*, P.G. 12, G.C.S. 29.

——— *Sel. in Ex.*, P.G. 12.

——— *In Lev. Hom.*, P.G. 12, G.C.S. 29.

——— *In Num. Hom.*, P.G. 12, ed. W. A. Baehrens, G.C.S. 30, Leipzig 1921.

——— *In Cant.*, P.G. 13, ed. W. A. Baehrens, G.C.S. 33, Leipzig 1925.

——— *In Jer. Hom.*, P.G. 13, ed. E. Klostermann, G.C.S. 6, Leipzig 1901.

——— *Sel. in Jer.*, P.G. 13.

——— *In Threnos*, P.G. 13, G.C.S. 6.

——— *Comm. in Mat.* P.G. 13, ed. E. Klostermann, G.C.S. 40, Leipzig 1935.

———— *In Luc. Hom.*, P.G. 13, ed. M. Rauer, 2nd ed., G.C.S. 49, Leipzig 1959.

———— *Fr. in Jo.*, P.G. 14, ed. E. Preuschen, G.C.S. 4, Leipzig 1903.

———— *C. Cels.*, P.G. 11, ed. P. Koetschau, G.C.S. 2, 3, 1899, trans. H. Chadwick, Cambridge 1953.

Polycarp, *Ep.*, A.F. I, Bihlmeyer-Schneemelcher.

Proclus, *Or.*, P.G. 65.

———— *Tome*, P.G. 65, ed. E. Schwartz, *Acta Conciliorum Oecumenicorum*, 4.2, Berlin 1914. Armenian text in *Girkᶜ Tᶜltᶜocᶜ*; see Armenian Sources.

Theodoret, *In Ps.*, P.G. 80.

———— *In Cant. Proem.*, P.G. 81.

———— *In Jer.*, P.G. 81.

SYRIAC SOURCES

Aphraates = Aphraatis *Demonstrationes*, ed. I. Parisot, *Patrologia Syriaca*, I, II, Paris 1894, 1907.

Ephrem, *In Genesim et in Exodum commentarii*, ed. R. R. Tonneau, CSCO 152, 153, Louvain 1955.

———— *Commentaire de l'Evangile concordant: texte syriaque*, ed. L. Leloir, Chester Beatty Monographs, 8, Dublin 1963.

———— *De Fide*, ed. E. Beck, CSCO 154, 155, Louvain 1955.

———— *De Nat.* = *De Nativitate*, ed. E. Beck, CSCO 186, 187, Louvain 1959.

SECONDARY SOURCES

N. Akinean, *Elišē Vardapet*, 3 vols., Vienna 1932–1960.

———— *Hay Matenagrunᶜean Oskedara*, *Handēs Amsorya*, 46 (1932), col. 105–128.

E. Beck, *Le Baptême chez saint Ephrem*, *L'Orient syrien*, 1 (1956), pp. 111–136.

B. Botte, *Le Lectionnaire arménien et la fête de la Théotocos à Jérusalem au Vᵉ siècle*, *Sacris Erudiri*, 2 (1949), pp. 111–122.

The Cambridge History of Later Greek and Early Medieval Philosophy, ed. A. H. Armstrong, Cambridge 1967.

R. P. Casey, *The Armenian Marcionites and the Diatessaron*, *Journal of Biblical Literature*, 57 (1938), pp. 185–194.

J. Catergian, *De Fidei symbolo quo Armenii utuntur Observationes*, Vienna 1893.

Conybeare, *Rituale* = F. C. Conybeare, *Rituale Armenorum*, Oxford 1905.

W. Cramer, *Die Engelvorstellungen bei Ephräm dem Syrer*, Orientalia Christiana Analecta, 173, Rome 1965.

Daniélou, *Bible* = J. Daniélou, *The Bible and the Liturgy*, Notre Dame 1956.

———— *Shadows* = *From Shadows to Reality*, London 1960.

———— *Theology* = *The Theology of Jewish Christianity*, Chicago 1964.

P. de Lagarde, *Agathangelus*, Abhandlungen der königlichen Gesellschaft der Wissenschaften zu Göttingen, 35 (1888), pp. 1–88.

H. Delehaye, *Les Origines du culte des martyrs*, Brussels 1912.

S. Der Nersessian, *An Armenian Version of the Homilies on the Harrowing of Hell*, Dumbarton Oaks Papers, 8 (1954), pp. 203–224.

———— *A Homily on the Raising of Lazarus and the Harrowing of Hell*, in *Biblical and Patristic Studies in Memory of R. P. Casey*, ed. J. N. Birdsall and R. W. Thomson, Freiburg 1963, pp. 219–234.

C. J. F. Dowsett, *The Penitential of David of Ganjak*, CSCO 216, 217, Louvain 1961.

Garitte, *Documents* = G. Garitte, *Documents pour l'étude du livre d'Agathange*, Studi e Testi, 127, Vatican 1946.

———— *La Vie grecque inédite de saint Grégoire d'Arménie (ms. 4 d'Ochrida)*, Analecta Bollandiana, 83 (1965), pp. 233–290.

———— *Le Traité géorgien "Sur la foi" attribué à Hippolyte*, Le Muséon, 78 (1965), pp. 119–172.

———— *Narratio* = *La Narratio de rebus Armeniae*, CSCO Subsidia 4, Louvain 1952.

Gelzer, *Anfänge* = H. Gelzer, *Die Anfänge der armenischen Kirche*, Berichte der königlichen sächischen Gesellschaft der Wissenschaften, 47 (1895), pp. 109–174.

L. Ginzberg, *The Legends of the Jews*, 7 vols., Philadelphia 1909–1938.

E. R. Goodenough, *By Light, Light*, New Haven 1935.

Grillmeier, *Christ* = A. Grillmeier, *Christ in Christian Tradition*, London 1965.

J. Gross, *La Divinisation du chrétien d'après les Pères grecs*, Paris 1938.

Hübschmann = H. Hübschmann, *Armenische Grammatik*, I, Leipzig 1897, 2. Auflage 1962.

James, *Apocryphal N. T.* = M. R. James, *The Apocryphal New Testament*, Oxford 1963.

H. Jensen, *Altarmenische Grammatik*, Heidelberg 1959.

J. N. D. Kelly, *Early Christian Creeds*, London 1950.

Lampe, *Lexicon* = G. W. H. Lampe, *A Patristic Greek Lexicon*, 5 vols., Oxford 1961–1968.

———— *The Seal of the Spirit*, London 1951.

Leloir, *Divergences* = L. Leloir, *Divergences entre l'original syriaque et la version arménienne du commentaire d'Ephrem sur le Diatessaron*, Mélanges Eugène Tisserant, II, Studi e Testi, 232, Vatican 1964, pp. 303–331.

———— *Ephrem de Nisibe, Commentaire de l'évangile concordant ou Diatessaron*, Sources chrétiennes, 121, Paris 1966.

H. Lewy, *Sobria Ebrietas*, Giessen 1929.

———— *The Pseudo-Philonic De Jona Part I*, S.D. VII, London 1936.

A. Luneau, *L'Histoire du salut, la doctrine des âges du monde*, Paris 1964.

Lyonnet, *Diatessaron* = S. Lyonnet, *Les Origines de la version arménienne et le Diatessaron*, Biblica et Orientalia, 13, Rome 1950.

Mariès, *Etude* = L. Mariès, *Etude sur quelques noms et verbes d'existence chez Eznik*, extrait de la *Revue des études arméniennes*, 8, Paris 1928.

———— *Le De Deo d'Eznik de Kolb*, extrait de la *Revue des études arméniennes*, 4, Paris 1924.

A. Meillet, *Altarmenisches Elementarbuch*, Heidelberg 1913.

Peeters, *S. Grégoire l'Illuminateur* = P. Peeters, *S. Grégoire l'Illuminateur dans le calendrier lapidaire de Naples*, Analecta Bollandiana, 60 (1942), pp. 91–130.

H. Rahner, *The Christian Mystery and the Pagan Mysteries*, in *The Mysteries*, ed. Joseph Campbell, Bollingen Series, XXX 2, New York 1955.

A. Renoux, *Lectionnaires arméniens et commémoraison de la sépulture du Christ le vendredi saint*, *L'Orient syrien*, 7 (1962), pp. 463–476.

———— *L'Epiphanie à Jérusalem au IVᵉ et au Vᵉ siècle d'après le lectionnaire arménien de Jérusalem*, Revue des études arméniennes, n.s. 2 (1965), pp. 343–359.

———— *Un Manuscrit du lectionnaire arménien de Jérusalem*, Le Muséon, 74 (1961), pp. 361–385.

M. Richard, *Acace de Mélitène, Proclus de Constantinople, et la grande Arménie*, Mémorial Louis Petit, Bucharest 1948, pp. 393–412.

Sargisean, *Agatᶜangelos* = B. V. Sargisean, *Agatᶜangelos ew iwr bazmadarean Galtnikᶜn*, Venice 1890.

K. Sarkissian, *The Council of Chalcedon and the Armenian Church*, London 1965.

H.-M. Schenke, *Der Gott "Mensch" in der Gnosis*, Göttingen 1962.

A. N. Srabyan, "*Yačaxapatum*" *čaṙeri helinaki harcᶜə*, *Telekagir*, 1962 no. 5, pp. 25–38.

W. J. Swaans, *A propos des "Catéchèses mystagogiques" attribuées à S. Cyrille de Jéru-salem*, *Le Muséon*, 55 (1942), pp. 1–43.

Tallon, *Livre des lettres* = M. Tallon, *Livre des lettres*, *Iᵉʳ groupe*, *Mélanges de l'Université Saint Joseph*, 32 (1955), fasc. 1.

E. Ter Minassiantz, *Die armenische Kirche in ihren Beziehungen zu den syrischen Kirche*, *Texte und Untersuchungen*, N.F. 11, Heft 3, Leipzig 1904.

Thomson, *Some Philosophical Terms* = R. W. Thomson, *Some Philosophical Terms in the Teaching of Gregory*, *Revue des études arméniennes*, n.s. 1 (1964), pp. 41–46.

——— *Vardapet in the Early Armenian Church*, *Le Muséon*, 75 (1962), pp. 367–384.

C. Toumanoff, *Studies in Christian Caucasian History*, Georgetown 1963.

J. Vogt, *Berichte über Kreuzeserscheinungen aus dem 4. Jahrhundert n. Chr.*, *Annuaire de l'Institut de philologie et d'histoire orientales et slaves*, 9 (1949), pp. 593–606.

A. von Gutschmid, *Agathangelos*, *Zeitschrift der deutschen morgenländischen Gesellschaft*, 31 (1877), pp. 1–60; reprinted in *Kleine Schriften*, III, ed. F. Rühl, Leipzig 1892, pp. 339–420.

R. McL. Wilson, *The Early History of the Exegesis of Gen. 1. 26*, *Studia Patristica*, II, 1957, pp. 420–437.

G. Zarpᶜanalean, *Matenadaran Haykakan Tᶜargmanutᶜeancᶜ Naxneacᶜ*, Venice 1889.

Index of Scriptural Quotations

Only direct quotations, not allusions, are listed here. For the Old Testament the numbering of the Armenian Bible (and the Septuagint) is followed. References are to the paragraph numbers of the *Teaching*.

General Index

References in italics are to the pages of the *Introduction*; those in roman type are to the paragraphs of the translation. Names which introduce scriptural quotations or are mentioned within them are omitted.

Aaron, 429, 431n5, 432; sons of, *8*, 541
Abel, 289, 290
Abraham, *5, 6, 7, 24*, 296n2, 298–300, 302, 305, 313, 316, 320, 323, 327, 433, 443, 468, 538, 580n1, 652
Abraham, bishop of the Mamikoneans, 564n1
Acacius of Melitene, *21, 36*, 368n1
Acts of Andrew, 489n1, 629n1, 685n3
Acts of Thomas, 685n3
Adam, *5, 6, 10, 17, 30*, 263n1, 264, 273–275, 277n3, 279, 287, 290, 291n1, 292, 295n1, 347, 350, 435n1, 585, 591–594
Agathangelos, *1, 2, 36–38*, 696n2; *History*, versions of, *3–4, 32n64*
Ages. *See* Seven ages of the world
Agriculture, similes of, 517–531, 617, 641–654
Altar. *See* Cross
Anahit, *1*
Anak, *1*
Ananias, 509
Anaximander, 267n3
Andrew, 448, 686
Angels, *28, 29*, 267, 276, 351, 381, 484, 490, 498, 692; appearances of, 323–325; dwelling-place of, 413–414; nature of, 262, 277, 322, 349, 360, 382. *See also* Man
Animals. *See* Creatures
Anti-Christ, 471
Aphraates, 267n1, 268n1, 441n1, 510n3, 529n1, 546n2, 638n1
Apocalypse of Peter, 471n1, 648n1
Apocryphon of John, 439n2
Apollinarians, 379n2
Apostles, *16, 26*, 361, 448, 457, 490–491, 512, 570n1, 607, 611, 614, 661, 664–666, 700, 713; as cupbearers, *8*, 507, 514; as a furnace, 638–639; as missionaries, *5, 31*, 609, 630–640, 663, 672, 674, 683, 685, 689; as torches, 683; as trumpets, 638, 640–641, 659; names and titles of, 685–686; number of, *5*, 612, 634; origins of, 684; relation of to Christ, 468, 632, 706. *See also* Baptism; Church; Disciples; Epistles; Gospels; Rhipsimē

Apostolic Fathers, *31. See also names of individual authors*
Archangels, 382. *See also* Angels
Arians, 369n1
Aristaeus, 503n1
Aristakēs, *2*
Aristotle, Armenian translations of, *11n15, 12n20*
Ark of Noah, 296
Arsacid monarchy, *38*
Artašat, *1*
Asia, 689
Assyria, 341, 577
Aštišat, *36*
Athanasius of Alexandria, *32*, 267n4, 268n1, 270n1, 275n1, 361n2, 367n1, 368n1, 386n1,4, 387n2, 399n1, 424n1, 465n1, 489n1, 566n5, 611n1, 616n1, 679n1, 684n4, 710n1; ps.-Athanasius, 274n2, 425n1, 433n1, 439n2
Atonement. *See* Redemption
Atticus, patriarch of Constantinople, *34*
Azot, 689

Babel. *See* Tower of Babel
Babylon, 341
Banquet, messianic, 508, 510
Baptism, *31*; by the apostles, 662, 679, 681–700; in name of Trinity, *16, 25*; in the church, *8*, 446, 679, 691; in *Yačaxapatum*, *27*; of Christ, *6–7, 24*, 408–422, 454, 552n1, 679; of John, *6, 24*, 408–409, 442
Barnabas, 543n1, 686; *Epistle* of, 473n1, 508n1, 668n2
Barsabbas, 686
Bartholomew, 521n1, 686
Basil of Caesarea, *31, 32*, 259n6, 260n4, 262n1, 267n4, 275n1, 424n1, 529n1, 633n1; ps.-Basil, 432n2
Bible. *See* Scriptures
Birds: as examples of the resurrection, 655–659; as nature's trumpets, 658; creation of, 260; named by Adam, 264
Birth: transmits sin, *17*; two births of Christ, 382, 388n1, 391

Main Themes of the Teaching